A NEW FREUDIAN SYNTHESIS

CIPS Series on The Boundaries of Psychoanalysis
Series Editor: Meg Beaudoin, PhD, FIPA

CIPS
CONFEDERATION OF INDEPENDENT PSYCHOANALYTIC SOCIETIES
www.cipsusa.org

The Confederation of Independent Psychoanalytic Societies (CIPS) is the national professional association for the independent component societies of the International Psychoanalytical Association (IPA) in the USA. CIPS also hosts the Direct Member Society for psychoanalysts belonging to other IPA societies. Our members represent a wide spectrum of psycho-analytic perspectives as well as a diversity of academic backgrounds. The CIPS Book Series, The Boundaries of Psychoanalysis, represents the intellectual activity of our community. The volumes explore the internal and external boundaries of psychoanalysis, examining the interrelationships between various psychoanalytic theoretical and clinical perspectives as well as between psychoanalysis and other disciplines.

Published and distributed by Karnac Books

When Theories Touch: A Historical and Theoretical Integration of Psychoanalytic Thought by Steven J. Ellman

Orders

Tel: +44 (0)20 7431 1075; Fax: +44 (0)20 7435 9076

E-mail: shop@karnacbooks.com

www.karnacbooks.com

A NEW FREUDIAN SYNTHESIS
Clinical Process in the Next Generation

Edited by
Andrew B. Druck, PhD,
Carolyn Ellman, PhD,
Norbert Freedman, PhD,
and Aaron Thaler, PhD

KARNAC

First published in 2011 by
Karnac Books Ltd
118 Finchley Road
London NW3 5HT

Copyright © 2011 by Andrew B. Druck, Carolyn Ellman, Norbert Freedman, and Aaron Thaler

The right of Andrew B. Druck, Carolyn Ellman, Norbert Freedman, and Aaron Thaler to be identified as the editors of this work has been asserted in accordance with §§ 77 and 78 of the Copyright Design and Patents Act 1988.

All rights reserved. No part of this publication may be reproduced, stored in a retrieval system, or transmitted, in any form or by any means, electronic, mechanical, photocopying, recording, or otherwise, without the prior written permission of the publisher.

British Library Cataloguing in Publication Data

A C.I.P. for this book is available from the British Library

ISBN-13: 978-1-85575-865-0

Typeset by Vikatan Publishing Solutions (P) Ltd., Chennai, India

Printed in Great Britain

www.karnacbooks.com

We dedicate this work to our loved ones: our parents, who live on in our memories; our spouses, whose love and support we count on every day; and our beloved children and grandchildren, who provide us with optimism about the future.

CONTENTS

ACKNOWLEDGEMENTS   xi

EDITORS AND CONTRIBUTORS   xiii

INTRODUCTION   xvii
Andrew B. Druck, Carolyn Ellman,
Norbert Freedman, and Aaron Thaler

CHAPTER ONE
Modern conflict theory: a critical review   1
Andrew B. Druck

CHAPTER TWO
Modern structural theory   25
Andrew B. Druck

CHAPTER THREE
States of consciousness   51
Sheldon Bach

CHAPTER FOUR
New developments in the theory and clinical application
  of the annihilation anxiety concept   65
Marvin Hurvich

CHAPTER FIVE
Breakdown and recovery in the analysis of a young woman   97
Aaron Thaler

CHAPTER SIX
On shame in narcissistic states of consciousness:
  clinical illustration   131
Mary Libbey

CHAPTER SEVEN
Anonymity: blank screen or black hole   157
Carolyn Ellman

CHAPTER EIGHT
Ferenczi's concepts of identification with the aggressor
  and play as foundational processes in the analytic
  relationship   173
Jay Frankel

CHAPTER NINE
Cultivating meaning space: Freudian and neo-Kleinian
  conceptions of therapeutic action   201
Neal Vorus

CHAPTER TEN
"Secretly attached, secretly separate" Art, dreams,
  and transference-countertransference in the analysis
  of a third generation Holocaust survivor   219
Michal Talby-Abarbanel

DISCUSSION OF "SECRETLY ATTACHED, SECRETLY
  SEPARATE"
Trauma in action: the enacted dimension of analytic process
  in a third generation Holocaust survivor   239
Gil A. Katz

CHAPTER ELEVEN
A new Freudian synthesis: reflections and a perspective   249
Norbert Freedman

REFERENCES   265

INDEX   287

ACKNOWLEDGEMENTS

The editors would like to give special thanks to Fredrick Perlman, past president of CIPS, Meg Beaudoin, and the CIPS board of directors, who had the wisdom and vision to create this innovative book series, which makes it possible to communicate recent developments in psychoanalysis to our colleagues, especially in North America. Further, we are thankful for the way that Meg, as the series editor and liaison with Karnac, has been with us throughout every step of this process.

We recognize the contribution of the IPTAR series of Controversial Discussions (created by Norbert Freedman), a component of the programme in pre-psychoanalytic education, which was the impetus for many of the chapters contained in this volume.

We are grateful to our teachers from the New York University Postdoctoral Program, our colleagues at IPTAR and at the New York University Postdoctoral Program, and the students and supervisees from both places that continually help us to formulate and change our ideas. We are especially grateful to our patients who are the true inspiration for our continual growth.

We also want to thank each other for the effort each of us put into the book, for the emotional support, intellectual contribution, and editorial work of each, without which we could never have done it.

Andrew B. Druck
Carolyn Ellman
Norbert Freedman
Aaron Thaler

EDITORS AND CONTRIBUTORS

Sheldon Bach, PhD, is an adjunct clinical professor of psychology at the New York University Postdoctoral Program in Psychotherapy and Psychoanalysis and a training and supervising analyst at the Institute for Psychoanalytic Training and Research (IPTAR) and at the New York Freudian Society. He is the author of *Narcissistic States and the Therapeutic Process*, *The Language of Perversion and the Language of Love*, and *Getting from Here to There: Analytic Love, Analytic Process*.

Andrew B. Druck, PhD, ABPP, (editor) is a fellow (training and supervising analyst), past president, former dean of training, and faculty member at the Institute for Psychoanalytic Training and Research (IPTAR). He is a clinical assistant professor of psychology, faculty member and supervising analyst at the New York University Postdoctoral Program in Psychotherapy and Psychoanalysis. He is the author of *Four Therapeutic Approaches to the Borderline Patient*.

Carolyn Ellman, PhD, (editor) is a training and supervising analyst at the Institute for Psychoanalytic Training and Research (IPTAR) and the New York Freudian Society. She is an adjunct clinical professor and supervising analyst at the New York University

Postdoctoral Program in Psychotherapy and Psychoanalysis, and a clinical associate supervisor at City University Clinical Psychology Department. She is the senior editor of *The Modern Freudians* and *Omnipotent Fantasies and the Vulnerable Self.*

Jay Frankel, PhD, is a faculty member at the Institute for Psychoanalytic Training and Research (IPTAR) and is an adjunct clinical associate professor and supervisor at the New York University Postdoctoral Program in Psychotherapy and Psychoanalysis. He is a supervisor at the Manhattan Institute for Psychoanalysis and in the Child and Adolescent Psychotherapy Training Program at the William Alanson White Institute. He is an associate editor of the journal *Psychoanalytic Dialogues,* and author of many psychoanalytic journal articles and book chapters on topics including play, trauma, identification, the analytic relationship, child psychotherapy, and the work of Sándor Ferenczi. He is co-author of *Relational Child Psychotherapy.*

Norbert Freedman, PhD, (editor) is a training and supervising analyst and former president at the Institute for Psychoanalytic Training and Research (IPTAR). He is an adjunct clinical professor and supervising analyst at the New York University Postdoctoral Program in Psychotherapy and Psychoanalysis, professor emeritus of psychiatry and former director of clinical psychology, SUNY Downstate Medical Center. He is the author of numerous publications on the clinical and empirical study of symbolization and transformations in the psychoanalytic process and he is co-author of the forthcoming psychoanalytic research volume, *Another Kind of Evidence* (2011, Karnac).

Marvin Hurvich, PhD, DP, ABPP, is a training and supervising analyst at the Institute for Psychoanalytic Training and Research (IPTAR), the New York Freudian Society, and the New York University Postdoctoral Program in Psychotherapy and Psychoanalysis. He is professor of psychology at Long Island University, Brooklyn Center, a diplomate in psychoanalysis, and a member of the International Psychoanalytic Association. He is co-author, with L. Bellak and H. Gediman, of *Ego Functions in Schizophrenics, Neurotics and Normals,* and his current writings are on theoretical, clinical, and empirical aspects of annihilation anxieties.

Gil A. Katz, PhD, is a faculty member, fellow (training and supervising analyst), and former dean of training at the Institute for

Psychoanalytic Training and Research (IPTAR). He is a clinical assistant professor of psychology, faculty member, and supervising analyst at the NYU Postdoctoral Program in Psychotherapy and Psychoanalysis. He is the author of psychoanalytic articles on enactment and the therapeutic action of psychoanalysis.

Mary Libbey, PhD, is a training and supervising analyst and faculty member at the Institute for Psychoanalytic Training and Research (IPTAR). She is a supervising analyst and faculty member at the NYU Postdoctoral Program in Psychotherapy and Psychoanalysis.

Michal Talby-Abarbanel is a clinical psychologist trained in Israel and a licensed psychoanalyst in New York. She is on the faculty of the New York Counseling Center and is an associate member of the Institute for Psychoanalytic Training and Research (IPTAR). She is in private practice in New York City.

Aaron Thaler, PhD, (editor) is a faculty member and supervisor at the Institute for Psychoanalytic Training and Research and the IPTAR Child and Adolescent Psychotherapy Training Program, and he leads the IPTAR Study Group on Winnicott. He is a faculty member and training and supervising analyst at the Psychoanalytic Training Institute of the New York Freudian Society. He is a supervising analyst at the New York University Postdoctoral Program in Psychotherapy and Psychoanalysis.

Neal Vorus, PhD, is a faculty member and supervisor at the Institute for Psychoanalytic Training and Research (IPTAR). He is an adjunct clinical assistant professor at the NYU Postdoctoral Program in Psychotherapy and Psychoanalysis, and an adjunct assistant professor of psychology at John Jay College of Criminal Justice.

INTRODUCTION

*Andrew B. Druck, Carolyn Ellman,
Norbert Freedman, and Aaron Thaler*

In every analysis, we arrive at critical moments, turning points that often occur far along into the work. These moments, which often replay significant traumatic biographical events, define the course of the analysis. They make it real, they actualize the verbal content, and the way in which they are navigated strongly influences the depth and success of the analytic endeavour. In this volume, we see how contemporary Freudian analysts have integrated different currents in Freudian theory and technique to deal with the challenges of these moments. Further, we see how, and why, the fabric of an analysis, the analytic frame within which these critical moments arise, the context that allows for these moments to emerge, is shaped first by the analyst and then by the analyst-patient dyad.

The work presented here demonstrates how modern analysts have translated and retranslated the contributions of analysts on whose shoulders we stand, including Freud, Winnicott, Loewald, Kohut, and others. The editors asked each contributor to show how they, in their unique way, have taken the work of first and second generation theorists and made it their own, specific to the kind of psychoanalytic work that is most often practised today. We see how our authors have deconstructed and then reinterpreted the work of our predecessors. These authors (representing three generations of analysts) are an out-growth of a series called Controversial Discussions at the Institute for Psychoanalytic Training and Research (IPTAR) in New York City. None of our authors had any knowledge of the other contributors' chapters. Thus, we, as editors, were curious to see what contemporary Freudian theory and practice would look like through the lens of these contemporary Freudians.

* * *

The opening chapters provide a theoretical overview, demonstrating the evolution of Freudian theory and the ways in which different founding analysts' work can be integrated. The later chapters, forming the bulk of this volume, translate that frame into clinical process and demonstrate different emphases in contemporary psychoanalytic work. We found that the papers demonstrate how analysts confronted with clinical dilemmas—for example, patients who cannot, for various reasons, use interpretations productively—find ways to address these dilemmas while deepening the analytic process. In this effort, we will see how central elements of psychoanalysis, such as interpretation and the nature of the patient-analyst relationship, have also been deconstructed and redefined as we enter a new century.

As you will notice, perhaps the greatest commonality between the various clinical papers is an intense focus on the subtleties of clinical process. We can see this in different ways. First, there is the discussion of the phenomenology of the patient's conscious experience and shifts in his or her affective state. Many of the analysts write of the mutative effect that results when the analyst enters the patient's conscious, as well as unconscious world, in one way or another. Further, we can understand some of our authors' focus if we take the common statement "I interpreted to the patient that …". Previous analysts focused on the content of what was interpreted; our authors look at the context of such statements. For example, to whom was the analyst interpreting? Is there a patient capable of appreciating the analyst's perspective, different from that of the patient? What kind of interpersonal action is an interpretation? What is the "meta-communication" in an interpretation? To what extent does it deepen an experiential process, or disrupt it? Why does the analyst choose to interpret at a given moment? From where does the interpretation come—to what extent is the analyst following the patient's clinical process and to what extent is the analyst following his or her theory? How much does an interpretation reflect joint discovery by the patient and analyst, and how much does it reflect the analyst finding what he or she believed must be there unconsciously?

Interpretation historically has been viewed as the major mutative factor in psychoanalysis, although its nature and role have been reworked over time by generations of analysts. In this volume, one finds further examination and reinterpretation of the concept and its mutative role. Many authors stress how the analyst offers interpretive space, that is, psychic space within which interpretations can be considered, played with, and taken in, perhaps in a transformed way, by the patient. At one point in time, the analyst offered an interpretation. Now interpretation is seen as something discovered by the patient. It may be an affirmation of the patient's newly-discovered voice, a statement reflecting the patient's, as well as the analyst's, creativity.

As the reader goes through the papers, he or she will see that many of the authors discuss patients with great difficulties in the sense of self, unintegrated self and object states, senses of self that feel false and inauthentic, annihilation fears, and struggles with humiliation and shame. The analysts describe working in an analytic regression that provides the context for emotional connection between analyst and patient, one that is, in a major way, mutative. One quickly sees that certain "classical" elements of psychoanalytic work are understated or missing, such as reliance on drive, defence, resistance, and interpretation. These traditional elements of Freudian theory and technique are not highlighted because, for most of our authors, they are assumed and taken for granted. They are seen here through the prism of a larger context of personal integration. It is this larger context that is highlighted, and traditional elements are subsumed or re-interpreted within it.

What is stressed is a developmental focus: how a sense of authentic self, a developed "mind", comes into being through the patient-analyst relationship. The analyst is often mostly a "subjective" object whose function is to reflect, affirm, bolster, and participate in some fundamental way in the needs of his or her patient's psychic structure. It is believed that a more developed mind and authentic sense of self comes into being through a complex and subtle interplay of internalization of the analyst and the patient's own creative process. Thus, "transference" is understood as much in terms of the current patient-analyst relationship as past relationships. The analyst looks at his or her current role in the patient's psychic state as much as his or her role as an object from the past. He or she attends to what the patient needs in the present as well as what he or she unconsciously repeats from the past. This way of thinking, along with different theoretical emphases, makes different observations and insights possible and the reader is treated to case presentations, which illustrate the work of contemporary innovative Freudian analysts.

The reader will find that a new synthesis has taken place in which the relationship with the analyst is a crucial element in setting the stage for patients to take a closer look into their own inner world. This detailed examination of the clinical techniques that were implied but not developed by analysts such as Winnicott, Ferenczi, Kohut, and Loewald has led to a new Freudian synthesis, which is the unique contribution of this volume.

CHAPTER ONE

Modern conflict theory: a critical review

Andrew B. Druck[1]

In this age of psychoanalytic pluralism, an age when, even within the broad contemporary Freudian framework, there is disagreement about essential aspects of psychoanalytic theory and technique, the practising analyst is faced with the problem of putting published material in some context. How is he or she to make sense of papers that state diametrically opposite opinions, often forcefully and dogmatically? Further, how is he or she to identify the commonalities as well as the differences between analysts? I propose to discuss two broad and overlapping ways of contextualizing the many papers and ideas facing us today. My aim is to make explicit major concerns, assumptions, and difficulties underlying basic Freudian points of view so that the clinician can place theoretical statements and technical recommendations within a broad framework. I will discuss modern conflict theory and an alternative emphasis within the continuum of contemporary Freudian psychoanalysis, which I will call modern structural theory. My emphasis here will be on modern conflict theory. I will save discussion of modern structural theory for the following chapter. I will make liberal use of quotes in my discussion to illustrate my points and to give the reader a greater "feel" for the analysts about whom I am writing.

Modern conflict theory

One obvious way to think about technique is to ask three interlocking questions: What is wrong with the patient? What will then "cure" the patient? And what, finally, is the optimal role for the analyst in facilitating this mutative process? Ideally, this all fits together, with one assumption flowing into the other. For example, in Freud's early writings, what was wrong with the patient was memories that were repressed; what would "cure" the patient was abreaction; the proper analytic role was then to facilitate abreaction, through the strength of the analyst's authority. These assumptions characterized the cathartic phase of Freudian theory, soon to be followed by the topographic emphasis and, finally, by Freud's structural theory, which is the basis for modern conflict theory.

According to Richards and Richards (1995), "[For modern conflict theorists], key theoretical constructs are conflict, compromise formation, and unconscious fantasy" (p. 429). Brenner (1976, 1982) has reformulated and essentially given operational definitions to the factors involved in unconscious conflict and compromise formation. Because of work by Arlow, Brenner, and others, the "classical psychoanalysis" of modern conflict theorists is different from the "classical analysis" of Freud.

Briefly, Brenner posits that any aspect of mental functioning should be understood as a compromise between four unconscious forces. First, there is the drive derivative, which is one's personal and idiosyncratic formulation of a sexual or aggressive drive. We all have sexual drives, but some of us want to do x in y way with person z while others have different conditions and wishes for drive satisfaction. As Brenner (1982) puts it, drive as a concept is "impersonal and general" while drive derivative is "personal and specific" (p. 26). Drive derivatives are not inherently dangerous and do not necessarily lead to opposition from the ego. To the extent that these derivatives are ego syntonic, the ego facilitates their realization. However, drive derivatives often do arouse unconscious dysphoric affect because they touch on an unconscious danger situation. In a second important contribution, Brenner (1982) adds depressive affect to Freud's focus on anxiety. Anxious affect refers to what may happen in the future; depressive affect refers to a "calamity" that someone believes has already happened to him and that he wishes to keep unconscious. When a drive derivative arouses unconscious dysphoric affect, one defends against this affect. In a third contribution, Brenner (1982) states that defences are not limited to the traditional "defense mechanisms" elaborated by Anna Freud. Any mental activity or action that serves to reduce dysphoric affect serves a defensive function. One drive derivative (angry feelings) can defend against the emergence of threatening opposite drive derivatives (loving feelings). Thus, Brenner objects to seeing defensive activity as situated in one designated area of the mind. Finally, Brenner points out that one must always attend to superego pressure, usually unconscious guilt for the drive derivative. This is the fourth component of intrapsychic conflict. These four aspects of mental functioning are in continuous unconscious interplay.

Drive derivative, dysphoric affect, defence, and superego pressure are the four independent variables of mental functioning. All else is viewed as the result of these variables in constant interplay. The result is a "compromise formation" between unconscious mental forces, which can shift from moment to moment, which is more or less adaptive, and which can be analysed back to the interplay of its constituent elements. No part of the mind is distinct. Every aspect of the mind is itself a compromise formation even as it participates in the process of internal conflict and compromise. Modern conflict theory is an internal systems theory of mental functioning (Boesky, 1994). Since every part of the mind, according to Brenner, is *itself* a compromise formation, Freud's distinctions between parts of the mind—id, ego, and superego—are no longer valid and it is misleading to speak of relatively distinct internal structures. Thus, he abandons classical structural theory (Brenner, 1994) and sees the mind comprised of compromise formations. Boesky (1994) comments that "... the new proposals seem to float without developmental anchors" (p. 512).

Classic examples of compromise formations are dreams, symptoms, and unconscious fantasies (Arlow, 1969). Unconscious fantasies are relatively stable. They are the "tinted" glasses through which we see the world, the internal filter through which we structure our subjective realities. They carry our unconscious wishes, fears, and our internal self and object representations. While an unconscious fantasy is itself a developmentally evolving compromise formation, it is also a concept somewhat distinct from the concept of compromise formation. As Richards et al. (1995) write:

> Thinking in terms of unconscious fantasy led to a more experience specific and explicitly narrative hypothesis, with the story of the unconscious fantasy fleshing out the bones of the compromise formation. The unconscious fantasy elaborates and specifies what the compromise formation outlines. Unconscious fantasy can be thought of as a synthetic, integrative concept whereas compromise formation is an algebra of the mind, enabling the analyst to tease apart separate strands of thought and feeling (p. 432).

Modern conflict theorists differ in their emphasis on each aspect. Uncovering the specific unconscious content and meaning of one's unconscious fantasy is a primary goal of analysis for Arlow (1995). In contrast, Gray (1973) and Busch (1995, 2001) focus on the process of unconscious conflict itself, especially on the ego's defensive efforts.

Modern conflict theory has probably been the most influential theory in "classical" psychoanalysis since the 1950s. The contributions of Arlow and Brenner led Freudian psychoanalysis to a supple framework of thinking, which resulted in a more experience-near, specific, here-and-now focus on the constant interplay of unconscious elements and shifting compromise formations at different moments in any psychoanalytic session. Abend (2005) writes, "For me, then, the analysis of unconscious conflict, and of the compromise formations to which it gives rise, is the quintessential feature of my way of understanding the patient's mental life and of the complexities of the clinical situation" (p. 24). Arlow and Brenner and their contributions have been justly celebrated in many forums (including, but not limited to, Richards and Willick (1986) and Blum, Kramer, Richards, and Richards (1988).

Yet, despite the great explanatory power and rigour found in this way of thinking, there is more to be said. As Loewald (1966) writes in his review of a book by Arlow and Brenner, "… they do present their views clearly and concisely and leave no doubt as to where they stand. But the reader is left with the impression that in their view issues are settled, concepts well defined and precise, problems well understood and in no need of further inquiry, of which many are neither as clear-cut nor as simple and one-dimensional as they are represented to be by the authors" (pp. 431–432). He continues, "… their own exposition of the structural theory which they consider superior, is … rigid, oversimplified, and final in tone and quality. There seem to be no open ends, debatable issues, genuinely obscure phenomena and meanings" (p. 433). In this chapter, I will discuss some difficulties with modern conflict theory. In the following chapter, I will discuss alternative approaches within contemporary Freudian psychoanalysis.

Critique of modern conflict theory

Modern conflict theory has evolved over the years, but before we move to its evolution it is worth discussing its narrow theoretical reach. Modern conflict theory focuses intensively and insightfully on a narrow range of data but leaves out much. First, modern conflict theory relies exclusively on verbal data obtained from classically "analysable" patients in "classical" psychoanalysis, as that is defined by Brenner and his colleagues. This method of psychoanalysis, Brenner (1982) writes, "… makes possible an independent, objective appraisal of those aspects of mental life" (p. 3). In making this claim, Brenner and most other modern conflict theorists do not consider challenges to such "independent, objective appraisal" from other Freudian psychoanalysts (Tuckett, 1994), or from the revisions that Brenner himself has made to modern conflict theory (Rothstein, 2005). Further, the theory leaves out "objective" data from "non-analysable" patients in psychoanalyses that are not "classical" and it leaves out subjective data from analysts' countertransference or from enactments in psychoanalytic work. For a theory that aspires to the understanding of all mental functioning, such data can be theoretically informative and might even illuminate aspects of traditional analysis with neurotic patients.

Second, Arlow, Brenner, and most of the early modern conflict theorists limit the elements involved in intrapsychic conflict and compromise. They include only the aforementioned four variables, each one of them conceived of narrowly. As modern conflict theory has evolved, many analysts comfortably use the overall framework of intrapsychic conflict and compromise formation but add elements to these initial four, while also expanding the range of phenomena included in these elements. One can be in conflict not only about sexual or aggressive drive derivatives but also about conflicted identifications, aspects of self experience, and difficulties with the self (Pine, 1988); dysphoric affect can include annihilation anxiety (Hurvich, 2003a); defences may involve the analyst in part-object transferences such as self object transferences (Kohut, 1971) or projective identification and associated defences under the rubric of splitting (Kernberg, 1975) or in action (Sandler, 1976; Katz, 1998; Smith, 2006; Busch, 2006); and the superego and its components may be made up of internalized objects, with some internal objects providing a source of support and strength in internal object relations systems (Jacobson, 1964; Asch, 1976). The framework of conflict and compromise remains essentially the same, but it is expanded. The elements change in kind and in nature.

Arlow and Brenner explicitly disavow such expansion, and this disavowal seems to have been maintained by those most closely identified with modern conflict theory (Abend, 2005, gives a clear discussion of modern conflict theory reflecting this approach). Arlow (1963) cautions that one should not take conflicts over identifications at face value; he emphasizes instead a focus on "… the drive component which the identification represents …" (p. 19). More striking is Brenner's statement limiting what he believes may be considered a danger situation. His statement is so strong that I will quote him as fully as I can within the confines of this paper, not only because of his particular views but also because the paragraph supports assertions I have made about modern conflict theory, as it is formulated by Arlow and Brenner. I urge the reader to read Brenner's (1982, pp. 67–68) remarks in full (see also Arlow, 1963, p. 15). Brenner (1982) writes the following:

> The factual correctness of Freud's four, typical calamities and their consequent practical importance in clinical work has been established by the collective experience of several generations of analysts. It should not be added to lightly. Any addition, if it is to be taken seriously, must be documented by pertinent clinical, i.e., psychoanalytic evidence. It is especially important that a patient's conscious complaint not be offered as evidence of the ideational content of the anxiety and/or depressive affect

which are involved in his or her pathogenic conflicts. A patient's complaint or report that he or she is empty, is merging with someone else, or is dissolving into nothing is not to be taken as a reliable report of the patient's psychopathology. It must not be taken at face value, as though it were a true, endopsychic perception of an aspect of the patient's psychic life. Such a report, such a complaint, is a symptom. It is a compromise formation .... Adequate analysis will reveal it to be a consequence of the patient's psychopathology rather than a description of it, a consequence that can be properly understood and evaluated only after such analysis has been done. In my own experience, I have found no evidence to support the propriety of adding another to Freud's list of typical calamities. The four he listed account satisfactorily for the initiation of conflict in every case I have observed or personally treated to date. Until evidence to the contrary is available, the calamities which figure importantly in psychic conflicts originating from childhood drive derivatives should be limited to object loss, loss of love, castration, and, after superego formation, various aspects of superego functioning, such as fear of punishment, remorse, self-punishment, etc. (pp. 67–68).

This paragraph offers us a snapshot of modern conflict theory as developed by Brenner (and Arlow). Note first how Brenner limits danger situations to those identified by Freud. His limitation disregards evidence by a great many psychoanalysts, including those identified with the British middle and Kleinian schools, those who have worked with psychotic patients, borderline, narcissistic, and schizoid patients, and those who have identified annihilation anxiety as an important danger situation even in neurotic patients (Hurvich, 2003). I believe that Brenner would respond that those patients were not treated in analysis, as Brenner understands it, that they were not really analysable, as Brenner defines analysability, and that much of this data was obtained through non-verbal means, evidence which he, and modern conflict theorists, do not consider valid psychoanalytic data. However, Brenner is making general statements about psychic functioning. To argue that the modes of data gathering were psychotherapeutic rather than psychoanalytic is, essentially, irrelevant to theory formation.

Note too Brenner's focus on understanding manifest content as a symptom, a product of unconscious conflict, whose latent content must be made conscious. While such an approach is certainly valid and perhaps quintessentially psychoanalytic, what does it mean to completely disregard manifest content, such as a patient's complaints? For one thing, it leads to some patients feeling, at least implicitly, criticized, dismissed, and unheard by their analysts, who are always conveying the message "What is he or she *really* thinking?". (In this context, the exchange between Arlow (1995) and Schwaber (1998) is fascinating, illuminating, and worthwhile.) Perhaps more to the point, this method of evidence gathering makes it impossible to determine whether, in fact, the patient's fear that he or she is dissolving or merging into the other has basis in the "reality" of his or her psychic life. Analysis of the patient's associations might determine that the patient is conflicted about castration anxiety. It might also lead to the conclusion that the patient does have substantial concerns about his or her psychic integrity, especially if the verbal material is supplemented by the analyst's evaluation of the patient's structural functioning (Pine, 1979; Druck, 1998; Akhtar, 2000). However, Brenner already concluded that annihilation anxiety cannot be one of the possible danger situations and both Arlow and Brenner concluded that a patient's manifest concerns about psychic regression are to be seen only as symptoms, as potentially analysable compromise formations.

Essentially, Brenner argues that what appears to be "pre-Oedipal" material can, and should, be understood as disguised Oedipal material. The further assumption is that any pre-Oedipal issues will become raised up and transformed into Oedipal material. However, Brenner, Arlow, and modern conflict theorists do not allow for the possibility that what appears to be Oedipal material may, in fact, be disguised pre-Oedipal material. Kernberg (1975), for example, has discussed how, for many patients, sexual promiscuity may have more to do with unconscious needs for concrete bodily contact with another person that alleviates unconscious fears about the integrity of the self, than with conflicted sexuality as such.

It is true, as Arlow emphasizes, that one can find a drive aspect to any internal object relational state or wish. One can also find a self component, a narcissistically regulating component, an ego component, and several other components. As Kernberg (1975) notes, one can also find an unconscious object relational component within what manifestly presents as a drive related conflict. Further, as

Brenner argues, one drive state can be defending against another drive state. This insight can easily be applied to any aspect of mental activity; any aspect, at any moment, can be both expressive and defensive, and these attributes are constantly shifting. My point is that there is no reason to privilege unconscious drives or any other component of mental functioning. The practising analyst does better looking for what is most pressing for a patient at any given moment. It is only theoretical fealty to Freud's focus on drives, an emphasis that is carried on in modern conflict theory (Abend, 2005) that leads us to concentrate on a disguised drive component.

The continuous unconscious process of conflict and compromise is assumed to take place within a developed structural context, a context that is assumed to develop as drive development proceeds. However, what happens to intrapsychic conflict in the many cases where structural development has not been optimal? Neglecting structural development is, perhaps, the most serious difficulty with modern conflict theory, especially as Brenner (1994) has continued to modify it in the direction of abandoning Freud's structural hypothesis. By structural development, I mean here the way in which capacities such as reality testing, self and object constancy, libidinal object constancy, signal anxiety, self esteem regulation, symbolic communication, the capacity for regression in the service of the ego, an authentic and coherent sense of self, and a host of what have been traditionally considered ego and superego capacities develop. These capacities form the context within which conflict and compromise formation take place and are crucial in traditional definitions of neurosis and analysability. It is adequate development of these capacities that defines someone as neurotic (as opposed to psychotic, borderline, and narcissistic, as examples of less fully-developed structures). For diagnostic purposes, the ubiquity of unconscious conflict is irrelevant. Because one finds intrapsychic conflict in everyone, at every level of development, conflict alone cannot be the final diagnostic criterion. It is assessment of structural development and analysis of conflict within a given level of structural development that leads us to accurate psychoanalytic diagnosis (Druck, 1998).

Modern conflict theory ignores the question of how conflict and compromise formation manifest themselves at different levels of structural development, and how these two variables interact. We see this in Arlow and Brenner's (1964) approach to psychosis, in Abend, Porder, and Willick's (1983) discussion of the borderline patient, and in comments such as the following by Arlow (1963):

> The disintegrative effect upon the ego of overwhelming anxiety is well documented from the experience with borderline and psychotic patients. *The interplay of forces here is the same as in neurotic symptom formation except for the importance of pre-phallic drives, aggression, and the ease with which ego functions, ordinarily outside the realm of conflict, are brought into the nexus of conflict and are reinstinctualized or regressively altered during the defensive struggle.* In many borderline and neurotic patients, symptoms characterized by severe, but transient, alterations of ego function (e.g. reality testing, sense of time, and identity) may be traced to defense against typical castration anxiety when one is able to translate the conscious psychological experience in terms of the ego's response to the unconscious phantasy (p. 16, italics added).

What does this italicized statement mean? Pre-phallic drives include strong, often overwhelming wishes (needs?) by the person to be with the other. It could be object hunger, it could be difficulty with object constancy so that the patient cannot separate from the other, it could be a form of love addiction, where earlier pre-Oedipal wishes manifest themselves as sexual promiscuity (Kernberg, 1975). In whatever way it is expressed, pre-phallic drives is a "drive theory" formulation that refers to strong wishes by someone for contact in order to feel whole, centred, coherent, and alive. Aggression, in this context, means overwhelming rage that must be defended against with defences that have been described as inherently ego weakening (Kernberg, 1975) or as leading to a paranoid-schizoid position. In traditional ego psychology, this sort of aggression leads to difficulties with neutralization, impairing ego development (Hartmann, 1964). When Arlow speaks of *"the ease with which ego functions, ordinarily outside the realm of conflict, are brought into the nexus of conflict and are reinstinctualized or regressively altered during the defensive struggle"*, he is telling us that structural development has not progressed to the point where intraspsychic conflict leads to a compromise formation that maintains structural integrity. Again using Hartmann's concepts, the autonomy of basic ego functions such as reality testing and rational thought in general, speech as symbolic communication, and eating for pleasure and nutrition, is compromised. Ego and superego functions on which the neurotic patient can ordinarily rely turn out to be fragile, severely compromised, or lost at moments of intense unconscious conflict in the more seriously disturbed patient. The structural context of intrapsychic conflict shifts in a way that severely impacts the process of unconscious conflict and compromise formation. These are giant "excepts" that are treated by modern conflict theorists as if they are parentheses in our conception of psychopathology. They are acknowledged but their implications are not considered.

Arlow (1991) writes as follows:

> Symptoms of the psychoses could be understood in terms of conflict, defense, and compromise formation. We [he and Brenner] suggested that there is a complementary series, a range of disturbance reflecting the ego's inability to effect adequate resolution of conflicts, from the severe pathology observed in the case of psychoses to the relatively mild disturbances observed in neurotics and the so-called normal. The problem in the psychopathology—not the aetiology—of the psychosis resides in the failure of the weak ego vis-à-vis the overpowering force of the drives. The aetiological considerations—namely how the ego came to be so weak and the drives so powerful—remain elusive (p. 54).

Here, Arlow comes close to acknowledging deficit (the "weak ego"), but he does not explore the logical and obvious next question: what is then the effect on the *process* (not just the result) of unconscious conflict and compromise of a structural context that Arlow acknowledges has not fully developed (what he calls the "problem in the psychopathology")? Rather Arlow throws up his hands: "The aetiological considerations ... remain elusive." But they are not so elusive. This question has been studied by major mainstream Freudian theorists such as Jacobson (1964), Mahler, Pine, and Bergman (1975), and Loewald (1978). Virtually everyone who has studied this issue concludes that parental internalization is a necessary condition for optimal development of structure (including drive development). Further, according to Loewald, the interplay of structural development and internal object relations is an ongoing process (analogous to continuing shifts in compromise formations). Loewald writes (1977) that "… during therapeutic analysis, especially with patients suffering from narcissistic disorders, we are able to observe the organization and dedifferentiation of psychic structure and object relations as ongoing processes. We can see that object relations and intrapsychic structure formation and then maintenance are intimately interrelated. And further, that there are psychic process-structures that are not intrapsychic but in an intermediate region as it were, analogous to Winnicott's transitional phenomena" (pp. 501–502). There are always two processes simultaneously at work: the process of compromise formation (a dynamic process) and the process of structure building or maintenance (a structural process). These are interwoven processes, highly determined by the patient-analyst relationship.

Loewald assumes that internalization is a major organizing principle of life, analogous to the pleasure principle. Our minds develop through separation and internalization, in continuing reciprocal processes (Loewald, 1951, 1973). Some degree of internalization—or support (Wallerstein, 1986)—has been shown to be a necessary and a mutative factor in every form of psychoanalysis as well as psychotherapy (see, for example, Gabbard & Westen, 2003). It is, I believe, this assumption that most threatens modern conflict theorists and forces them to disregard the implications of what they know or to sharply define the boundaries of psychoanalysis and psychotherapy so that the gold of psychoanalysis will remain uncontaminated by psychotherapeutic factors. Thus Arlow (1981) writes that focusing on development and on what are commonly (and inaccurately) termed pre-Oedipal factors will lead to a failed attempt at a replacement therapy.

How, then, does modern conflict theory deal with structural difficulty? There are several related responses. One, as we have seen, is to deny such difficulty and to assert that what seems to be structural difficulty can be understood as the product of conflict. As Busch (2005) writes, "… conflict as the result of internal processes *only* was promulgated in awkward ways through the 1980s …" (p. 31, italics in original). Another response is to acknowledge such a difficulty but to de-emphasize it in analysis. Kaplan (1984), for example, says that we are best off focusing on what psychoanalysis does best—analysis of conflict—rather than broadening our emphasis to considerations that will lead us away from our therapeutic strength. Abend (2005) states this a bit differently, but in a way that leads to a similar therapeutic strategy. He writes:

> Those of us who subscribe to the view that the analysis of instinctual conflicts, and of the compromise formations to which they give rise, is the centerpiece of psychoanalytic therapy look on the infinite variability of our patients' individual mental qualities as most significant *insofar as they lend particular shape and color to the fate of their important instinctual conflicts*. Although we cannot fail to notice the effects of those qualities on our patients' lives, for better and for worse, we believe that the analytic task is to try to understand and modulate the disadvantageous outcome of conflicts (p. 13, italics in original).

Finally, some modern conflict theorists, exemplified by Brenner (1982), have tended to disregard what we have learned from working with patients of the widening scope, by asserting that these are data obtained from psychotherapy rather than psychoanalysis.

The analyst's role in modern conflict theory

I have emphasized the minimalist focus of modern conflict theory, as originally developed by Arlow and Brenner, because it is precisely the specific and narrow focus of this theory of aetiology—of what is wrong with a patient, any patient—that has led to a specific, narrow, and sharply defined focus on what is necessary to "cure" a patient and then to the optimal analyst's role. Brenner, and most modern conflict theorists, see "cure" as unattainable. What is attainable are more adaptive compromise formations. It is the patient's insight into how his or her mind works that leads to more adaptive compromise formations. Given this single mutative factor, the analyst's role is clear: to structure a psychoanalytic situation that will facilitate the emergence of unconscious conflict and defence in as clear a manner as possible and to then interpret this unconscious material with the patient. There are, of course, differences in approach between classical analysts, and I will be discussing developments in modern conflict theory following Arlow and Brenner's contributions, but I cannot over-emphasize the influence of Arlow, Brenner, and their colleagues on how a "classical" analysis has been defined, along with the prescribed and proscribed role for the analyst in such an analysis.

"Classical" analysts have traditionally been suspicious of the analyst's influence on their patient, on the mutative aspects of the analyst-patient object relationship, especially internalization of the analyst, and of what they have considered "transference cure" (a presumed result of this internalization). That concern has continued through the thinking of modern conflict theory innovators such as Paul Gray (1987, 1991). He argues that even if a patient believes that his analyst likes him, this belief must be challenged. This belief, one should understand, is not viewed as primitive idealization (a defence against trusting and working with the analyst). The belief may be accurate. It may come from an atmosphere of safety in the analysis and it may facilitate the patient's communicating difficult material. Still this belief must be challenged and analysed. Gray believes that to the extent that a patient feels emboldened to share conflicted thoughts because he believes that his analyst will not condemn him, the patient is using a transference fantasy to sidestep experiencing his own (now projected) internal unconscious superego conflict about expressing that piece of uncomfortable thought. If this transference fantasy—a fantasy that facilitates the patient's expressing uncomfortable feelings and thoughts—is not challenged and understood, the patient is seen as missing an opportunity to fully understand his mind in conflict. Any part of psychoanalysis, then, that relies on un-understood patient-analyst experience, on non-verbal data (such as enactment or the analyst's unconscious thoughts, feelings, or reveries), and, especially, that allows for unanalysed internalization, is seen as psychotherapeutic rather than psychoanalytic because it bypasses a patient's insight into his unconscious mind. It is this insight that leads to structural change and that is presumed to have the most lasting effects.

Given this belief in what is most mutative in psychoanalysis, the analyst's optimal role assumes a narrow understanding of the psychoanalytic situation. Traditional concepts such as free association, neutrality, the psychoanalytic frame, transference, countertransference, and interpretation are understood in their most restricted way (Adler & Bachant, 1996; Busch, 1995). The analyst's role is expressed most succinctly and evocatively by Tarachow

(1962), who coined the term "therapeutic barrier" to describe the relationship between patient and analyst that defines psychoanalysis as opposed to psychotherapy. Through the therapeutic barrier, "... the *real* situation is transformed into an *as if* situation ..." (p. 379, italics in original). Tarachow adds: "The difference is that in psychotherapy the real events are treated as *a reality*, while in analysis they are treated as expressions of the patient's fantasies and as determined by the inevitable needs of his solutions of his unconscious conflicts ... . The critical concern is the status and function of the relationship between therapist and patient. If it is taken as real, then the symptoms and life events are also taken as real, and both therapist and patient turn their backs on the unconscious fantasies and anxieties. If the real relationship is set aside, then both therapist and patient turn towards an understanding and working through of the unconscious fantasies" (p. 378, italics in original).

Maintaining this sort of situation is difficult and imposes a burden of loneliness on the analyst. Tarachow is quite serious about this. He writes: "Loneliness is not to be regarded in a naïve sense. A casual remark about the weather breaks the loneliness and establishes real object relationship" (1962, p. 381). It is, perhaps, relevant to our discussion that Tarachow, in the same paper, writes that this "rigorous conception of the ideal therapeutic relationship" is only partially accurate, cannot be "experienced as sharply as I put it here", and leaves out other important aspects of the relationship such as the "real relationship" which is a major aspect of the analysis (1962, p. 383; see also Druck, 1989). We see this often in modern conflict theorists—an elegant, clearly-formulated theory turns out to have many parenthetically-stated or unstated exceptions whose theoretical implications are never elaborated but which prove that the original elegant theory is overly simplistic when applied to actual clinical experience.

Let us return to our original three questions. We have discussed thus far: "What is wrong with the patient." It is conflict organized around repression—as opposed to what Kris (1985) has termed "divergent" conflict, or what analysts such as Kernberg (1975) and Bromberg (1994) have considered as dissociation (or splitting) of self and object units. The "cure" is presented as the patient having insight into how he defends against drive derivatives based on unconscious fears that date back to childhood and can now be given up as they are affectively recognized. As the patient realizes how his past lives in, and narrows, his present, he is able to tolerate more aspects of the elements in unconscious conflict, and his compromise formations become more adaptive. The analyst is the medium through which the patient's ego is able to negotiate intrapsychic change. I stress that it is the synthetic function of the ego that is seen as the agent of change, through insight provided by the analyst. The analyst, then, is expected to stay as much out of the "real" field as possible. Thus he or she is expected to listen neutrally to what the patient says from all aspects of mental functioning (equidistant from the ego, id, and superego), so as not to identify with one aspect of the conflict and influence the patient's resolution in one direction or another. Neutrality and abstinence are seen as protecting the patient's autonomy and individuality and as providing an analytic frame in which the patient's idiosyncratic construction of the world can emerge.

Concepts such as a "working alliance" as reflecting a "real" (i.e., non-transferential) relationship between patient and analyst have been successfully challenged, primarily in a classic paper by Brenner (1979). However, Brenner's paper speaks to the question of separating "real" and "transferential" elements of this relationship. It does not address questions such as why a patient comes to analysis and listens to the analyst as he or she challenges basic assumptions of a patient's internal world. What keeps him going? This question has been at the heart of analysis since Freud's time (Friedman, 1969) and has never been successfully addressed because discussion of a *real* closeness between patient and analyst works against classical psychoanalysis, which is interested in seeing how a patient turns a relatively anonymous analyst into part of his or her internal fantasy world. Bringing into consideration those aspects of the patient-analyst relationship that are relatively "real" leads to questions about the analyst's influence and about transference cure. The patient-analyst relationship becomes more complicated, muddy, and less "scientific".

To focus on the "real" events in an analysis *as real*, to look at a patient's structural weakness *as such* makes more difficult a focus on the patient's idiosyncratic moulding of these events, given his or her structural strengths and weaknesses. The analyst's concentration on unconscious conflict leads to suspicion of "reality" interactions and consideration of these as manifest content. The analyst prefers to understand what these interactions *really mean*, that is, what is their unconscious meaning. "Cure" via internalization bypasses the patient's full awareness of all elements of the mind in conflict. Gray (1987, 1991) and Levy and Inderbitzen (1997) are especially sensitive to these "transferences of authority" (Gray, 1987). Attempts by the analyst to establish a climate of safety in which the patient feels more comfortable speaking (by, for example, empathic remarks or modifications in the analyst's posture) are seen as attempts to bypass transference concerns. The analytic situation is, paradoxically, seen as inherently unsafe (Levy & Inderbitzen, 1997) because it provides the patient with the anxiety-filled opportunity to explore dangerous and feared aspects of his or her mind and to put into play adult conflicted capacities. The analyst optimally establishes "safety" through the interpretation of defence rather than through attempts at a "working alliance" (Zetzel, 1956; Greenson, 1965; Brenner, 1979). The de-emphasis on "reality" cuts two ways. Brenner (1979) writes that whatever the analyst's actual behaviour towards his patient, it is only the patient's idiosyncratic transference reaction that is important and needs to be considered. Further, to the extent that the patient, because of structural difficulty, may require more than interpretation from the analyst, then this is considered to be a transference wish more than a structural need (Pine, 1979; Akhtar, 2000). Thus the analyst's role—what he attends to, how he responds and, perhaps as important, does not respond—is closely determined by theoretical assumptions about aetiology and what is mutative.

While all Freudian analysts see insight through interpretation of transference as a crucial mutative element in analysis, to some extent interpretation is both idealized and taken out of its analytic context by modern conflict analysts. They tend to disregard the underlying analytic atmosphere and analytic connection that make it possible for an analyst to conceive of certain insights and interpretations and for the patient to consider them when they are offered. To the extent that an analysis, any analysis, rides on an underlying patient-analyst connection, one that has been discussed in different ways by many analysts including Akhtar (2000), Bach (1985, 2006), Jacobs (1991a, 1997, 1999), Katz (1998), Kohut (1971), and Ogden (1991, 1994), then an interpretation and its effects cannot be considered without simultaneous consideration of the analytic atmosphere within which the interpretation is made and that interpretation's effect on the patient-analyst relationship as well as on the interplay of unconscious mental elements. The way, for example, an interpretation is both empathic and distancing, simultaneously gratifying and frustrating, the way in which it encourages and also titrates regression and transference development, the way that it may reflect a mutative interaction that has already taken place as well as opening the path for a different kind of analytic relationship—all these issues and others make interpreting a complex interaction, one that cannot be viewed as only (or even primarily) conveying content (insight) from one person to another.

One last criticism remains to be made about "classic" modern conflict theory. Several key aspects of modern conflict theory, including its emphasis on verbal material from the patient, its emphasis on Oedipal conflict, its de-emphasis (and fear of) therapeutic regression and of the mutative aspects of the patient-analyst relationship, and its theoretical insistence that every manifest complaint by a patient is to be understood as a symptom and to be interpreted from this viewpoint, have led many patients to leave their analyses feeling that they did not go "deep" enough, that what are considered pre-Oedipal issues such as feelings of emptiness, inauthenticity, identity difficulties, and narcissistic issues, were not adequately grappled with and were instead interpreted and organized by the analyst upwards into more verbal and theoretically acceptable Oedipal material. Such patients have often reported leaving analysis feeling criticized (Silverman, 1984) by the analyst's interpretive focus. They view it as implicitly or explicitly insisting that the patient accept reality. That is, they respond to the focus, ultimately, on their reality testing rather than on their experience of themselves and of "reality" as a subjective creation.

Recent developments in modern conflict theory

I have stressed the minimalist focus of modern conflict theory, in its understanding of the interacting variables in compromise formation and in its conception of the patient-analyst relationship. With regard to the former, modern conflict theory (dare I call it *modern* modern conflict theory?) has become more integrative. It accommodates a greater variety of elements in the interplay of intrapsychic conflict and compromise formation and in the analyst-patient relationship. Busch (2005) writes: "The contemporary clinician would find it difficult to understand his patients without a conceptualization of unconscious conflicts between and among object representations, self-representations, self object representations, and so on. Such an understanding indicates that we have come a fair way from the time when true conflict was thought to occur only in the Oedipal phase, and only between particular agencies in the mind fueled by energy sources" (p. 30). There are many conflicted variables in addition to sexual and aggressive drive derivatives; there are other types of dysphoric affect in addition to anxiety and depressive affect such as annihilation anxiety (Hurvich, 2003), and these affects vary in amplitude and in disruptive effect (signal anxiety as compared with panic anxiety, for example); there are more primitive forms of defence such as defences organized around splitting and part-object relationships (Kernberg, 1975); and the superego has a much more complex role in unconscious functioning than primarily as a conveyor of unconscious guilt.

With regard to the patient-analyst relationship, several analysts have given greater consideration to the analyst's subjectivity. By "subjectivity" I am referring to several interrelated issues: who a particular analyst is vis-à-vis his or her "theoretical" orientation as he or she decides on a technical approach to a given patient (Akhtar, 2000); how a given analyst attends to his inner thoughts and feelings as a source of data about his patient, in what can be described as an expanded view of countertransference (Jacobs, 1999, 2001a; Smith, 2000); how a particular patient-analyst experience has an informative effect (Sandler, 1976; Jacobs, 1997; Katz, 1998; Smith, 2006); and how particular patient-analyst experiences in themselves, along with (and underpinning) insight through interpretation, have a mutative effect. Modern conflict theory has traditionally not acknowledged the analyst's subjectivity in these ways, and has certainly not explored its implications for the psychoanalytic process.

There has been a great deal written within the Freudian corpus (for space reasons, I am not including here relational writers) on the analyst's relationship to his theory as he or she makes technical choices. It has become clear that an analyst does not dispassionately choose a theory based on evidence, nor does he make his technical choices based primarily on his theoretical framework. Lasky (1993) has discussed how our character influences the theory we choose. Eisold (1994) has emphasized the role of theory in supporting professional and group identities. Rothstein (2002) has shown how decisions about analysability can be affected more by the consultant's countertransference than by "objective" assessment.

Jacobs (2001a) has discussed how the analyst can make what appear to be "correct" technical decisions that are also countertransference enactments. Finally, Fonagy (2003) has written about how we can make differing inferences and clinical "rules" based on the same theoretical overview. Fonagy argues against the idea that there is a tight connection between our theory and our technique. He writes: "… it has been impossible to achieve any kind of one-to-one mapping between therapeutic technique and theoretical frameworks. Interestingly, it is as easy to illustrate how the same theory can generate different techniques as how the same technique is justified by different theories" (pp. 25–26).

While the traditional Freudian conception of the neutral abstinent analyst has been challenged from outside Freudian theory (and while this relational challenge has undoubtedly forced consideration of this issue within Freudian psychoanalysis), I want to stress that one major challenge to the analyst's objectivity has come from modern conflict theorists. Boesky (1990) writes how resistance is:

> the joint creation of patient and analyst in a number of instances that are not necessarily a manifestation of a disadvantageous countertransference. I do not refer to all resistances, nor do I suggest that the analyst creates the transference. I am referring to certain forms of resistance to which the analyst inadvertently contributes in every successful analysis as an unavoidable expression of the essential emotional participation of the analyst in the interactional definition of the psychoanalytic process which I favor. I consider the "purity" of a theoretic analytic treatment, in which all of the resistances are created only by the patient, to be a fiction. If the analyst does not get emotionally involved sooner or later in a manner that he had not intended, the analysis will not proceed to a successful conclusion (p. 573).

Jacobs (1991a), speaking of an analysis' opening phase, writes:

> Reacting spontaneously with responses that inevitably include a mix of some personal as well as more objective elements, the analyst uses his intuitive understanding of the patient's present state of mind and character to make unconscious adjustments in his technique … the messages sent and received by patient

and analyst as they begin to work together and enter upon the initial period of mutual exploration that becomes the basis for the establishment of an unspoken contract that goes beyond formal arrangements or technical procedures. Certain rules and limits are established and certain values communicated. Moreover each party discovers a good deal about the other (p. 12).

Greenberg (1995) (not a modern conflict theorist) has illustrated how both the patient's and the analyst's personal characterological predilections affect the analytic ambience in what Greenberg terms the "therapeutic matrix". He writes: "… in the final analysis, the interactive matrix—not the psychoanalyst's textbook—is the crucible within which technical procedures are forged (p. 21).

Another challenge to the idea of an "objective" analyst has emerged from modern conflict theory itself. Rothstein (2005) discusses how Brenner's (1994) belief that all mental functioning is based on more or less adaptive kinds of compromise formations has challenged the idea of the objective analyst. To the extent that nobody is ever completely rational and objective, one inevitably encounters two subjective beings in the psychoanalytic situation, both of whose mental functioning is based on an ever-shifting balance of unconscious factors. This inevitably affects analyst-patient interaction. Rothstein (2005) stresses the "shaping" effect of the analyst's "personality" on the patient's transference.

While Rothstein's contribution is important in outlining how the analyst's subjectivity is a natural outgrowth of modern conflict theory, his equating the analyst's subjectivity with the analyst's countertransference betrays a certain developmental lag. It is true that Freudian analysts have repeatedly used a broad definition of countertransference as a way to discuss the analyst's character and subjectivity as it contributes to the evolving psychoanalytic situation. Still, the term "countertransference" implies some degree of pathology (distortion in the analyst's optimal role due to the interference of unconscious factors). The term "subjectivity" seems a bit more neutral, avoiding pathological implications and indicating that the analyst's subjectivity is an expectable, integral, and necessary aspect of optimal listening and responding. Smith (2004) uses the term "subjectivity" in just this way, as he writes the following:

> I want to comment that some who have read earlier versions of this paper have felt that I am describing an analyst who works from too "subjective" a point of view, while others, by contrast, are puzzled by my continuing use of what they see as the more "objective" model of conflict and compromise ... . I would suggest that subjective and objective aspects of analytic listening can and do coexist harmoniously both on different levels of clinical theory and in the mind of the analyst at work ... . The model of conflict and compromise, as it applies to the patient, reveals a rich intrapsychic life in all its particularities, which is our primary focus. Apply the same model to the mind of the analyst, however, and we discover the continuous interaction of two intrapsychic lives at a degree of complexity that can only be described as "radically subjective", ... one that functions both as a fundamental underpinning of the work and a source of considerable data. Whether this data is accessed through the compromise formations we observe on the surface of the patient's material and infer in its depths, or through the subjective reveries of the analyst, our ultimate goal is the further definition of the unconscious life of the patient (p. 650).

As the number of variables included in the process of unconscious conflict and compromise formation has broadened, as we recognize ubiquitous subjectivity in the way we listen (Smith, 2000), as we see that experienced Freudian analysts attend to different factors in the way they listen, as we see that we may be enacting countertransference issues even while making the "correct" technical response (Jacobs, 2001a), as we learn more about unconscious communication through action and enactment (Sandler, 1976; Katz, 1998; Smith, 2006), our perspective on the analyst's role has broadened. Our understanding of what it means to think about unconscious conflict and compromise has changed considerably, so much that earlier formulations by Arlow and Brenner seem hopelessly dated. We have moved from Arlow (1969), who wrote that every unconscious object representation must ultimately be understood from a drive perspective, to Brenner, who limited the factors implicated in unconscious conflict, to analysts such as Smith, Jacobs, and others, who certainly look for, and analyse, unconscious conflict, but whose focus on examining everything from the sole perspective of four variables in unconscious conflict seems less intense. Busch (2005), a major contributor to modern conflict theory and to a developed theory focusing on analysis of defence, concludes a paper by stating that "... the analyst of today might best be known as the 'contemporary Freudian, countertransferentially aware, self psychological, relationally interested, Kleinian- inspired, ego psychologist'" (p. 43).

I may have given the impression that modern conflict theory has evolved from the insightful contributions of Arlow and Brenner to a commonly held broader view of modern conflict theory. This impression would be wrong. Abend (2007) has insightfully and cogently discussed the range and clash of opinions within the Freudian "mainstream" today. He asserts that the more traditional approach within modern conflict theory is most preferable and he argues against many of the propositions that I have been discussing. Abend supports the approach discussed by Arlow and Brenner, which focuses on the patient acquiring insight into his unconscious fantasies and inner mental life via analysis of his transference onto an abstinent and neutral analyst. An example of Abend's (2002) thinking:

> A sharp division exists between those analysts who are convinced that relational distortions resulting from early, even preverbal developmental difficulties can be correctively influenced by the very nature of the new relationship that forms between patient and analyst, and those who question this fundamental premise. As one of the latter group, I see this relational emphasis as consistent with the long-standing historical trend to deemphasize the central importance to analysis of sexual and aggressive conflicts in favor of increased attention to pre-Oedipal developmental issues. To some analysts, including many in the expanded mainstream, this shift is an advantageous advance in analytic understanding, while others of us still hold to Freud's revolutionary focus on the complex consequences of the Oedipal period on both normal and pathological human development (p. 1433).

If modern conflict theory can be compared to a religion, then Arlow, Brenner, Abend, and others would be "orthodox" practitioners, while Boesky, Smith, and Jacobs are from the "reform" wing, accepting the overall rubric but less committed to the minimalist drive and

Oedipal-dominated premises of Arlow and Brenner. They are more open to integrating influences from other aspects of psychoanalytic theory. These later conflict theorists are interested in how the analyst's subjectivity influences his or her diagnostic formulations, his or her listening, and the overall unfolding of the psychoanalytic process. They are more connected to Arlow and Brenner than to relational or Kleinian theory, but they are open to influence from these perspectives. Perhaps their most important innovation, as a group, is to consider how the analyst's subjectivity can be used to increase sensitivity to aspects of non-verbal communication in the analytic hour and, then, to bring more material into the interpretive mix. Thus they look at the mix of "reality" and "transference" within both patient and analyst and in the analytic field. The patient-analyst relationship in all its verbal and non-verbal complexity takes on a much greater focus than it had years ago.

None of these considerations fundamentally alters the traditional paradigm of change in psychoanalysis. The analyst's role is still fundamentally interpretive and the major mutative role remains insight into all aspects of the patient-analyst experience, an experience that, in itself, may also contain mutative aspects. However, with all this, what these analysts do *not* consider is the role of the patient-analyst experience in structural maintenance and growth. It is only within what I am calling "modern structural theory" that there is a theoretical reason to consider this aspect of the patient-analyst experience. This brings us to another challenge to modern conflict theory, that of patients in the "widening scope" who have not fully developed structural capabilities. Even if we choose to accept that unconscious conflict and compromise is ubiquitous, what happens to this process when the assumed structural context for this process is flawed? How does conflict within a psychic structure that is compromised affect an analysis, including the analyst's role? I will discuss this issue in the following chapter.

Note

1. The author would like to thank Beverly Goldsmith Druck and Gil Katz for their helpful comments on this paper.

CHAPTER TWO

Modern structural theory

Andrew B. Druck[1]

I have discussed modern conflict theory and its emphasis on unconscious conflict and compromise. Some of the difficulties with this focus revolve around its narrow definition of aetiology (*only* conflict and compromise between four narrowly-defined variables), its narrow view of mutative effect (insight into the dynamics of an already developed inner world) and its narrow view of the analyst's role (receiver of transference distortions and interpreter of them). I have stated that one major challenge to this position revolves around the question of what happens to conflict in an inner world that is not fully developed. Under these circumstances, is there a change in the analyst's optimal posture? A second major challenge, then, one that follows from the first, revolves around differing conceptions of the patient-analyst experience. This takes many forms, from the effect of this experience on establishing and maintaining a patient's reflective capacity, to how the analyst uses non-verbal data that he or she receives (often through awareness of countertransference affect or enactments), to questions regarding the mutative role of this experience.

Responses to these questions have shaped a contemporary Freudian emphasis that I will attempt to describe. This overview is meant to provide an overall integrative context for the contributions of many analysts. (Relational analysts have made important contributions to these issues and have probably influenced the direction of contemporary Freudian theory, but these are beyond the purview of my topic.) While modern conflict theory is relatively easy to name and describe because of its sharp focus, what I am calling "modern structural theory" is more difficult to name and characterize. I have tried to be inclusive, looking for what is common in different emphases of what Busch (2006) terms "... an unrecognized force within contemporary psychoanalysis" where different writers are "... integrating trends from a variety of psychoanalytic schools into what I would call an expanded Freudian clinical theory" (pp. 83–84). What seems central in all these emphases is a developmental focus, and belief in some form of internalization as crucial in the evolution of an inner world and inner structure.

While most of those whom I will describe essentially share a common focus, some choose a general term to describe this Freudian approach, for example, "the American Middle School" (Chodorow, 2003), or "intersubjective ego psychology" (Chodorow, 2004). Others use a general term, but pair it with another to highlight the contrast between this overall emphasis and modern conflict theory, for example, the "right wing" and "left wing" of Freudian psychoanalysis (Druck, 1989); the "classical" and "romantic" points of view (Strenger, 1989; 1997; Akhtar, 2000). Others focus on the patient-analyst relationship and highlight it in terms such as "self and object Freudians" (Ellman, 2005). The term I am proposing, "modern structural theory", focuses on the constant interplay and effect of the patient-analyst relationship on structural capacities at any given moment. "Modern structural theory" is a term originally used by Boesky (1990, p. 556) in a different context. Since Brenner (1994) has abandoned structural theory, the term is open for use and it fits my focus.

There are difficulties with this overall term. Many analysts who I would consider as working within "modern structural theory" would object to the emphasis on structure. They believe that the emphasis on the "self" and its vulnerabilities (Kohut, 1971, 1977) and the sense of authenticity (Winnicott, 1965a, 1975) are more experience-near. I agree. It is clinically useful to think in terms of shifts in self and object states. Another possible objection to the term "modern structural theory" is that it is too evocative of ego psychology, that it is, in fact, a continuation of ego psychology. While ego psychology began to address many of the issues discussed by modern structural theorists (Bellak, Hurvich & Gediman, 1973; Blanck & Blanck, 1974, 1979; Knight, 1953; Schlesinger, 1969; Wallerstein, 2002, as examples discussed in Druck, 1989), these theorists did not directly address problems such as a sense of emptiness, inauthenticity, false self, or narcissistic difficulties. These are issues of the self that may be better understood within a theory of the self and its development. They are not as easily formulated within a structural framework, although Pine (1988) has demonstrated that it can be done. Ego psychologists also advocated a precision in their conceptualization of analytic work that did not fully appreciate the analyst's global role in internalization and its overall impact on ego and superego functioning. While ego psychologists attempted precise interventions and precise modulation of the analytic relationship to shore up what they perceived as ego or superego difficulties and attempted to limit full transference development and analysis (this was almost the definition of what made a treatment psychotherapeutic and supportive), modern structural theorists see a global attachment and internalization process in the context of a more complete transference regression as effecting change. Here too, I agree with the more contemporary formulations. What I will attempt to describe differs significantly from the 1950s ego psychology.

Still, all that said, "modern structural theory" is a broader and more integrative term than a term focused almost exclusively on object relations and the self. These latter terms sometimes neglect consideration of intrapsychic conflict and of factors less directly connected to vicissitudes of the self. If modern conflict theory can become "conflict-only", then some variations of the approach I attempt to describe run the risk of becoming "self and object relations only". Some major influences on this approach, particularly those from Kohut and self psychology, minimize the aetiological role of internally generated intrapsychic conflict so much that, for all intents and purposes, they do not consider it at all. While they are sensitive and brilliant at describing narcissistic experience and narcissistic transferences, their understanding of aggression as largely a form of narcissistic rage or disruption of the self precipitated by an analyst's misattunement seems to leave out a major aspect of the human condition, that of internally generated intrapsychic conflict. Following Pine (1988), I believe "psychologies" of self experiences can be integrated within the broad rubric of conflict and deficit, without losing the diagnostic and dynamic sensitivity that a broad structural approach provides.

I also find that the term "structure" provides a way of discussing more precisely the many areas of psychic functioning that develop well or poorly. While terms that emphasize the self focus on a framework that emphasizes differences from classical psychoanalysis, this term maintains continuity with recent developments in modern conflict theory and easily integrates influences from disparate points of view such as those of contemporary Kleinians, self psychologists, and some modern conflict theorists.

As I begin, I would like to state that the views expressed in this paper are mine alone and not the consensus of all four editors. Second, I am aware that, in attempting this synthetic overview, I am casting a wide net. I emphasize points of possible convergence between many differing points of view and I do not mention major differences in their approach. My point is to demonstrate how these different points of view *can* be integrated into an overarching set of assumptions. In this effort I follow the model of relational theory, which integrates many approaches that are, in important ways, in conflict with each other, in order to emphasize a shared outlook.

Deficit and conflict

My argument can be stated as follows. First, not everyone has fully developed psychic structure. Many of our patients have *demonstrable* structural deficits (Pine, 1974; Akhtar, 2000). Second, conflict, in one form or another, is ubiquitous, even in patients with deficits. Third, it then becomes important to understand what happens to intrapsychic conflict when the structural context for compromise formation is itself compromised in a major way. Finally, most analysts who accept the idea of developmental deficit (whether or not they use the term "deficit") see structural development occurring as a function of the patient-analyst relationship, in tandem with insight.[2] Internalization and the analytic experience move to a greater place of importance.

I use the term "structural deficit" to refer to an aspect of mental functioning that is fragile or lacking in a patient (Pine, 1974, 1994; Druck, 1998). There are many examples of deficits. Some of these have been discussed by ego psychologists, including difficulties with fluid ego boundaries and reality testing, difficulties in capacity for libidinal object constancy, capacity for signal anxiety, capacity for signal guilt (Modell, 1965), and capacity for stable reality testing. Others stem from the findings of Kohut and self psychology, including difficulties in capacity for optimal self esteem regulation (Kohut, 1971, 1977), capacity for evocative memory and for holding introjects (Adler & Buie, 1979), and capacity for shifting between viewing oneself as a self and as an object (Bach, 1994). Winnicott and the British Middle School have emphasized the difficulties of a "false self" versus an authentic sense of self (Winnicott, 1965a, 1975; Balint, 1968). While all these stem from different traditions and frameworks, they can be understood as aspects of "normal" drive, ego, and superego development (or, using a different framework, development of the self and its capacities) that generally develop fully and optimally in the interplay of child and parent (Jacobson, 1964; Mahler, Pine & Bergmann, 1975). Thus I am including under this rubric phenomena emphasized by different schools of psychoanalytic thought—or, as Pine (1988) might point out, different "psychologies". All, however, see psychic (structural, self) development as an integral goal of psychoanalytic work and all see this as occurring through the analyst-patient relationship. Further, all see the presumed "deficit" as being an ongoing state of the patient, rather than a symptom that is the product of underlying variables in conflict and which may be ameliorated by correct interpretations of this unconscious conflict.

When I speak of deficits, I am not negating the ubiquity or importance of internal conflict. I want to emphasize that the patient's "deficit" is not simply that the patient "lacks" the capacity in question. The deficit may be variable and result from dynamic factors, such as unconscious anger at the analyst for "abandoning" him, in combination with developmental lacks. Thus deficits are part of a constantly shifting internal *process*. The structural regression that we often see is highly variable and fluid and often dependent on the patient's experience of a positive internal connection with his or her analyst. The patient's attempt to "hold" and to be held by an internal image of someone, to maintain a consistent positively cathected self or object representation is something that is tenuous and that he or she may fail to maintain in the face of increased internal conflict pressure. *Whatever the aetiological reason*, the patient cannot hold this internal conflict with relatively adaptive compromise formations. Instead, he or she regresses structurally—what Freud (1900, p. 548) termed "formal" regression—becoming more concrete (for example, seeking actual contact rather than maintaining an inner symbolic representation of the absent object) and more indiscriminate (any object may suffice).

It is the interplay between inner conflict and structural difficulty that concerns me here. My emphasis moves from the process of intrapsychic conflict to the context in which this process of conflict and compromise takes place. As Loewald (1966) writes, "... the role of defense and conflict is justifiably a center of attention in any psychoanalytic consideration, theoretical as well as clinical. But the more we advance in our understanding of psychoanalytic problems, the more, I believe, we become impressed with the importance of deeper problems of deficiency and deformation of the psychic structures themselves, over and above the problems of conflict between the structures and defenses against it" (p. 435).

For diagnostic purposes, it is not the conflict itself that is crucial. Rather, it is the patient's capacity, at a given moment in time, to tolerate that conflict, to be able to maintain structural attributes such as separation of self and object, signal anxiety, signal guilt, and higher-level defences in the face of internal conflict. To put it differently, adequate development of psychological structure becomes the defining trait of neurosis; it is not conflict, which is found at every level of development (Druck, 1998).

The concept of unconscious conflict, in which drive derivatives, dysphoric affects, defensive attempts, and superego concerns continually affect each other and lead to shifting compromise formations (Brenner, 1982), views its four mental components as relatively discrete elements of the mind in conflict. These are the independent variables of the mind, and what they lead to—any other psychic phenomenon—is understood as a symptom, a result of these variables in unconscious conflict. However, each of these variables is itself affected by the overall structural context. In a patient who has not reached the capacity for signal anxiety, for example, a disruptive stimulus, internally or externally induced, brings about annihilation anxiety (Hurvich, 2003), which leads to more massive, blunt, and maladaptive defences. Moreover, the impulses themselves are experienced as more peremptory and global, and thus more threatening. A conflicted wish for sexual contact in the context of a neurotic structure becomes experienced, in a patient with less well-developed structure, as a conflicted and self-threatening pull and force towards merger. Or, as Kernberg (1975) notes, the sexual urge may reflect a patient's attempt at an "upward" displacement, a sexually-experienced and contact-dominated wish for emotional or interpersonal contact or experience, or self-definition, or to shore up a fragmenting self state. One can only experience oneself or others physically and concretely, through touch and sex. I could elaborate further (see Druck, 1998), but, for the moment, my point is that we cannot consider conflict and compromise formation without simultaneously considering that person's level of structural development. Conflict and compromise are affected by this structural context, both in the ultimate compromise and also in the way each of the variables in this process of conflict and compromise is itself shaped and experienced. In the same way, we cannot consider a particular deficit, without simultaneously considering how it is affected by inevitable intrapsychic conflict. (This is to understand the matter broadly; there are many patients who cannot experience themselves as separate objects. For them, intrapsychic conflict cannot be contained and experienced as coming from their own self and inevitably is experienced as located, at least partially, in another person.) These theoretical considerations lead to a clinical stance that considers a patient's conflicts—for example, the role of drives and defences against them—not only in its own right but also in the larger context of building and maintaining structural (or self) coherence. This, then, is one way to understand the constant interplay of internal unconscious intrapsychic conflict within a psychic context where full development has not occurred.

Despite the contention of modern conflict theorists, understanding and interpreting the patient's actions in this situation as due to *only* intrapsychic conflict (whether from a "classical" or Kleinian point of view) often proves insufficient and can severely alienate a patient who is subject to *only* interpretations of this sort. While the patient's difficulties can be understood in various ways, one aspect that must be included and communicated to the patient is the patient's attempts at finding, in a flailing manner, an adaptive solution to what is, to him or her, a "real" and (psychologically) life-threatening problem. For example, with "neurotic patients", who, by definition, have a developed structural psychic system, the analyst may look at unconscious conflict around aggressive drive derivatives with the goal of modifying too strict compromise formations and permitting more access to these derivatives and to their associated sequelae, such as assertiveness, ambition, and other traits that can be inhibited by conflicts around aggression. In patients where structure has not been fully developed, aggressive drive derivatives may destroy fragile holding mental representations of the object, so that to be angry with the analyst leads to the patient feeling alone, panicked, or affectively dead. In other situations, aggression against the analyst can serve to strengthen or re-create fragile boundaries between patient and analyst or to accompany nascent attempts at separation and individuation. Here the analyst's task is not to "interpret" defences to these (barely) unconscious aggressive drive derivatives, because doing so decreases the patient's global attempts at achieving structural coherence and leads to further regression. It is preferable for the analyst to acknowledge to himself the necessary adaptive aspects of these drive derivatives and either to remain silent or to say something that acknowledges and accepts the adaptive aspect of the patient's aggression. As part of this process, it becomes important to communicate to the patient that what the patient is actually saying, the manifest content, the patient's perspective, is heard and taken seriously in its own right, rather than as material to be interpreted for its latent content and "real" meaning (Arlow, 1995; Schwaber, 1998).

There is, perhaps, also a more complex way to understand the interaction between conflict and deficit. Loewald (1951) writes as follows:

> In the formation of the ego, the libido does not turn to objects which, so to speak, lie ready for it, waiting to be turned to. In the developmental process, reality, at first without boundaries against an ego, later in magical communication with it, becomes objective at last. As the ego goes through its transformations from primitive beginnings, so libido and reality go through stages of transformation, until the ego, to the extent to which

it is "fully developed", has an objective reality, detached from itself, before it, not in it, yet holding this reality to itself in the ego's synthetic activity. Then the ego's libido has become object relationship. Only then does the ego live in what we call an objective reality. In earlier stages of ego-formation the ego does not experience reality as objective, but lives in and experiences the various stages of narcissistic and magical reality (p. 18).

Loewald is pointing out that one's experience of reality is not a constant, but that it shifts with development. Experience of reality changes with the child's evolving experience of object relationships. We know this from a cognitive point of view, as Piaget (Flavell, 1963) and others have taught us, but Loewald stresses this from an experiential point of view. Not only is one's experience of an "objective" reality a developmental achievement; it is subject to regressive shifts at times of conflict, as well as lacunae, such as superstitions. We have also learned this from the contributions of Winnicott, Mahler, Jacobson, and Kohut, who, along with Loewald, form the parents and major intellectual trailblazers of what I am terming "modern structural theory".

From this perspective, it is not only the internal structural context of intrapsychic conflict that must be taken into account; it is the manner in which one's experience of reality constantly shifts in tandem with these "internal" vicissitudes. When we acknowledge the common clinical observation that experiences of a positive connection with one's analyst increase one's ego and superego capacities (defined broadly to also include a more vivid and authentic sense of self), we are also asserting that one's experience of oneself, of others, and of the world itself constantly shifts depending on one's experience of connection to internal loving and affirming object representations. The song "When you're smiling, the whole world smiles with you" (Fisher, Goodwin & Shay, 1950) is not only addressing an interpersonal truth. It may be heard as reflecting how one's subjective experience of the world, one's state of being mirrors one's internal affective state. We are inevitably led to consideration of an intersubjective dimension of treatment. It is not only the analyst who is experienced by the patient; the environment within which patient and analyst are situated shifts in affective tone in line with shifts in patient and analyst. This is similar to an unconscious group process dynamic and is one way of understanding Ogden's concept (1994) of the analytic third. Processes such as splitting and projective identification—stressed by Klein and modern Kleinians— which are defences and communications that assume permeable boundaries between patient and analyst, and which are saturated with affect that permeates a room, become important aspects of this intersubjective environment. Analytic interventions suggested by Bion and Winnicott, such as containment and holding, become crucial, non-verbal therapeutic interventions in this affectively charged, highly porous therapeutic atmosphere. The analyst as provider of an environment becomes a crucial aspect of an optimal analytic stance in helping patients develop structural capacities within which they can begin to experience an authentic and stable sense of self and other and then tolerate intrapsychic conflict long enough to begin to understand (symbolize) it.

Freudian analysts influenced by this broad perspective will focus on developmental processes facilitated in such an environment. They will highlight the patient's developing capacities for symbolizing (Freedman, 1985), or reflecting; being able to view themselves from different perspectives (Bach, 2006); becoming more self-esteem regulating, and insightful (Sugarman, 2006); capable of hearing an interpretation (Akhtar, 1998; Tuch, 2007); or having more of a sense of authenticity, a "true self". There is more of a sense of ongoing developmental *process*, rather than on the analyst deconstructing (analyzing) what is viewed as a product of unconscious mental functioning, otherwise known as a symptom. The analyst working this way calibrates himself and his interactions to attune himself to what he sees as his patient's structural requirements. The analyst may interpret conflicts impeding what is understood to be necessarily mutative internalization (Buie & Adler, 1982). He or she may also interpret internal conflicts for patients in areas where they want to understand something that is ego dystonic. However, interpretations, whatever effect they may have in terms of insight, also serve to help regulate the analytic environment and a regressive process that may sometimes blur the patient's experience of internality and externality.

To approach this a bit differently, according to Loewald, Winnicott, and others, we emerge from an experienced situation of merger and unity. These authors focus on the ways in which we learn to experience ourselves as separate people, with our own individual inner minds. Such a focus leads to an emphasis on the role of early object relations and the way in which these help the child become separated. The interactions also give form and shape to the child's inner world. Aspects of this nascent inner world, including drives and their psychological representation, become ways in which the child, and then the adult orient themselves vis-à-vis others, the environment, and reality itself. A drive (derivative) is a push for instinctual satisfaction, as Freud and modern conflict theorists have emphasized. However, it is also a way to sometimes establish, and other times dissolve, boundaries between ourselves and others, a way to establish a form of reality experience, a way to test or bolster a weakened self, a way to discover who we, and others, are. Drives are important as content and as process. Our focus, then, necessarily becomes a bit more developmental, looking towards the patient-analyst environment to see how each aspect of mental life works towards forming, stabilizing, and destabilizing inner mental life, as opposed to our assuming a constant inner and external world and looking at vicissitudes of already developed aspects of that world. One does not replace the other: we can maintain a traditional emphasis on drive derivatives and the vicissitudes of unconscious conflict (including many other variables in the mix) but also look at how these elements function from a developmental perspective. Depending on the patient's diagnostic level, and depending on the different moments in treatment, one emphasis becomes figure, the other ground. Thus analysis of conflict and deficit is not *sequential*, in the sense that one first helps a patient grow structurally (deal with deficit) and only then helps them understand their internal conflict; rather, deficit and conflict work in a continuous and simultaneous interplay and must be worked with in this manner.

I have been discussing patients with deficits, and the question of how intrapsychic conflict in these patients can be best understood. However, I believe that structure and conflict must interact, to some extent, even with neurotic patients (who are considered neurotic precisely because they have developed most structural capacities). It is this constant interplay where unconscious and conscious elements interpenetrate that Loewald (1973) sees as healthy in the neurotic patient. Perhaps we are referring to a similar process when we speak of regression in the service of the ego, or of the analyst becoming part of the patient's internal world (Bird, 1972; Bach, 1985, 2006), or when we speak of the non-verbal "enacted dimension" (Katz, 1998; 2002) of psychoanalytic work, or of the intersubjective analytic third (Ogden, 1994). In all these circumstances, there is some form of analytic regression that affects the permeability of patient and analyst boundaries and the nature of their connection. When a patient hears and resonates with an analyst's interpretation, perhaps he is doing more than considering it intellectually. I would argue that he must also be taking in his analyst, and that optimal conditions for hearing an interpretation involve some loosening of patient-analyst boundaries. I should also add that I have been stressing similarities between thinking of a patient in structural terms and thinking of the patient in terms of vicissitudes of the self. However, this is one circumstance where the differing ways of thinking about patients may diverge. Patients may be considered "neurotic" from a structural point of view, but may feel a sense of emptiness, meaninglessness, and a "false self" from a different theoretical point of view. Certainly from this latter point of view, the patient's finding himself in the context of an analytic holding environment anchored by his analyst is crucial, whatever his structural diagnosis.

The analyst's role

I have stated that patients' difficulties can often be understood as the result of intrapsychic conflict in a context where the psyche is incompletely or unevenly developed. The goal of treatment is structural development through some combination of insight into intrapsychic conflict and concomitant development of structural capacities that enable such insight. The mechanism for achieving this goal is the patient-analyst relationship, and that will be my focus in this section.

I would like to begin by discussing why a patient works in analysis. This is a question that Freud often discussed and that was carried forth by many Freudian thinkers over the years (Friedman, 1969, 1992, 1997). There is always an effective working alliance between patient and analyst, one that is manifested by the simple fact that the patient arrives, speaks to the analyst, and considers what the analyst has to offer. In this sense, "working alliance" is a descriptive term. But why does the patient do this work? Is this alliance separate from transference? Must the analyst behave in a certain way to facilitate such an alliance? Zetzel (1956) and Greenson (1965) believed that the analyst must attend to maintaining this alliance, which they saw as separate from the transference relationship, but Brenner (1979) effectively demonstrated that transference and alliance could not be separated. He, and other modern conflict theorists, took the position that a patient's reaction to their analyst was less based on the analyst's actual behaviour and more on the patient's specific transference fantasies. This led some modern conflict theorists to conclude not only that the analytic relationship was experienced solely through a patient's idiosyncratic transference disposition, but also that "[t]he psychoanalytic setting is a dangerous situation" (Levy & Inderbitzen, 1997, p. 380). Safety in this situation is an "illusion" (Levy & Inderbitzen, 1997, p. 380) because the situation stimulates powerful fantasies, which may, in fact, be verbally actualized and enacted by the patient, whose analyst will not be completely able to control or own his reactions, subject as he is to his own unconscious conflicts. Helping a patient experience a sense of safety in the analytic situation is best accomplished through interpretation of a patient's unconscious transference fantasies. They believe that an analyst's actual behavioural attempt to promote safety is ineffective and could impede analysis of what is truly important, the patient's unconscious fantasies.

Parenthetically, the interesting paper by Levy and Inderbitzen highlights one central difference in technical emphasis between modern conflict theory and modern structural theory. Many analysts whom I am grouping under the broad rubric of modern structural theory, such as Kohut, Winnicott, and Bach, delay analysing major aspects of the transference until late in the analysis, since they see the transference experience, through which a whole and vitalized self with the capacity for symbolization and reflective awareness emerges, as mutative in its own right. Premature transference interpretations are viewed as disrupting or impinging on what is, for the patient, a sought-out and necessary developmental experience. Modern conflict theorists see no good reason for this approach, since they see the major difficulty for the patient as unconscious conflicts that are manifested in both the positive and negative transference and that need analysis. This is why the former analysts focus on the analyst's provision of an adequate holding environment as facilitating safety, while the modern conflict theorists see analysis of unconscious transference fears as providing safety. To put it as starkly as possible, modern structural theorists focus on the transference (technically pre-transference, since the analyst is not experienced by the patient as a separate object) interaction between the patient and a variety of self objects, an experience that provides a holding environment within which the patient can regress and internalize aspects of the analyst in order to resume necessary structural development (whether it is in the realm of narcissism, or in development of a "true self"). Modern conflict theorists focus on the patient's transference distortion of the analyst (experienced as a separate object) and on the analyst's analysis of the unconscious meanings of this distortion, including attempts to see the analyst as a "safe" object (Gray, 1987, 1991). Stolorow and Lachman (1980), discussing differences between Kohut and Kernberg, make a similar point when they write: "The essence of Kohut's technical suggestions is to focus emphatically on the *state which the developmentally arrested patient needs to maintain and achieve*, whereas Kernberg strongly emphasizes interpreting *what* the defending patient needs to ward off" (1980, p. 99, italics in original).

This entire discussion and controversy deals with the question of whether there is such a thing as an alliance separate from transference and whether the analyst should behave in a specific way—a way contrary to traditional understandings of an optimal analytic stance—to maintain such an alliance. What if we do not assume separation of reality-based alliance from unconscious primary-process-based transference? What if we ask, simply, why a patient working in what is commonly accepted as the usual psychoanalytic posture (Winnicott, 1954) does the analytic work? Modern conflict theorists would say that the working alliance is based to a large extent on the patient's capacity for autonomous ego functioning and regression in the service of the ego. These capacities are based on his firm achievement of secondary process functioning and whole object relations; his sense of a real and vivid self; his capacity to express his inner life verbally; and his acceptance of the reality principle, which here is that the "rules of the game" established by the analyst will help him most productively address his presenting problems. This patient works within the rigours of the analytic situation because he is psychically able to do so, and because he understands and accepts his analyst's rules just as another patient will cooperate with his physician's treatment plan in areas of physical illness.

Here motivation for the patient-analyst alliance is reality-based and provides the background for the foreground of analytic work. Traditionally, this is conceptualized as "... the patient's identification with the analyst's analyzing functions" (Lasky, 1993, p. 148). Note that, even here, in this "classical" position, there is acknowledgement of the patient's identification with the analyst's "analyzing functions". This theoretically limited and strictly defined identification, which is probably impossible in real life, is not considered to be part of the larger patient-analyst relationship (which is primarily transferential in nature), and its larger implications are not explored. Patient-analyst relations are not seen as, in themselves, having therapeutic effect. This area of interaction is just there, like the air we breathe. The moment that we need to focus on the patient-analyst relationship is the moment when we see it as an area of transference that we must understand through interpretation. The very act of noticing it, of having to remark on it, makes it something needing analysis. Thus working alliance is here a term that does not involve boundaries of the stance or really address issues of why the patient chooses to do the work. Both patient and analyst do their respective therapeutic jobs, as the job is defined by the therapist and accepted by the patient.

One might ask, however, whether that same analytic relationship *in its own right* keeps the work going and motivates the patient. As part of this question, I need to distinguish between Freud's understanding of the positive transference as a motivating force and what I am about to describe. For Freud, the patient worked because he wanted the analyst's love (Friedman, 1969). To work because you want the analyst to love you and approve of you is a transference issue. As Friedman (1969, 1992, 1997) has often and eloquently described, the therapeutic problem here is that the analyst has a different goal from the patient-insight rather than reciprocating the patient's love. While the analyst may use the patient's positive transference to power the patient's motivation to look at certain difficult issues, at some point the analyst must analyse that same motivating positive transference, dashing the hopes that sustained a patient through the analysis.

I am describing something different here: at what point does the patient's *capacity* to do analytic work, to self-reflect, to communicate verbally, to feel whole and alive—capacities that are assumed in descriptions of "analysable" patients who have working alliances—become enhanced or even established by his or her experience of *connection* to the analyst? We know from clinical experience that patients invariably work better analytically when they feel such connection. Thus, rather than experience competing with insight, we see that it facilitates the capacity for insight and reflection. This, however, is not the object-related transference situation that we described above. It is more of an ego (or self) state, an experience of the analyst within a traditional analytic stance. It is this kind of experience and relationship that is described by analysts such as Loewald, Kohut, Balint, Bach, Ogden, and others, who see the analytic situation as a holding environment within which a patient can find himself in the analyst's presence. As Loewald (1960) writes, successful analysis depends not on the analyst's scientific objectivity and distance but on the analyst's closeness and involvement. In an extended discussion of this issue, he writes, "The transference neurosis, in the sense of reactivation of the childhood neurosis, is set in motion not simply by the technical skill of the analyst, but by the fact that the analyst makes himself available for the development of a new "object relationship" between the patient and the analyst" (p. 17). Loewald considers this new object relationship to be a critical mutative factor and terms it the "positive nature of neutrality" (p. 20).

To suggest that the analyst-patient relationship might have inherent structure-promoting effects is not to attempt parsing out "reality" or "transference" aspects of such an alliance. On the contrary, it assumes, as Loewald (1973) suggests, that these elements are inextricably intertwined. Here one might see both the capacity and the reason for the patient's cooperation in a quiet and background object relationship. In this context, the term "working alliance" does not only acknowledge the obvious fact that patient and analyst work in a certain reality context. We go further and state that it is *because* of certain inherent background and unanalysed (at the moment) factors in the treatment that the patient both chooses to work in analysis and has the capacity to do the analytic work. In fact, these factors may ultimately be unanalysable because one cannot completely eliminate the patient's natural identification with his analyst that is the product of a good analysis, even if one systematically analyses these factors.

Here the term "working alliance" is not synonymous with the positive transference. Nor is it the result of an analyst attempting to behave in a way consistent with a theoretical model of development and re-parenting (Abend, 2007; Arlow, 1981) and ignoring transference meanings that the patient assigns to the analyst's behaviours and interventions. Notions of re-parenting and corrective object relationships refer to the analyst attempting to facilitate a certain kind of object relationship that he believes is optimal for that given patient, based on his theoretical model of optimal development. This is something different, although it certainly involves a new object relationship for the patient. Theorists discussed here attempt to facilitate a psychoanalytic situation within which the analyst may be used by the patient as needed to develop a more authentic sense of self and for other kinds of structural development. The analyst, who through much of this treatment is not experienced as a separate object, mostly anchors that therapeutic situation, although he or she may, according to his or her temperament, theory, and the particular clinical situation, interpret patients' conflicts around what is seen as necessary use of the analyst (Buie & Adler, 1982). These conflicts involve fears around merger, envy, and other such difficulties.

This entire approach rests on a theoretical assumption about the inherent connection between object relationship—any object relationship—and ego functioning (Loewald, 1978). We assume that ego functioning and the working alliance is most optimal under conditions when it is nurtured in some way by the existence of an object relationship, both in the actual analytic situation and as internalized by the patient. For patients with deficits, the analytic work, in any given analytic session, is facilitated by structural holding and nurturance provided by the analyst in the analytic environment. Thus the analyst is constantly gratifying as well as frustrating. Further, we assume that, in the long term, structural development as well as eventual analysis of intrapsychic conflict is achieved through internalization of the analyst and the holding environment (Bach, 1985, 2006; Balint, 1968; Loewald, 1960; Winnicott, 1965a, 1969, 1975). So, if we understand the working alliance as a reflection of a patient's capacity to look inward and imagine possibility while also fully accepting and internalizing the demands of external reality, we can understand that the working alliance, rather than being a precondition for analysis, is a capacity that develops and is strengthened over the course of an analysis. Like the capacity to free associate, a working alliance signifies an achievement that heralds the beginning of a termination phase.

Loewald (1951, 1960, 1973, 1978, 1979) discusses the way in which a patient's *motive* for structure formation and *capacity* for higher levels of structure come together. *The joining of structural capacity (including development of the self in all its aspects) within which intrapsychic conflict may be tolerated, symbolized, and analyed, and the patient-analyst object relationship is perhaps the major difference in emphasis between modern conflict theory and modern structural theory, in conception of what is wrong with the patient, how that difficulty emerged, and model of an optimal analysis. The working alliance becomes the manifest representation of this theoretical assumption.*

Who then is the analyst and how can we understand what is mutative in psychoanalysis? We have moved far from early ideas of the analyst as a neutral abstinent interpreter. The analyst's role is complex. The analyst is always a paradoxical figure, one who is simultaneously experienced in different dimensions, within which foreground and background aspects of the analyst are in constant dynamic relationship. We are in the patient's mind and outside it, as an object and a subject, in an unconscious primary process universe as well as a conscious secondary process world, as a part object and a whole object, as a past figure pulling and structuring reality as well as a new object who stands for what can be possible in the future. The analyst is always in and out, new and old, in the past and in the future, all at once. He is a "provocateur" of "disjunctive experiences" at "the prerepresentational level" as well as "… the facilitator of the synthesis at the representational level" (Freedman, 1985, p. 336) "under the hegemony of a libidinal object relationship" (Freedman, 1985, p. 335). He awakens and soothes (Rosegrant, 2005), interprets, holds, contains, mirrors, and enacts—at least. Different analysts in the Freudian spectrum emphasize different aspects of this complex role.

All of these parts of the analyst potentiate one another. It is because the analyst transferentially and actually (Sandler, 1976; Katz, 1998, 2002) resonates with past objects that the analytic situation gains such affective intensity. This is one way a new experience can touch past experience and help shape its effect. Loewald's (1960) distinction between "new discovery of objects" and "discovery of new objects" is relevant here. We are always involved in a paradox: the analyst, as a new object, facilitates his being experienced as an old object, and this experience itself becomes a new discovery of this old object rather than a new discovery of a new object.

Interpretation is simultaneously an expression of empathic closeness and connection as well as of reflective separation. This is why interpretation of unconscious conflict, regarding a transference issue that the patient himself sees as problematic, can be experienced as a form of empathic understanding. This is why the question of insight *versus* experience misses the point: insight is a form of experience between two people. It is one way in which they connect. Interpretation becomes a complex act rooted in the moment-to-moment relationship between patient and analyst, where it connects the pair on one level even as it opens new, and often conflicted, areas between them on another. An interpretation simultaneously stabilizes a patient's inner world and the patient-analyst relationship in one area, even as it destabilizes it in another. It brings about new ways of being even as it acknowledges areas that have already been enacted and experienced. Interpretation rides on a current of experience, one that facilitates certain insights on the part of both patient and analyst even as it closes off capacities for seeing other insights at those moments.

Interpretation is not a matter of supplying unconscious content that a particular theory specifies in advance. Interpretation is part of a broader process, one in which the patient develops curiosity and the capacity to allow for and consider different perspectives on himself and others. Development of this capacity, in itself, is what is mutative in analytic work. It is not the realization that we love our mothers and hate our fathers. Rather, it is our capacity to consider this and other perspectives that opens us up to ourselves and to others. It is like falling in or out of love or separating from a parent, internally as well as in reality. Suddenly you can see yourself and others through what feel like different eyes, in a more rich, complex, and differentiated way, along with access to greater and more varied affect. So insight is not a matter of discovering content or "truth". It is part of a continuing process of developing a capacity for multiple perspectives.

Interpretation, then, is much more than the analyst making the unconscious conscious. As the analyst interprets to his patient who he is now, he is also, as Loewald (1960) writes, communicating to his patient a vision of who he can become. He is engaging with his patient in an "integrative experience" (p. 25). This is a satisfying experience for the patient. Friedman (1969) concludes that it is with Loewald's contribution that the question of why a patient works in analysis is resolved. It is in these satisfying integrative experiences that we find a unity of aims between patient and analyst:

> Satisfaction, in this context, is a unifying experience due to the creation of an identity of experience in two systems, two psychic apparatuses of different levels of organization, thus containing the potential for growth. This identity is achieved by overcoming a differential … . Analytic interpretations represent, on higher levels of interaction, the mutual recognition involved in the creation of identity of experience in two individuals of different levels of ego organization. Insight gained in such interaction is an integrative experience (p. 25).

This is what I mean when I speak of internalization of the analyst as a major mutative force. It is a broad and global process, encompassing, in many forms, mentalization (Fonagy & Target, 2000; Myerson, 1979, 1981a, 1981b), transmuting internalization (Kohut, 1971), finding one's true self within a holding environment (Winnicott, 1965a, 1975; Balint, 1968) and the general process of developing a self-reflective mind of one's own, capable of seeing one's self from different perspectives and tolerating unconscious wishes and internal complexity (Bach, 2006; Tuch, 2007).

What, then, is mutative? I think we should, first of all, acknowledge that nobody really knows. Our theories tell us what should work and then, if the analysis is successful, we believe that it succeeded because of what we anticipated would work. If we ask analysts about their experiences and then patients about their experiences, we often discover that patients were affected by aspects of the work that the analyst may not have thought were important. However, we do theorize about this issue. Many have, from their own theoretical contexts, described similar processes, where the analyst first becomes experienced as part of the patient's inner world, where there is then some kind of disjunction or frustration, or psychic gap that creates space for reflection and insight, and then some kind of resumption of connection, but on a higher level. We see descriptions of such a process in Loewald (1960), Kohut (1971), Freedman (1985), Druck (1989, 2002), Ellman (2005), and others. Even the classical psychoanalytic formulation of treatment reflects such a process: there is regression to the transference neurosis, where, according to Bird (1972), the analyst becomes part of the patient's mental structure. Then disjunction and resolution at a higher level occur through interpretation. In what seems like a universally agreed-upon process, patients use the analyst for structural development, to understand how unconscious conflict and compromise have affected, and still affect, their life, including their experience of themselves, others, and "reality" itself, and then they mourn: mourning old objects, mourning early versions of their self and what they might have become, mourning what the analysis did not fully provide, and, finally, mourning their analyst. In this process, it is important to think about simultaneity rather than sequence. It is not that one element of the analytic process happens first and is then followed by the second element. Rather, interactions between patient and analyst, including interpretations, reverberate on different levels simultaneously.

Conclusion

I have focused on two broad issues: conflict in the context of structural deficit and the structure—promoting aspects of the patient-analyst relationship, because I see these as two broad principles within which much of the current work in contemporary psychoanalysis can be grouped. The focus on development of one or another aspect of structure (including an authentic sense of self) is shared by theorists such as Winnicott, Loewald, Mahler, Jacobson, Kohut, and Bach. These all consider the process through which mind emerges from an early relational matrix, culminating in the Oedipal situation. Such processes become themes in the psychoanalytic situation, where, instead of caricatured "re-parenting", analyst and patient understand the patient's struggle to attain what he or she missed and is now conflicted about getting. I have focused on internalization of the analyst and the analytic environment as major mutative factors, especially for patients with deficits of different kinds. However, I do not mean to slight the role of interpretation of unconscious conflict as it emerges in the transference, especially with patients for whom a stable sense of internal world and self has become established.

Within this overall context, our understanding of the analyst's inevitable subjectivity, along with how patients (and analysts) often communicate through action has led us to study the informative aspects of countertransference (Jacobs, 1991a, 1997, 1999a, 1999b; Smith, 2000); the intersubjective field (Ogden, 1991, 1994); and the entire "enacted dimension of psychoanalysis" (Katz, 1998; Sandler, 1976), which operates alongside the verbal dimension. We now have an expanded view of the analyst's function, as an interpreter, container, holder, mirror, aid in mentalization (Fonagy & Target, 2000; Sugarman, 2006); facilitator of the patient's capacity to think (Tuch, 2007); and protector of a certain optimal analytic environment. The focus of Kleinian and modern Kleinian theorists on splitting, projective identification, and other defences, which operate in an environment where self and object boundaries are permeable and where communication is often non-verbal, fits within this emphasis, as does their focus on envy and its destructive effects on internalization. Modern structural theorists also focus on specific aspects of the patient-analyst process, to understand better how the relationship works in expanding the patient's capacities for interpretive work. Finally, analysts such as Smith and Jacobs, who identify themselves as modern conflict theorists, fit easily into this overall rubric in their focus on the continuing effect of countertransference on the analyst's listening and intervening.

As I conclude the second of two chapters devoted to outlining two overarching and overlapping theoretical emphases within contemporary Freudian psychoanalysis and their influences on conceptions of the analyst's optimal role, I would like to register a comment about the role of theory in our clinical work. For far too long, analysts have been too focused on theory. We have passionately argued about theoretical differences and we have assumed that our theories should, and do, guide technical interventions. This has led to a superego-dominated view of technique, within which interventions that go against a particular theoretical view are seen as incorrect (Lipton, 1977). Analytic honesty, openness, and innovation are thus discouraged (Fonagy, 2003). Elements of a given psychoanalytic interaction that fit an analyst's predisposed theory are attended to and emphasized; those that do not are not noticed or are seen as irrelevant to the analytic process. Analysts speak of how their years of "clinical experience" have convinced them that their approach is the best one; yet they do not even attempt to explain how other analysts of similar prominence and years of clinical experience employ diametrically opposing assumptions and interventions yet also claim excellent results. Presumably every analyst has some treatments that work out less well than others, but we know nothing about these cases. Do they demonstrate that a given theoretical emphasis does not work for a given kind of patient? Do different kinds of approaches work differently for different kinds of patients? We have no idea.

Schafer (1979) has discussed how our theories are "fictions" which are useful approaches to reality rather than being reality itself. Theoretical schools evolve within themselves so that the truths of one era become modified by later generations of analysts. The loose integrations of theoretical propositions, our fictions, often are turned into "myths". Schafer writes:

> As myths they are ultimate unchangeable assertions about reality pure and simple. Like primitive religious beliefs, they claim direct access to one and only one clearly ascertainable world. Then they are beyond comparable analysis; other conceptions of the order of things are discredited (pp. 347–348).

The theoretical schools selectively find clinical phenomena (facts) that bolster their beliefs. Each school focuses on different clinical data (in all areas: how they understand what is wrong with the patient, how they understand the analyst's optimal role, and in what they attend to in the clinical encounter). Theoretical schools ultimately work within "... a more or less closed system" (Schafer, 1979, p. 348), one often developed with, and geared towards, a schematic paradigmatic patient. All this could teach us to take our theories and their assertions as provisional hypotheses. Unfortunately, an analyst's theory often becomes used to defend himself from the inherent ambiguity and uncertainty inherent in any analytic encounter (Friedman, 1978a; Eisold, 1994).

In my overall review, I have stressed the close theoretical connection between a given theory and the prescribed analytic role. However, in practice, the connection is not as close as it may appear. As Fonagy (2003) has shown, analysts do what makes sense to them and then rationalize it on the basis of their theory. Akhtar (2000) has shown that decisions are made and changed as much as a result of the analyst's internal shifts as on the basis of his "diagnosis" of the patient and what the proper stance should be. That is, his decision is based as much on his internal affective "countertransference" state as it is on his cognitive theory. Years ago, Wallerstein's (1986) research demonstrated that support had a prominent mutative role in all types of analytic treatment, including psychoanalysis proper where the analyst attempted to minimize support. What are the implications of these findings for our clinical theories of psychoanalysis? All this suggests that we are concentrating on the wrong thing. I believe theory has an important role as an orienting point for an analyst as he navigates the close emotional encounter with a patient in analysis. However, it seems to me preferable to shift our concern from disagreements about theoretical issues for which we will never have evidence one way or the other, to a focus on issues that emerge from inherent difficulties in the analytic task itself.

All psychoanalytic work, for example, must involve patient and analyst in some affective connection, but with some gap, some degree of optimal frustration. It is this combination of connection and inevitable mis-attunement and distance that leads to psychic space and to the opportunity to feel something that has been in the background. We always see a shifting equilibrium of closeness and distance between patient and analyst, and all theoretical systems see both as crucial. In self psychology, for example, it is moments of mis-attunement that form the figure for the ground of a merged or idealizing transference; the moments of mis-attunement create the gap, the opportunity to notice that patient and analyst have been in a certain kind of relationship. Traditional Freudians used concepts such as abstinence and neutrality to highlight that gap. In traditional work, these concepts were placed within the context of psychoanalytic theory of mind. Neutrality and abstinence were necessary for full development of the transference neurosis. However, these concepts can be understood as related also to the inherent demands of an analysis. They offer a way of the analyst placing himself, a centering position where he puts a bit of drag on a constantly evolving system of transference and countertransference, of closeness and separation. These concepts help stabilize the analyst, they offer theoretical orienting points, especially within an intersubjective context, so that he is more able to establish or maintain an optimal gap in which psychic possibility and psychic space, and therefore new insight and experience, become possible. These concepts of abstinence and neutrality anchor the interpersonal balance between a patient and their analyst, in the same way that, as Winnicott has famously noted, the beginning and end of a session are the structural anchors of closeness and distance, of love and hate.

Note that I have tried to take traditional concepts, rooted in demands of theory of mind, and place them into a theory of what an analytic process inevitably demands of patient and analyst. Friedman (1997; 2002; 2005) has been a pioneer in such a focus. It is time that we begin to examine the complex connection between a particular analyst's understanding of his or her broader theoretical outlook; his or her particular character; the given patient; the given time in treatment; and the unique challenges that this particular patient poses to this particular analyst at this particular time.

This leads me to the question of what actually happens in a psychoanalysis (rather than what is supposed to happen) and to the role of non-specific elements in treatment—those elements that we all acknowledge exist and have great power but that do not fit into our theories. Study of these non-specific elements has led us to identify aspects of the clinical situation that we now see as central to the work. Factors such as empathy, holding, containing, enactment, internalization, and even helping someone name what he is feeling or thinking are now seen as specific mutative elements in analysis (Gabbard & Westen, 2003). Who knows what there is yet to learn about the analytic encounter? I can do no better than to end with a quote from Jacobs, who has done so much to broaden the scope of modern conflict theory.

Jacobs (1997) writes:

> This subject—the uninterpreted and, given the current state of our knowledge, often uninterpretable aspect of the analytic situation—is a vast one, far too large for me to do more than touch on here. It is an important issue, however, because much of what is happening in analysis today represents an effort to broaden the database we can effectively draw on in conducting an analysis. Our interest in detecting and interpreting nonverbal and paraverbal communications; our attempts to tune into subtle

> manifestations of countertransference and other subjective experiences of the analyst; our exploration of actions, enactments, and fantasies jointly created between patient and analyst—all are attempts to broaden our canvas and, in doing so, give our patients fuller pictures of themselves.
>
> In its understanding and use of these so-called uninterpreted aspects of analysis, our traditional approach has, in my view, served us less than satisfactorily. We tend to refer to such features of the analytic situation as nonspecific factors or therapeutic elements and leave their elucidation to other theoretical systems. We then often ignore or dismiss what those other systems offer by way of explanation, in part because we do not really consider these factors to be essential parts of the analytic process. As a result, we are left the poorer for having no better understanding of what, like it or not, are inherent parts of the analytic situation (p. 1042).

I believe that the broad group of analysts working under the rubric of "modern structural theory" —and I include analysts such as Jacobs—are engaged in just that effort in their integrative focus.

Notes

1. The author would like to thank Beverly Goldsmith Druck and Gil Katz for their helpful comments on this paper.
2. For many patients, the capacity for self-reflection is a product of psychoanalytic work.

CHAPTER THREE

States of consciousness

Sheldon Bach

We all think we know the difference between being awake and being asleep but that is, among other things, the difference between two states of consciousness. When we wake up or go to sleep we have altered our state of consciousness. We can also alter our state of consciousness by taking drugs that lower our state of excitation or drugs that raise our state of excitation or drugs that are hallucinatory; or by exercising (endorphins), by falling in love or having sex, by meditating, by getting angry, by being in isolation or being inebriated, by fading out listening to a boring lecture or by getting enthusiastic about an exciting one. You can see that almost anything we do may involve changes in our state of consciousness.

It is also clear that we often react to people and describe them by their apparent or publicly visible states of consciousness: "He's a space cadet", "He's so uptight", "She's a dizzy dame, out to lunch", etc. I believe that some diagnostic categories are abbreviated descriptions of certain characteristic states of consciousness, and more than 30 years ago I wrote an elaborate description of the narcissistic state of consciousness, some elements of which have been paralleled by the DSM IV diagnosis (Bach, 1977). But when we try to actually define what we mean by a state of consciousness, we run into considerable difficulty.

There seem to be multiple parameters to a state of consciousness, including certain patterns of affect, different kinds of body schemata, different organizations of time and of thought, and different degrees of awareness of self and object. There is also often some personal categorization of the state such as: *this feels like my real self*, or *this feels like my social or assumed self*, or *this feels out of sorts, depersonalized or even feels like someone else*. But the idea of a state of consciousness is a conceptual crossroads because it integrates both physical and mental parameters. We can imagine that each person has a normal or usual state of consciousness that can be frequently altered but that returns eventually to its normal state. This normal state can be expressed as a diagnostic classification, so that we might imagine a typical hysterical state of consciousness, an obsessive-compulsive state of consciousness, the narcissistic state of consciousness that I described, and even an alternation between manic and depressed states of consciousness. Other people prefer to think not of a normally unified state of consciousness but of various states of consciousness that are more or less dissociated.

I myself was trained in those olden days when nobody even thought to question that people had a unified sense of self, which they quaintly Latinized as their ego. Nowadays, when everything around us is being so rapidly deconstructed, many people are hard put to believe that they or their neighbours have a unified sense of self, and many even question the value of such a hypothetical attribute.

But even in those olden days, that very same manic-depressive patient who in his manic state would characterize me as "Dr. Bach/Beethoven/Brahms", in his depressed state would seemingly not know who I was. Clearly the alterations in his affect pattern had been accompanied by alterations in his awareness of self and other as well. In a certain sense one might imagine psychoanalytic therapy with this patient as an attempt to modify his usual states of manic and depressed phases to a more regulated state that encompassed and attenuated these extremes. Although the parameters of affect, body schema, time and thought organization, and self and object awareness all interact, sometimes therapy succeeds in modifying some of them far more than others.

But to my way of thinking, the process of modifying the patient's ordinary state of consciousness can only really begin from the inside, that is, by the analyst's attempt to enter into the patient's world in a particular way. Ideally, this would involve "meeting" not only the patient's parameters of emotional arousal but also his parameters of body schema and orientation, of thought and memory organization, and of self and object awareness.

I remember that decades ago, early in my practice, I would often find myself moving my body in the same rhythm or conformation as the patient, and I used to puzzle about what this meant. Nowadays we have considerable research by Norbert Freedman and collaborators (Freedman, Barroso, Bucci & Grand, 1978; Freedman & Berzofsky, 1995), by mother-infant researchers (Beebe & Lachmann, 1988; Stern, 1985), and also by neuroscientists investigating mirror neurons (Di Pellegrino, Fadiga, Fogassi, Gallese & Rizzolatti, 1992) to help us understand these very important imitative phenomena. But going into this now would take me too far from my topic.

So when I suggest that we try to "meet" the parameters of the patient's state of consciousness, I mean, not necessarily an attempt to match or to regulate nor yet to deliberately change these parameters, but rather an attempt to recognize and accept them and thereby bring them into a larger system of which the analyst forms a part. I believe that ultimately the analyst's attentive presence in this larger system does indeed lead to increased mutual trust and to mutual assimilation and interpenetration in ways that I have described elsewhere (Bach, 2006). Since most of this accommodation and assimilation goes on either unconsciously, preconsciously, or in ways that the Boston Change Group (Stern et al., 1998) is calling implicit, I think that it all forms a small part of what Freud meant when he referred to the unconscious of one human being acting and reacting with that of another.

So we can have states of consciousness involving a single person such as the normal waking state, sleeping state, trance, ecstasy or drug highs. A famous example of the latter is the state that Coleridge (1816) was in when these lines just seemed to pop into his mind:

> In Xanadu did Kubla Khan
> A stately pleasure dome decree
> Where Alph the sacred river ran

> Through caverns measureless to man
> Down to a sunless sea ... .
> And all who heard should see them there
> And all should cry, Beware! Beware!
> His flashing eyes, his floating hair!
> Weave a circle round him thrice
> And close your eyes with holy dread
> For he on honeydew hath fed
> And drunk the milk of Paradise ... .

Well, Coleridge had not fed on honeydew or milk but he had swallowed two grains of opium to relieve an attack of dysentery. And these lines and the rest just came to him in this drugged state but the poem was unfortunately never finished because "a person from Porlock" rang at his doorbell about some business matter and interrupted things, forcing him back into his usual waking state of consciousness.

So that is an example of an individual state of consciousness, a state of creativity in this case, but we might also have given examples from states of psychosis or ordinary humdrum states. James Joyce's *Ulysses* is a fascinating attempt to record the state of consciousness of one Leopold Bloom, who turned out to be not so ordinary after all. Or perhaps no one is ordinary when viewed closely enough.

Interestingly, even the simple drug state that I described is not as simple as it seems. You may recall the work of Stanley Schachter (1964) who demonstrated that our emotional experience is a function of both a physiological state and a cognitive interpretation of that state. Thus, when he gave his subjects adrenalin to produce arousal, they could interpret that arousal in contradictory ways depending upon the cognitive set he induced in them. Since writing this I have learned that Art Spielman and Steve Ellman, at the City University of New York, did even more impressive experiments (Ellman, personal communication, 2009). Working in a sleep lab, they gave three groups of students sleep medication, a placebo, or no treatment and measured sleep onset. Sleep onset was very impressively shorter in the sleep medication group, but here also the medication turned out to be adrenalin! So much for so many experiments with antidepressants and placebo, for example. As Schachter suggested, with an active medication the subjects can feel that *something* is happening to their body, but precisely what that might be is subject to great cognitive variations. We might imagine that a better-designed trial would test medications against an *active* placebo, that is, something that actually makes subjects feel that their body is being affected in some way or another.

As a young graduate student I participated in experiments where we gave large doses of LSD to groups of artists and groups of obsessive-compulsives. As a gross generalization, the artists tended to lend themselves to the experience and produce primary process, whereas the obsessives actively *defended* themselves against the same experience and became increasingly logical even in the drug state.

But we are now also beginning to think of states of consciousness that include the dyad, or expanded states of consciousness as Tronick et al. (1998) call them. These generally refer to that special state that mothers and infants can get into when nursing, for example, but at other times also; a special state that seems more than the sum of the two component states. Mutually shared states of consciousness are commonly found in the early nursing couple, but shared states that might be analogous can be seen in couples in love, in small improvised jazz combos and in many other situations as well.

Some of you may remember that wonderful scene in Tolstoy's *Anna Karenina* (1877) when Levin first discovers that Kitty, who had previously rejected him, now loves him. Levin writes down only the *first letter of each word* of a long, complicated sentence, but Kitty immediately understands his meaning and responds with an initialled sentence of her own, whose meaning, in turn, he immediately comprehends. Their minds are in that state of perfect sympathetic resonance so characteristic of love, and Levin, neither eating nor sleeping, spends all that night and the next morning in a trance. When he walks through the streets to her house to speak with her parents, the world seems magically enchanted. He watches the children going to school, the pigeons on the street, the rolls in a bakery window covered with flour, and everything he sees takes on a significance of unearthly beings which makes him laugh and cry for joy (pp. 397–403).

Anyone who is lucky enough to have known the magic of love will recognize this enchantment of the world and understand why people will risk their lives to attain it. It is also understandable why less fortunate people will spend their days in altered states of consciousness—like being high on drugs—to mimic or parody this state. Of course, unlike fairy tales, this re-enchantment of the world may not last forever, but as long as it does last it is marvellous and astonishing, and it revitalizes the world in a way that amplifies its meaning and makes it seem wonderfully worthwhile to be alive.

We know very little about mutually shared states of consciousness, but the importance of the subject cannot be overestimated. Unfortunately, it includes not only experiences of love and joy and positive religious communion such as Pentecostal revivals, but also experiences of mutually shared hatred such as lynch mobs, pogroms, and whole nations caught up in a wartime frenzy in which the enemy has lost human qualities and has been reduced to the status of a thing. While some of this has been investigated by those interested in group psychology and some touched on in studies of sado-masochism, it has never been in the mainstream of psychoanalytic thought.

But nowadays we are also beginning to think of the analytic couple as working within a shared or mutually constructed state of consciousness that is being called the "third", that is, not a monad or a dyad but a third state that the analyst and analysand have constructed together (Green, 2004; Ogden, 2004).

Presumably this third does not arise in every analysis because, for one thing, it implies the suspension of disbelief that we experience when we go to the opera or theatre and allow ourselves, as the curtain rises, to be caught up in another world that has different parameters of reality. We must *permit* this willing suspension of disbelief, and some people have imagined the analytic situation as a small two-actor theatre production that opens when the analysand rings the doorbell and concludes when the door is finally shut. Personally, I feel that once the play has started it goes on day and night, whether the actors are present or absent, until the final curtain. But certain people are unable to enjoy the theatre or to allow themselves to fully engage in therapy because they are too literal or too concrete, too defended to permit any sort of regression in the service of the ego. Some of these people become challenging patients, and I have written at length about how one can try to go about permitting or inducing a regression to occur. But this also leads off in another direction.

Some of you may remember the Charlie Chaplin film *City Lights* in which Charlie saves a drunken millionaire from committing suicide and when the millionaire is drunk he becomes Charlie's greatest friend but when he sobers up he cannot remember who Charlie is and he throws him out of the house. This is a striking example of state specific memory, but that is something that we also find quite frequently in shared states of consciousness. For example, some analysts might have difficulty in remembering facts about certain patients outside the consulting room, but when the patient is there in the room with them it all seems to come back effortlessly. One might say that the shared state of consciousness along with its memory parameters has been re-established.

Analogously, certain patients cannot remember any of the details of the previous session—it may sometimes seem as if the session had never happened, and this may be pervasively true in their life as well as in therapy. I have called this a lack of state constancy and described how, as the treatment progresses and as mutual trust and self and object constancy increase, such memories become more structured and established.

Indeed, I believe that one of the evolutionary advantages of a shared state of consciousness is that the child remains in the caretaker's mind even when the couple is separated. Of course this is also true of lovers and, to my way of thinking, it also becomes true of therapist and patient when the treatment is working well.

In my last book (Bach, 2006) I devoted the opening chapter to the subject of keeping the patient in mind and the tremendous importance to some patients of knowing that someone is keeping them in mind. I would go so far as to say that for certain patients who have been traumatized by not being kept in their parents' mind, the most important mutative factor in the treatment is their gradual realization and growing belief that they actually are being held in the therapist's mind, even over weekends and long breaks. This feeling of existing in someone else's mind is absolutely crucial to the sense of existence itself, that is, one develops a sense of *"I am"* through learning that *"I exist in the mind of someone else"*.

Paradoxically for many people, being abused or mistreated, that is, being thought about negatively, often seems preferable to not being thought about at all. This paradox can constitute an important element of masochism, for the masochist frequently elicits mistreatment in order to avoid the even worse danger of being forgotten or not existing in the mind of someone else. I am not going to venture into the arena of sado-masochism, for that would lead us away from the subject and I have written about it extensively elsewhere (Bach, 1994).

But the question of existence, of what is I or self, of what makes one feel alive and together and real, is a very important element of states of consciousness and one that is still being hotly debated. I cannot go into a history of this but I just want to remind you that from the very advent of psychoanalysis, from the time of Breuer and Freud, there was disagreement between the two about how their clinical findings should be conceptualized. Freud favoured the idea of anxiety-provoking impulses being repressed to the unconscious, with resistance to their uncovering, whereas Breuer, along with Janet and Charcot, favoured the idea of hypnoid states (Cranefield, 1958; Gottlieb, 2003). Thus from the beginning there was a disagreement about whether to imagine a single self in conflict or a multiplicity of dissociated selves, and this disagreement or confusion has persisted to this day. Classical Freudian and Kleinian theory still maintains the unity of the self in conflict, even if that self is split, whereas Relational theorists such as Sullivan (1953) and Bromberg (1995) subscribe to a view of multiple dissociated selves, while self psychologists view the developmentally fragmented self as trying to heal itself via selfobjects. Ferenczi (1932) also seems to have had a view of dissociated states that was clinically different from Freud's, and even the old-timers like Helena Deutsch (1942) described patients with as-if personalities. Winnicott (1955) openly postulated a True and a False self in everyone, with the True self feeling real and alive and the False self containing those experiences that had been imposed without assent and therefore deprived of the stamp of self-authenticity.

Contemporary neuroscience has made some of the most amazing contributions in this area, but to my mind they raise more questions than they answer. Among others, I am referring to Sperry and Gazzaniga's (1967) work with commissurotomy patients that seems to indicate that the separate hemispheres could be inhabited by different "personalities"; I am also referring to Libet, Gleason, Wright, and Pearl's (1983) work on action potentials that shows that movement begins well before the conscious decision to move, and to LeDoux's (1996) work that suggests that traumatically intense stimuli can bypass the higher mental processes and influence bodily responses directly. Neuroscience is still at that tantalizing stage that holds immense promise but currently serves to show us how little we really understand.

Most of the theorists I have mentioned might agree on the existence of self-states, that is, various states of consciousness that might exist in one person over time, and some would say even at the same time. These theories interest me mainly because their metaphors so strongly influence how we view the therapeutic enterprise and therefore how we talk to our patients.

With a particular patient at a given phase of treatment, it makes a world of difference whether we see ourselves as a detective or an archaeologist trying to gather the facts, as a soldier struggling against his enemy's resistances, as a surgeon making a clean incision, as a mother tending to an upset baby, as a gardener watering a growing plant, as a blank slate on which the patient is writing, or as a container for unwanted garbage; as a co-participant in a mutual enactment, as a co-constructor of a shared state of consciousness, as one person fighting another in a life-or-death struggle, or as any of the other metaphors that have so permeated our thinking.

It also seems to make a difference whether we see ourselves as primarily analysing the mind into component parts or as primarily synthesizing them—whether we interest ourselves in small details or try to take a holistic view. All these actions will be very much influenced by our theoretical models. For example, if we see people as composed of multiple shifting states of consciousness that can never be completely reconciled or even comprehended, we might tend to emphasize tolerance for our ambiguities, acceptance of our multiple realities, and we might make interpretations that would elicit and amplify these strands. On the other hand, if we see people as possessing an ego that is besieged by unconscious conflicts, we might tend to emphasize the conscious and unconscious factors that interfere with our agency, and we might make interpretations that tend to decode the unconscious into a conscious language. Not that we cannot have multiple models, and many of us do, but in my experience the primary mutative factor seems to be the model that our own analyst employed and our identification or dis-identification with this experience.

Originally Freud saw conflict as occurring between the ego and some repressed, unconscious instinctual forces, although he later recognized intrapsychic conflicts and also noted conflicts between two ideas consciously held, such as in perversions where the patient feels both that he *is* castrated and that he is not. This defensive use of splitting was eagerly taken up by Melanie Klein (1946) and her group, and later by Kernberg (1967) and others. Kohut and Wolf (1978) postulated both horizontal and vertical splits in the self, the horizontal being the classical split between the conscious and the unconscious, whereas the vertical is a split in the self where both parts of the split may be conscious.

Yet another attempt to handle this was Kris's (1985) recognition of two kinds of conflict which he called convergent and divergent conflicts. The convergent conflict is the traditional head-to-head convergence of a drive motivation and a repressing force, and it is usually handled by interpretation, that is, by repeatedly pointing out the conflict, which may very often be unconscious.

In contrast, the divergent conflict appears as an oscillation between two poles of a dilemma, such as a rapprochement conflict in which the subject is relatively aware that he wants both to merge with and get away from his object. Whereas convergent conflicts are typically resolved by insight or understanding, divergent conflicts are typically resolved by a process of mourning, that is, by moving back and forth between the two poles without denying the existence of the other pole until some resolution occurs.

In my own experience, divergent conflicts are the kind that predominate in our challenging patients, and the nature of the conflicts and the need for mourning explains to some extent why these cases are so difficult to manage and take so much more time.

But once again I have been seduced into straying from my topic. I suppose one of the reasons for this is that "states of consciousness" is such a broad subject that it can include almost anything one wants. But at this point I will just review some points in a way that I hope might be clinically useful.

We have seen that the patient arrives at your office bringing with him certain motivations and his particular everyday state of consciousness, just as you arrive at your office with the same accoutrements. I imagined this as the beginning of a play with at least two principal actors, although many more may appear on the scene in the course of time. Once the play has started it continues day and night, over weekends and vacations, whether you are having direct contact with the patient or not. The vehicle that carries the play is the transference, both in the patient and in yourself, and it continues unbroken in *his* unconscious and in yours whether or not you are actually seeing each other or even consciously thinking about each other.

Although at the beginning the patient may feel observed and criticized by you and may possibly feel afraid and ashamed because of this, our hope is that in the course of analysis we can slowly establish a mutually shared state of consciousness. We do this generally by staying as close to the patient's feelings as we can and not attempting to observe critically or to bring in extraneous material. This includes not imposing our personal psychoanalytic theory on the patient's material so that he finds himself in a Procrustean bed of our making, rather than on a mattress stuffed with his own material that merely amplifies and organizes the motions of his mind. It was to Kohut's great credit, in my opinion, that he closely studied a class of narcissistic patients who were incapable of ingesting standard psychoanalytic interpretations, and in the process discovered the specific types of transference *experiences* that they actually needed. Of course, I believe that this paradigm extends to most patients at the beginning of treatment and that an interpretation of material unknown to the patient is only useful after an authentic self is available to digest it.

For at the beginning we are trying to enter into the patient's emotional world; to learn to trust his feelings and to allow him to begin to trust ours. If we are even fractionally successful, the patient's emotions and our emotions begin to slowly interpenetrate, and we begin to see the occasional emergence of a mutually shared or expanded state of consciousness.

In this expanded or transitional state, which for a long while may exist only for moments at a time, the question of who is observing whom or who is judging whom, or even who has said what, becomes no longer important or even relevant: it no longer makes sense. In such a shared transitional state the patient is no longer ashamed or afraid to say whatever comes to mind and the analyst no longer has to worry about tactics or technique because this also has become irrelevant.

Of course I am describing an ideal state that rarely exists in such a perfect form, but Balint (1968), Winnicott (1953) and many others have also described variants of this third state. One could also call it a state of mutual trust, a subject that Ellman (2007) has been dealing with for a long time. Not to suggest that it will last, because as the transference inevitably goes through its cycles, it may again become defensive, paranoid, schizoid, or filled with rageful enactments. But once such moments are achieved they are never entirely lost, and they become part of the loving and hating or trusting and distrusting of a primary object that I have described as the process of mourning in divergent conflicts.

I suppose I should say a word about regression here, because mostly I have been describing the psychoanalytic situation in which the patient comes three to five times a week and is usually lying on the couch with the analyst out of sight. For most patients who are able to tolerate this arrangement, it has generally proved to allow for the widest flexibility of expression and states of consciousness in both patient and analyst and, paradoxically, for the most intimate of connections. The reasons for this are manifold but to mention just two:

1. The recumbent position is closer to the sleep state and to the child state and so facilitates the emergence of archaic states and material; and
2. It bypasses the usual social conventions of conversation and throws us back to a level in which affects, sensations, and neurophysiological reactions come to the foreground while words tend to lose their customary symbolic meanings and remain in the background.

There are of course many patients who at the beginning are not sufficiently trusting or stabilized enough to use this arrangement, but I try to work towards it *especially* with them because in my experience psychoanalysis is often the only real cure for many of the most challenging and disturbed patients.

One of the great advantages of having the patient use the couch is that it allows him the possibility of making you into whoever or whatever he wants and needs you to be, regardless of who you actually are. Now of course that happens even when the patient is sitting up, but it often makes it harder for him to imagine you as what he needs if he is constantly confronted by a dissonant visual image. And of course the shame implicit in revealing our needs is more difficult to deal with when you feel stared at and observed. Certain patients may habitually look away when they are seated across from their therapist, and this is often a sign that they want, consciously or unconsciously, to be lying on the couch.

I think by now I have said enough about states of consciousness so that the next time you notice a shift in consciousness you might be more curious about what is happening. Not that I suggest you interrogate people about this, because I do believe that the most therapeutic approach is to join in their state, to the extent that that is possible. But entering into another person's world, whether patient or friend, can be extremely difficult. If the other world is very different, the parameters are changed so much that questions which seemed absolutely crucial in one world may appear totally irrelevant in the other. To take the most obvious example, in a court of law it is critical to know who said what, but in certain mutual states in analysis it is of no importance if something was said by the analyst or the patient; both parties may feel this is simply irrelevant, and if the question were to be pursued it would spoil the situation.

By analogy, a superficial dream with lots of secondary process may be easy enough to describe, but something from the depths may be almost impossible to express in logical words and categories. We might imagine that one of our jobs as therapists is to help organize the multiple worlds in which all of us live and to integrate them in some meaningful way.

Many years ago I pointed out that there are two general kinds of consciousness that everyone shares, which I called subjective and objective self-awareness (Bach, 1985). In subjective awareness, we are lost in ourselves and oblivious to others, like in a daydream, whereas in objective self-awareness we are acutely aware of observing ourselves as if we were another person, sometimes to the extreme of feeling depersonalized. Compare in your mind the stereotypes of an hysterical person who is walking through the streets lost in fantasy with the stereotype of an obsessive who is walking through the same streets acutely aware of every movement of every limb and of the gaze of every onlooker.

But in fact we all oscillate between these two states of consciousness to a greater or lesser degree depending on what seems appropriate. It is conventionally inappropriate to be lost in your own fantasies while I am giving a lecture, just as it would seem less functional to be acutely observing your own and your partner's every movement while you are making love. Many people have great difficulty either in finding the state of consciousness appropriate to a particular situation or else in shifting appropriately back and forth. Fonagy (1991) has written extensively about the difficulty borderline patients have in arriving at reflective self-awareness, but that is only a small part of the larger issue of flexible shifting between states of consciousness.

And that is why I want to mention the therapeutic effects of simply permitting oneself to enter, whether on or off the couch, into a state of consciousness that promotes free association. We have generally thought of free association as useful in permitting unconscious material to rise into consciousness. But a related and perhaps even more important function is that "it facilitates the patient's learning to integrate and to shift flexibly among states of relatively objective self-awareness and reality adherence, and states of relatively subjective self-awareness and disregard of reality" (Rosegrant, 2005, p. 765).

Just as we must all shift between sleeping and waking every single day of our lives, even when awake we all oscillate between being relatively asleep in subjective awareness or acutely awake in objective self-awareness. Some people do this more easily and more successfully than others. It is an important part of our therapeutic work to help our patients bring their multiple worlds of sleeping and waking into a more coherent and more meaningful integration.

CHAPTER FOUR

New developments in the theory and clinical application of the annihilation anxiety concept

Marvin Hurvich[1]

My interest in annihilation anxieties (AA) goes back to a 1980 clinical observation that recalcitrant symptoms in more disturbed patients are often underlaid by defended anxieties concerning annihilation and threats to survival. Analytic scrutiny revealed that these anxieties included apprehensions of being overwhelmed, dissolved, invaded, or going insane. In addition to constructing a research instrument to measure the extent of these anxieties in clinical populations (Benveniste, Papouchis, Allen & Hurvich, 1998; Hurvich, 1989; Hurvich, Benveniste, Howard & Coonerty, 1993; Hurvich & Simha Alpern, 1997; Hurvich, Allen, & Mcguire, 2006a; Levin & Hurvich, 1995), I embarked on an intensive study of the psychoanalytic literature that revealed a consequential incongruity concerning annihilation fantasies and anxieties (Hurvich, 2003). On the one hand, there were hundreds of references to the correlates of survival-related apprehensions. On the other, formulations of such anxieties tended to be relatively undeveloped, and accorded little conceptual status in standard current mainstream theoretical works. Recent compendia of psychoanalytic theory and practice (Goldberger, 1996; Gray, 1994; Moore & Fine, 1995; Nersessian & Kopff, 1996; Person, Cooper & Gabbard, 2005) rarely mention these phenomena, or refer to them only in passing. I concluded that an important set of anxiety contents and experiences were either being overlooked or remained undeveloped in serious mainstream theorizing. Although these compendia did deal with *psychic trauma*, a closely related concept, they neither related psychic trauma to the psychoanalytic theory of anxiety nor reached any kind of consensus regarding its definition. Exceptions include the work of Krystal (1968, 1988) on *Massive Psychic Trauma* and volumes edited by Furst (1967), and Rothstein (1986), among others. A recent statement by Andre Green (2006) is congruent with my observation that there has been a failure to develop the implications of annihilation anxieties. Green wrote that issues such as fears of annihilation, primitive agonies and nameless dread are mentioned "in relation to theory with regard to a hypothetical appearance during the childhood of patients, *but their clinical description in the adult has been given little detailed attention in clinical psychoanalysis*" (p. 42, italics added).

In 1926, Freud wrote, concerning his evocative concept of the *traumatic moment*: "*Anxiety is the original reaction to helplessness in the trauma and is reproduced later on in the danger situation as a signal for help*" (pp. 166–167, italics added). The anxiety that Freud refers to here reflects all the hallmarks of terror, or of what some writers had been referring to as *annihilation anxiety* (Little, 1958). This connection further motivated me to look for ways to interrelate, and additionally connect anxiety theory and trauma theory. In previously published work, I have presented a detailed consideration of the annihilation anxiety concept (Hurvich, 1989, 1991, 2000, 2002a, 2002b, 2003, 2004). The current chapter highlights my specific contributions to the construct, the writers whose ideas I utilized, elaborated, and attempted to connect, and the presentation of new applications that explore annihilation anxiety as a process variable in a psychoanalytic therapeutic framework.

My contributions

Here are what I believe to be my additions to psychoanalysis in the area of anxiety theory:

1. A specification of six annihilation anxiety Dimensions and sub-Dimensions, which highlight central components and major manifestations of these survival-related fantasy contents/anxieties.

I consider the bringing into focus of these survival-related apprehensions to be part of this contribution. The Dimensions comprise a range of psychic dangers associated with threats to the sense of safety, and specifically, to mental survival, to apprehensions over being destroyed or being unable to function, to self cohesion, and to fears over intimacy in interpersonal relations. These six overlapping Dimensions are at the level of *clinical generalizations*. They provide a succinct framework that highlights major areas under which most of the *clinical observations* regarding survival apprehensions may be included. Psychoanalytic writers typically have specified one or another of the manifestations of survival anxieties (Hurvich, 2003), but, rarely a series (i.e., Winnicott, 1974; Laing, 1959).

I have also related the Dimensions to the famous four basic dangers (Freud, 1926; Brenner, 1982), and have claimed that annihilation fantasy contents and anxieties may go beyond these four to include states of being Overwhelmed, Merged, Disorganized, Invaded and Destroyed, which may be triggered along with any of them as secondary reactions (see Proposition 14, Hurvich, 2003). This may be based on the disorganization of self or of ego functioning due to the intensity of the initial anxiety, or when the initial anxiety elicits additional frights, i.e., secondary anxiety (Hurvich, 1997; Schur, 1953). Freud (1926) described each of the four dangers in terms of *loss*: of object, of love, of genital integrity, and of superego support. Annihilation fantasies and anxieties can, in this regard, be seen as concerned with *a loss of the capacity to function and/or exist*. There is also an important contrast here. The four previously recognized basic dangers centre on the *anticipation* of being harmed by an avenging external or internal other, which is what leads to fear of the anticipated loss of the object, etc. While annihilation anxieties can also be engendered by apprehensions of being threatened by the retaliatory intentions of others, they are uniquely concerned with threats to, or disturbances of, the capacity to function or to exist. In this regard, Freud (1926) added that the real essence of the danger goes beyond the loss of object and involves, for the infant, intolerable tension which he or she is unable to alleviate alone (p. 137; see also Schur, 1953, p. 71).

The Dimensional approach allows a more specific delineation of the clinical manifestations under scrutiny, such as, whether the emphasis, in a given case, is on the threat of *Invasion,* or the threat of *Abandonment*, etc. Similarly, in relation to the sub-Dimensions, when the major relevant Dimension is being *Overwhelmed*, is the fantasy about being *Smothered, Swept away, or Overstimulated*? When the apprehension is about being merged, are there indications that this is serving as a defence against the terror of *Abandonment, or something else* (Lewin & Schulz, 1992)? This elucidation also has therapeutic implications. For example, containment and reflection are especially appropriate forms of intervention (while confrontation and interpretation would be more likely to trigger substantial defensiveness) in patients whose invasion apprehensions (Dimension 4) are especially strong.

Dimensionalizing annihilation anxieties, as just described, allows the raising and exploring of questions that have theoretical, diagnostic and therapeutic implications. For example, to what extent and under what conditions are high penetration fears associated with riddance mechanisms such as externalization and projection? To what extent and under what conditions does the repeated use of these defences interfere with containment, identification with the analyst, and taking in the analyst's interventions? Under what conditions do annihilation anxieties in both patient and analyst influence manifestations of transference and countertransference? What are the relations between a wish for or fear of merger, of penetration, and of being overwhelmed? What are the relationships, in a given patient and for groups of patients, between fears of falling forever, fears of shattering into bits, and fears of fading away? How do these relationships connect to such factors as specific traumatic history, dominant unconscious fantasies, high or low levels of aggression, high or low ego strength in general, and particular ego functions, such as stable reality testing and capacity for synthesis? In relation to what considerations do fears of catastrophe, merger, and penetration constitute survival concerns, and when do they not (Hurvich, 2003, pp. 605–606)?

2. A second contribution is proposing annihilation anxieties as a bridge between the psychoanalytic theory of *anxiety* and the psychoanalytic theory of *psychic trauma*, both refining and further delineating Freud's 1926 assertion that anxiety is the first reaction to a trauma. This is also consistent with Compton's (1980) view that the traumatic state was always at the heart of Freud's anxiety theory. Relevant here is the proposal that

[A]nnihilation anxieties constitute psychic trauma markers. And, conversely, that experiences of psychic trauma increase annihilation fantasy apprehensions. Thus, annihilation anxieties are centrally involved in the experience of psychic trauma, and comprise major traumatic residua (Hurvich, 2003, p. 591).

A traumatic situation response, often associated with helplessness and panic anxiety, may induce or be a response to annihilation concerns. This is supported by frequent reports from panic attack victims regarding fears of going crazy, losing control, and/or dying (Hurvich, 2002b, 2003).

I am further proposing that this elaboration of the annihilation anxiety concept, and the designation of annihilation anxiety as a trauma marker, answers Sandler, Dreher and Drews (1991) call for finding a *relevant concept that could "represent the whole spectrum of traumatogenic disturbances"* (p. 140). The dimensional approach to annihilation anxieties complements the trauma concept, by providing greater specificity concerning the anxieties involved.

3. A third contribution builds on the two propositions just delineated. This is a proposal to *expand the basic danger series to include annihilation apprehensions, while retaining the distinction between a traumatic situation and a danger situation.*

Once the trauma has occurred, experiences of being overwhelmed, a signature of the traumatic moment, subsequently can be anticipated and the anticipation itself constitutes a danger situation. In addition, when the affective component is *controlled* and *attenuated* (Hurvich, 1996), it is consistent with a key definition of signal anxiety: a "recognized, remembered, expected situation of helplessness" (Freud, 1926, p. 166). This is the justification for proposing that annihilation fantasy anticipations be included in the basic danger series (Hurvich, 1989, 2002a, 2002b, 2003).

This is also true for experiences of being invaded, merged, disorganized, abandoned, and destroyed. Thus, issues related to being overwhelmed or annihilated (Freud, 1923, p. 57) may be part of a traumatic moment in present time, or may characterize a danger situation that is anticipated in future time: concerns about being overwhelmed, etc., may thus reflect either present, actual, or potential threat (Hurvich, 2003; Schur, 1953). This formulation is somewhat at odds with Kohut's (1984) closely related concept of disintegration anxiety, which he *differentiates from the basic dangers*.

To suggest an extension of the basic danger series to include survival concerns constitutes a step in the direction of greater integration of the psychoanalytic theory of *anxiety* and the psychoanalytic theory of *psychic trauma*. This rapprochement enhances and enriches both concepts, and renders them more relevant to the range of issues that arise in the consulting room, the psychiatric ward, and beyond. The annihilation dangers reflected in the six Dimensions enrich clinical understanding and expand the focus of anxieties that are seen as important and noteworthy. They constitute an attempt to further delineate the psychoanalytic formulation of anxiety, a concept Freud (1917) asserted to be central to the psychology of neurosis (i.e., of psychopathology).

An objection might be raised that putting traumatic-annihilation anxieties in the basic danger series blurs Freud's valuable distinction between traumatic and signal anxieties. On the contrary, what is being underscored here is that traumatic anxiety and overwhelmed helplessness, i.e., the traumatic moment, can subsequently be anticipated, and associated with psychic content. And while in the traumatic moment, the anxiety response tends to be *uncontrolled*, when it is later anticipated, it may become associated with *controlled* affect. In this regard, it is useful to distinguish annihilation *anxiety* from annihilation *content*, the former usually implying *uncontrolled* anxiety, the latter, *controlled*. Annihilation content may thus be connected with a traumatic moment, but it may be the anticipation of a traumatic moment. As an anticipation, annihilation fantasies meet all the requirements Freud specified for a danger situation, as quoted above: a "recognized, remembered, *expected* situation of helplessness".

Currently, there is a tendency to emphasize the essential similarity between traumatic and other anxieties (Brenner, 1986; Compton, 1980). But the substantial regression and disorganization that often accompany traumatic anxieties lead to outcomes that are consequentially different from those associated with non-traumatic anxieties. The difference is clinically meaningful. Defences against traumatic anxieties include dissociative, catatonoid, paranoid, and/or compensatory mechanisms (e.g., identification with the aggressor, abuse of alcohol and other drugs), and encapsulation (Hopper, 1991). Traumatic experiences may shatter fantasies of invulnerability and the person's sense of safety in the world (Zetzel, 1949). When the anxiety signal is deranged or put out of action, the ability to anticipate psychic danger is compromised. Indeed, Compton (1980) posited a negative correlation between helplessness and anticipation: "Roughly, the less anticipation, the more helplessness" (p. 755). These reactions are rarely found in non-traumatic anxiety responses.

4. A related contribution is the identification of annihilation anxieties as central to the more severe psychopathologies, in cases which extend beyond the neurotic range (Hurvich, 2002, 2003a, 2004). These survival apprehensions are especially prevalent in more disturbed patients. They include psychoses, borderline and narcissistic personalities, perversions, many psychosomatic conditions, and many addictions. Full-blown annihilation anxieties are seen most dramatically in panic attacks, nightmares, acute suicidal crises, and fulminating psychotic breakdowns.

The famous four basic dangers are also relevant for these more disturbed patients, where they tend to be found in conjunction with, and to trigger annihilation apprehensions. Even here, additional distinctions can be made. For example, borderline and psychotic patients may deal with annihilation anxieties differently. Borderline children have been reported to retain awareness of threats of psychic fragmentation, while psychotics are more likely to mask such awareness with delusions (Frijling-Schreuder, 1969).

Additionally and consequentially, highlighting the centrality of annihilation anxieties in psychopathology beyond the neurotic range could lead to improvement of psychoanalytic psychotherapy with these more disturbed individuals by stimulating increased awareness in clinicians of the significance of these anxieties and their inter-relationships. Awareness should also be raised regarding the relationship of annihilation anxiety to ego and superego functioning, particularly with character defences as well as with defensive processes more generally, and with how they affect transference and especially countertransference reactions (Wallerstein, 1997).

5. Another contribution involves elaborating the meaning of annihilation anxieties in psychoanalytic theory by utilizing a propositional approach focused on specifying the essential features of these

anxieties (Freedman, Hurvich & Ward, 2007; Hurvich & Freedman, 2006b). The major components of this approach to psychoanalytic concepts are Coreness, Dimensions and Modifiers (Hurvich & Freedman, in preparation). This endeavour includes delineating the major assumptions and implications of the construct in succinct, declarative statements, cast in plain English, that are potentially testable. It is proposed that any psychoanalytic concept can be clarified by applying such a propositional approach.

Propositions related to annihilation anxieties

The following illustrate the Propositional Method in relation to the central topic of this chapter.

a. The danger associated with annihilation anxieties is survival threat;
b. Annihilation concerns constitute early danger, but can be engendered throughout the life cycle whenever there is a perception-fantasy of survival threat;
c. Annihilation anxieties comprise a fifth basic danger, which interrelates with the four generally accepted basic dangers in various ways;
d. Annihilation anxieties are centrally involved in the experience of psychic trauma, and comprise major traumatic residuals;
e. Excessive annihilation anxieties, especially during developmental years, increase the likelihood of ego function weakness and self pathology. Conversely, ego weakness and self pathology increase the likelihood of excessive annihilation anxieties;
f. Annihilation concerns may be encoded in a concrete somatosensory, affective, pre-symbolic form;
g. Annihilation apprehensions, as with the four typical dangers, may be identifiable as dynamic psychic content, and constitute a component in a conflict-compromise matrix.
h. Annihilation anxieties may occur with or without anticipation;
i. Annihilation-related themes/fantasies may be accompanied by uncontrolled or controlled anxiety;
j. Annihilation fantasies and affects constitute motives for defence;

k. Fears of being overwhelmed by aggressive as well as by libidinal impulses associated with self and object representations are a repetitive finding in relation to annihilation anxieties;
l. Annihilation anxieties are found in psychotics and in non-psychotics;
m. Anxiety and symptoms may be experienced as psychic danger, and can trigger annihilation anxieties as secondary phenomena;
n. Symptoms, beliefs, affect states and behaviours are especially resistant to change when they are defending against annihilation anxieties (Hurvich, 2003a).

6. The last contribution involves a programme of empirical research which focuses on measurement of annihilation anxieties with objective and projective tests (see references already cited), and from the clinical interview. This material is not included in the current chapter.

Six annihilation anxiety dimensions and sub-dimensions

The *Dimensions* involve different degrees and qualities of *helplessness*, and variations on how central the threat is anticipated to be for ego functioning, for the integrity of the self, and for the stability and predictability of the person's object relations. As already stated, the six *Dimensions* are related to and sometimes overlap with Freud's (1926) basic dangers (loss of the object, loss of love, of castration/bodily harm, and loss of super-ego approval), and may be triggered along with them, but also go beyond them. In their briefest designation, the annihilation *Dimensions* are:

1) OVERWHELMED   2) MERGED   3) DISORGANIZED
4) INVADED   5) ABANDONED   6) DESTROYED

A number of clinical observations are subsumed under each of these dimensions, such as apprehensions over disappearing, of leaking out, of being devoured or engulfed; of smothering, being trapped; of vertigo, of falling, fear of regression, of losing control of urges, and of going insane. Also included are fear of fear itself, as well as fright, terror, horror, and dread.

OVERWHELMED

		MERGED
Buried Alive	Smothered	Devoured/Swallowed
Drowned	Swept away	Absorbed
Flooded	Trapped	Trapped
Loss of Control	Inability to Function	
Overstimulated		

FRAGMENTED: SELF/EGO

		INVADED
Split off	Immobilized	Persecuted/Tortured
Disappeared	Melting	Intruded upon
Dehumanized	Mortified	Penetrated
Evaporated	Negated	Body Complaints
Falling apart	Nothingness	
Going Insane	Shattered	

ABANDONED

		DESTROYED
Cast out	Falling	Killed
Cut off	Excluded	Poisoned
Deserted	Rejected	World Destruction
		Catastrophic
		Mentality
		Demoralized
		Immobilized

While these psychic *contents* go a long way in defining annihilation anxieties, there is also a *formal* aspect, related to ego strength, that plays an important role in differentiating when "going to pieces" does or does not lead to "falling apart" (Epstein, 1998). These formal factors are set forth as variables in relation to traumatic (annihilation) and signal anxieties (Hurvich, 2004).

TRAUMATIC ANXIETY　　　　　　　**SIGNAL ANXIETY**

Desymbolized <----------------------------------> Symbolized
Uncontrolled <-----------------------------------> Controlled
Intolerable <--------------------------------------> Tolerable

NEW DEVELOPMENTS IN THE THEORY AND CLINICAL APPLICATION

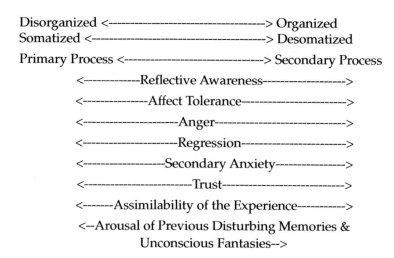

```
Disorganized <--------------------------------> Organized
Somatized <----------------------------------> Desomatized
Primary Process <-------------------------------> Secondary Process
           <-------------Reflective Awareness------------------>
           <----------------Affect Tolerance--------------------->
           <------------------------Anger----------------------------->
           <----------------------Regression----------------------->
           <------------------Secondary Anxiety---------------->
           <-------------------------Trust------------------------->
           <--------Assimilability of the Experience----------->
           <--Arousal of Previous Disturbing Memories &
                   Unconscious Fantasies-->
```

While all these add additional specificity to annihilation anxiety manifestations, the most central are Desymbolized/Symbolized (Freedman et al., 2007), Uncontrolled/Controlled (Hurvich, 1997; Schur, 1953), and Intolerable/Tolerable (Freud, 1894; Krystal, 1988).

When annihilation fantasies are accompanied by markers characterizing the more pathological, maladaptive, and primitive pole, the reaction is more likely to qualify as a traumatic response. Conversely, when the markers found along with annihilation content are on the more adaptive side (controlled anxiety, presence and utilization of reflective functioning, etc.), there is a greater likelihood that it is an anticipation of a traumatic situation. The important issues of time of recovery and residuals, including the possibility of a traumatic neurosis or post-traumatic stress disorder are relevant here. Time of onset whether infantile, childhood, adolescence, or adulthood is also a key variable. Severe childhood trauma tends to result in a permanent expectation and dread of a return of the traumatic state. In these cases, fear of emotions develops and thus increases the likelihood of an impairment of affect tolerance (Zetzel, 1949; Krystal, 1988). Under debate is the contribution of psychic trauma to pathogenesis more generally, and how to distinguish pathological influences of trauma from other patholog-ical effects (Baranger, Baranger & Mom, 1988). While his conception of psychic trauma changed as his theories evolved, Freud (1940) attributed a key role to psychic trauma in all symptom formation.

Psychoanalytic theorists who have influenced my views

In the framework of this chapter, the current section must be substantially abbreviated. From Freud, most essentially, I utilized the two-fold view of traumatic and signal anxieties, and the "traumatic moment", the subjective sense of helplessness, the idea that anxiety is the first reaction to the trauma, and that danger situations develop hierarchically. From Anna Freud (1952), there was the description of an early anxiety triggered by perceived threats to the intactness of the mental organization, a key basis for annihilation anxiety experiences. There was then Max Schur's (1953) emphasis on the distinction between *controlled* and *uncontrolled* anxiety, with some nod to Freud's distinction between bound and unbound energy; and between evaluation of the danger and the reaction to that evaluation; Silber (1989) additionally differentiated experiencing the danger, and its evaluation. Schur (1953) further focused on loss of the time sense due to regression in reality testing, resulting in earlier anxieties potentiating current ones; and eventuating in loss of the ability to restrict anxiety to a signal; and that resomatization is a regressive response to danger, which tends to reinforce the subject's sense of actual danger, and often triggers secondary anxiety. I also learned from Krystal's (1968) early elaboration of massive psychic trauma, his identification of alexithymia as a key sequela of psychic trauma, and his elaboration of Max Stern's depiction of the catatanoid response to trauma. Stern (1988) additionally defined the basis for signal anxiety as the ability to ascribe meaning to one's states of tension, implying a degree of tension binding combined with subjective awareness.

Zetzel identified the issue of anxiety tolerance, and underscored the importance of experiencing some anxiety as a prophylaxis against future traumatic overwhelming. She also emphasized the place of aggression in the anxiety arena, as had Melanie Klein, Heimann, Issacs, and Riviere (1952), and Flescher (1955). Rangell (1955) made the important point that the psychic danger, in the sense of helplessness, leads to the fantasy-anticipation that things will get worse, never stop, and move towards total psychic and motor paralysis. Compton (1980) added the distinction between a danger situation and an anxiety response, and also recognized that anxiety experience is based on a fantasy of disaster, possibly a memory or repetition of an earlier state of helplessness, and that a time correction constituting the reality-testing component is needed. Compton further clarified that the components in the pathogenesis chain can occur in different temporal orders, but especially that perception of danger is what triggers anxiety, rather than the more popular view that anxiety signals danger. The perception of danger view comes from early Freud (1917), Stewart (1967), Waelder (1967), Schafer (1983a), Gillette (1990), and Lazarus (1966). Additional Compton contributions I have utilized include his assertion (1980) that the traumatic state was always at the heart of Freud's anxiety theory, which is the opposite of the view taken by Brenner (1953), who rejected Freud's evidence for *traumatic anxiety*. I have found no challenge in the psychoanalytic literature to Brenner's 1953 position, which suggests this key change of Freud's anxiety theory has been insufficiently recognized. Brenner also decisively rejected the inclusion of psychic dangers beyond the famous four (1982, 1997). It has further been inadequately appreciated that Brenner's widely embraced formulation of the calamities of childhood both collapses and confounds the distinction between a danger situation and a traumatic one, as did his 1953 definition of anxiety as "an emotion (affect) which the anticipation of danger evokes in the ego" (p. 22). He claims this definition allows us to "avoid the *unwelcome necessity* of assuming that there are two kinds of anxiety" (p. 22, italics added). In contrast to this idea of "unwelcome necessity", Freud's presentation of the *two* sources of anxiety constitutes the essence of his revised anxiety theory of 1926, re-iterated in 1933. In my view, Brenner's more parsimonious formulation cuts out the heart of Freud's 1926/33 revised theory, and virtually blocks further integration of the theories of anxiety and of psychic trauma, as already emphasized.

I have also learned from and utilized the insights of Winnicott (1960a), especially his "primitive agonies" (Going to pieces, Falling forever, Having no relationship to the body, and Having no orientation). Other influences include Laing's (1959) Ontological Insecurities (Engulfment, Implosion/Impingement and Petrification/Depersonalization), and Margaret Little's (1959) assertion that when annihilation anxiety prevails, everything is linked with survival and non-survival, and Bion's (1952) evocative concept of nameless dread.

Clinical application section

The patient is a 56-year-old white, female, Christian-born college graduate with advanced degrees in her chosen field. She is from an affluent, non-East Coast family, with a financially successful father and an artistically talented mother, socially prominent community leaders involved in civic and religious activities; a power-couple, who projected a public image of the perfect family. The patient is the third of four, with a brother five years older, one three years older, and a sister, six years younger. This is a selective case report included to illustrate the concepts delineated in earlier sections of this chapter.

Presenting complaints

When we began seven years ago, the patient described herself as a "ball of pain", with frequent anxiety and chronic feelings of dread, alarm that she was unravelling, and a pervasive sense of sadness, guilt, and low self-esteem. She was ashamed and discouraged over her weight. She had a tense and conflictual relationship with her parents. While socially popular, they showed little respect or empathy for others, and deeply resented being told anything about how they conducted themselves. Their façade of graciousness was underlaid by manipulative and blame-avoidant trends. Domineering towards their children, the father had beaten them, especially the boys, and both parents used the silent treatment and ignoring when the children displeased them, up to the present day.

The patient also described an ongoing childhood disappointment and feeling of deprivation and rejection in the relationship with her mother, who "sucks all the air out of the room", whose refrain was, "You are hateful and ungrateful"—a mother whom she felt spoiled every day of her childhood. There was the quality of a narcissistic trauma, with the mother demanding attention and adulation but ignoring and devaluing the patient's needs for consideration and recognition. The patient regularly felt depleted, unhappy, alone, and exhausted. She did not feel loved for herself by her mother. A replay of this trauma has been central to the patient's difficulties in her chosen profession, where she has been struggling to make something happen. Since the age of five, the patient had felt her mother wanted to crush her self expression and wishes for attention. She also expressed concern that her boyfriend might kill himself, that she could not bear his dependence on her, and that she did not know how to handle him.

As I later learned, for years the patient had an uncertain sense that something had happened with her father when she was little. She recalled no details, and the topic was off limits. Things were so terrible with her mother that she could not bring herself to question her relationship with her father and possibly risk losing him as well. She did not have enough security with her sense of self to move in that direction. Reflecting back on that, she said, "As time went on, I developed a sense that you could help me with this, and then it took over three years of our hard work for it to fully come out. I had a vague sense that something was there, but allowing the rest of my mind to see the picture was slow in coming. There was guilt, fear of punishment, retaliation, and the dread of hurting my parents." For years, she had felt ashamed, guilty, and infuriated over how they treated her, and she was unable to deal with their overt and subtle criticism in ways that allowed her to experience good feelings about herself.

The patient acknowledged great difficulty entering intimate relationships with men, stating that when a man showed interest in her, she felt *cornered*, and when she yielded to him, it felt like she was *"in free-fall, like falling off a cliff"*. "Sex ruined things," she said. And it was only with her current boyfriend of 20 years that sex was eventually successful, but they had not been sexually active for the past five years due to mutual agreement, and more recently due mostly to his disinclination. Reports of childhood sleepwalking and, during her early 20s, awakening in the beds of men she hardly knew and not remembering how she got there, pointed to *dissociation* and a likely history of sexual abuse. As the analysis proceeded, repetitive psychic trauma from childhood sexual relations with the father came to be recognized as a significant psychic organizer.

Course of treatment

This on-the-couch psychoanalytic treatment began at two times a week, and later increased to three. The patient's dreams and fantasies have been dominated by sexual and aggressive imagery. She has had many fantasies of hurting her father painfully and severely, without clearly understanding why, until the reasons surfaced during the analysis.

Dead girls in the closet dream

The first dream, reported after four months, was one she had dreamt at the age of 35 while in a previous therapy. This earlier treatment had been sought following her being sexually seduced by a Swami, as reported below:

> There's an empty house, and I'm desperately looking to save someone. I'm going from room to room, opening closets, and in every one I find a dead girl. It looked more like a Halloween skeleton, but I knew it was a dead girl.

She associated the dream setting to her female cousin's bedroom where, as an adolescent, she thought she saw the girl's father fondling her breasts, and the cousin looked unhappy.

In exploring the dream, the patient associated herself to the dead girls in the closets she was trying to save. The Halloween skeletons "are supposed to be scary, but they aren't real. Still, in the dream, it was really scary." This decades-old dream, remembered in the treatment, hinted at incest via the uncle. *I pointed out that, in the dream, she discovered that something had killed her long ago, perhaps psychically, and that skeletons in the closet, suggested hidden family secrets. I noted that she had strong motivation to rescue herself and that, while she felt very afraid, she attempted to deny the scariness* (via the Halloween skeletons).

In the earlier therapy the patient had been unable to say the dead girls dream aloud, and the therapist then asked her to write it down, while commenting that she thought the patient was being melodramatic. She dated the high level of anxiety she had suffered for years to the dead girls in the closet dream. The patient told me that the secret was ready to come out then, but the therapist did not know how to handle it or help her bring it out. As a result, it "left me with 20 years of anxiety before we got to it here".

A few sessions later she described another dream of having gone to the bathroom, where she pulled out a tampon, and tampons kept coming out. Her association was to *secrets*. The dream imagery suggested the secrets related to extruding things from her genitals. After reporting this dream, she recounted a long forgotten memory of how, while baby-sitting at the age of 12, in a semi-trance-like state, she had sexually stimulated a four-year-old boy while he slept. This is an example of the obligatory repetition found in many trauma victims; the urge/tendency actively to perpetrate what had been passively suffered.

Once the patient recovered this memory, following the report of the dead girls in the closet dream, she postponed, for three weeks, telling me of a freshly remembered episode from when she was 30. At that time she had been seduced by a Swami from an Eastern spiritual community to which she had become attached. She lost her will when the Swami unexpectedly made physical advances. Following the event, she was unable to stop crying, felt like killing herself, and had to sever her ties with the group. For months she felt mystified at her state of mind, gained weight rapidly, and sought therapy. She recalls being so pent up and frightened at the time, that on her way to the early sessions she rolled up her car windows and screamed to release the virtually unbearable tension.

Remembrance of the Swami molestation, following the recovery of the episode where she had fondled the four-year-old boy, led to a gradual awareness, described by her as a *series of snap-shots that slowly became a more continuous memory*, which led to the connection that her father and she had long engaged in sexual activity, between the ages of four and 12. As she said, "The idea that father had a deeper connection with me that I hadn't remembered was cracked open. What I did to the little boy, and what had happened with the Swami felt real, and opened the memory that father had done things to me, and that they were real also." Here the recall of what she had actively perpetrated—turning passive into active—preceded and likely expedited uncovering of the father-incest memories, as did the recall of being passively seduced by the Swami.

An additional, *recent* event also seemed related and facilitative: the patient had successfully headed off a habitual fault-finding/blaming ritual to which the parents regularly subjected her when they visited New York. We came to see this as a pattern: other therapeutic breakthroughs, especially recovery of memories and the making of significant connections, followed experiences of active mastery in her current life. Here is an example of the working through of the traumatic memories, repeated many times with related imagery and different details; and here again, including active fantasy responses, alternating with the accompanying annihilation anxiety:

> I'm his little girl [crying] and if he realized and thought of that, he wouldn't have done all these things. Now I'm switching it around, because I used to be afraid he was stabbing me and splitting me through the middle. Now, I want to put my fist through his throat and split him all down the middle, and then, bleeding and split open, I want to walk on him. She continued: "Remembering being close to him, I feel like I'm *falling off a cliff, falling into nothingness*. (What emotion?) I'm terrified, diving, running away. My mind goes, like over the cliff, so I won't be there .... (More detail?) I'm lying down, and I can't get away, flat on the bed, and the only thing that can get away is my mind [dissociative defence]. So diving off a cliff allows me to get away. It becomes a happy escape, like jumping into a lake from a rope tied to a tree branch, like I did with my brothers at grandpa's farm.

The carnival dream

Several years into the treatment, as she was recovering some disconnected fragments of the incest episodes, the patient reported the following dream. The sexual explicitness stands in marked contrast to the more disguised imagery of the earlier dead girls dream, and is consistent with the view that dreams with such content suggest efforts to master childhood traumatic experience (Fine, Joseph & Waldhorn, 1969) *Here is the dream as she reported it:*

> A bedroom turned into a children's carnival. There were three women there with no clothes on, but they were wearing makeup. I'm an adult and am told to sit on the edge of the bed and spread my legs. I said, "I've never done this before." The most grotesque woman starts stimulating me with her tongue, it's bizarre. I allow it but I am not enjoying it. She looks up at me and says, "I'm a virgin giving head." I thought, "Now I've been to whore's camp." There's a hula-hoop and I am supposed to throw a plate through it into a basket. People come

into the room, shine a spotlight on me, and someone says, "It's F's [the patient's] turn." Another says, "No, she already had a turn." I get a plate as a prize and I recognize it as Aunt B's plate [the mother of the girl whose room was associated to the dead girls in the closets dream].

The patient now reveals that the cousin's father had chronically abused the cousin sexually. It's the cousin she had seen being fondled by the girl's father, as reported earlier.

"The grotesque woman's tongue was very specific, a strong sensory feeling. I've never seen a tongue like that! Thick, and too red, and too big for her mouth. I watched her go back and forth over the inside of my legs—it felt real, *like I'd experienced that before*. The feeling, it was all grotesque and wrong, but I was supposed to be polite, not say anything or protest. In the dream it seemed like a routine thing, like the dead girls in the closet.

Carnival dream associations

The faces of the naked women running the carnival were distorted because of their sexual arousal, and reminded me of an X-rated Fellini film [such distorted facial expressions were later connected to her father's unfamiliar look when he was sexually aroused]. They asked me to throw another plate, and my father yells, "No, she's already misfired." (Misfired?) It's the man that misfires. (What occurs to you?) An explosion, like a bomb going off in my face, from the ejaculation, too close to my face.

This traumatic memory surfaces as an association to the dream. These are the kinds of traumatic memories recovered in the analysis. Others were of father drying her off after her bath, of his face and body being very close to her, and of feelings of excitement, vulnerability, disorientation, and dread.

Several sessions after telling the carnival dream, the patient revealed for the first time that she had followed stimulation of the little boy with pleasuring herself, and believes the incident took place when she was around 12, the time she earlier reported that the incest activity stopped. The incident had been unrecalled for years, but its meaning, together with the recovery of the Swami experience, were instrumental in facilitating the gradual recapture of the incest memories. The comment about pleasuring herself provided an "in context" opportunity to ask about her masturbation fantasies.

Masturbation fantasies

Masturbation fantasies regularly provide clues to the person's preferred conditions for sexual pleasure and indications of object-relational dispositions, the ideal adult version being an integration of sex and object love. This patient's masturbation fantasies have been strongly influenced by her sexual traumata and the meanings those had for her, and are a clear example of how the sexual traumas constituted psychic organizers. The two repetitive scenarios she told me were:

> When I touch myself, I imagine I am working in a brothel, but I'm behind a board—I give the men sex but they can only see the bottom half of me … [and] I'm in a large room, sitting on a sacrificial table, waiting for the king, and the whole town is watching, and trying to get me excited by their presence. The king comes in, has sex with me, *but I win*, because I do not get excited. He loses control of himself, and I do not. I'm the one in the centre of things, and I am in control. Here it's not secret, it's public. I receive great public acclaim because I'm the winner.

The patient later added another basis for the resistance to getting excited, and connected it with childhood headaches she chronically suffered. "I resisted the pleasure I now seek because it was related to something that was morally WRONG." The deliberate pleasure inhibition subsequently resulted in her losing control of the excitement, and, for some years, she had not been able to get excited over sex with her boyfriend. That seemed to be changing.

In both masturbation fantasies, she was a victim: in the first, a prostitute in a brothel who provides sex but limits her participation to her bottom half—it is sex without loving or being loved by the partner, while she hides and withholds herself. The second fantasy involved submission to being sacrificed to the sexual desires of the king (father), but here she turns the tables, "stoops to conquer", as she appears to submit to being sacrificed, and triumphs by resisting successfully the sexual excitement, in contrast to the man/father—

who "loses" because he cannot control his sexual desires. In these prototypical fantasies, constructed to enhance her sexual arousal, the patient described sexual dynamics centering on the issue of control over sexual abandon, i.e., in sado-masochistic terms, rather than in terms of mutuality. It is a kind of obligatory fixation in a person who has been chronically sexually seduced and betrayed by her father, and, later, by other men, with her unconscious compliance. Also worth noting is the series of reversals in this fantasy: it is public, not private, and she gets community praise for not giving in to the sexual excitement. She was able to recall that she was terrified that the secret might become known by family members, while, at the same time, she had had a strong urge to reveal it.

While the direct traumatic impact of the sexual violation has been demonstrated, another sequela of the incest was the way in which identity integration was impeded. The patient came to realize, in the course of the treatment, that she could not bring together the image of herself as an ordinary girl and the image of herself as her father's sexual partner. Further, she had a parallel difficulty with achieving an integrated mental image of her father: she could not bring together memories of him in the family situation of her day-to-day life with memories of his unfamiliar visage in the now partly-remembered sexual situation, which she currently recalls as having been distorted, vacant, and unrelated to her. Another indication of compromised self-integration was her split-off partial self-representations described below.

Facilitative external events

The analytic work was aided, complemented, and potentiated in the fifth year of the analysis, when the patient's niece, while psychiatrically hospitalized for suicidal ideation and for a serious eating disorder, accused her grandfather (the patient's father) of having molested her repeatedly. When the patient's sister, the girl's mother, expressed serious doubts concerning her daughter's accusation, my patient then revealed to the niece's therapist that she herself had been molested years earlier by her father. This account was leaked by the therapist to the niece's father, who confronted the patient's parents. The patient's father stated that since his daughter and granddaughter had made these accusations they must be true, but that he remembered nothing. He apologized to both, went into personal therapy, and made what the patient initially thought were efforts at reparation.

The effect of getting the secret out, the subsequent support the patient received within the family, and the details of her parents' responses as the situation unfolded, were followed in the months ahead by a substantial lessening of the patient's intense shame and guilt. This clinically significant series of events was represented in a subsequent dream reported during this period in the treatment.

"I am in a clean, light apartment, and notice a vile, black, mould-like substance leaking out of the wall at the baseboard. The super says that if we remove the outer wall layers, the mould will be detoxified when it is exposed to the light and to the air."

An additional facilitative factor was the realization, as a result of reading an article in *The New Yorker* on psychopathy, that her father had psychopathic traits. This led to her understanding better why his cold behaviour and changed appearance during the sexual encounters threw her into such a frightened state of mind. It clarified that he wanted a physical intimacy that did not signify his love for her. This, for the patient, constituted a rejection that paralleled her mother's ongoing rebuff. In addition to the directly traumatic aspects of the paternal sexual behaviour, the patient, as already mentioned, experienced this intimate liaison as a compensation for the lack of being made to feel special and loved by her mother. It was when the patient realized that her father otherwise treated her in no special way, that his manner was devoid of tenderness, that he was satisfying himself without regard for the consequences to her, and that his remembered facial expression was blank and unloving, that it all changed into a traumatic betrayal, a second trauma on top of the first. "It was my recognition of being used that hurt the most."

The patient's mother went into a depression following the incestual news, and made a serious suicidal attempt. The patient's father subsequently sustained several physical injuries from accidents. Now, less afraid of her father and less intimidated by her mother, she was more able to believe that what had happened was not her fault. She began to recognize that she had in fact not hurt others the way she believed/fantasied she had. She does still feel guilty about stimulating the boy, however, and appreciated my comment that she very likely did not do him any lasting harm.

The deeper level of these issues was being simultaneously pursued in the analysis. The patient had described a painful repetitive fantasy while growing up, of being trapped in a box-like room where she bounced from one wall to the other, feeling like she was spinning out of control. This was associated with a feeling of confusion that was followed by an anticipatory dread of disintegration. We were able to put these experiences together with her difficulty in integrating disparate images of herself and of her father as follows: both the bouncing sensation and the dread were related to the virtually intolerable disjunctive conflict created by a detail of the incest. At night the patient would lie in bed with a combination of sexual excitement and dread that her father might come in. The excitement was both of the anticipated exquisite bodily sensations, as well as of the implications of the Oedipal victory over the rejecting mother. It was the confusion in her mind created by this conflict that threatened to drive her mad. Also of central importance was the conviction that it was all her fault. This was found to be based on the undeniably thrilling sensations that suffused her body during the actual incest. Recovery of the memory of the molestation of the boy, and the Swami seduction both strengthened her awareness that the incest was truly initiated and controlled by her father and not by her, as she had feared.

The recent revelations in the family that he had molested his granddaughter, and his subsequent attempts at some apparent repair, in conjunction with her even more recent realization that her father had psychopathic traits, further strengthened her belief that she was not the guilty one in the secret childhood liaison. Her feelings of specialness and superiority over her mother, and the idea that she was winning were additional factors making it difficult for her to overcome the belief that it was all her fault.

As we worked through these issues, the patient demonstrated significant improvements in professional and personal achievements, together with noteworthy increases in self-esteem and a greater subjective tranquility. "I'm in a new phase: more ease, more fun, more discipline, and less pressure from within. I enjoy the little things much more." Of special note is the decrease in experiences of being overwhelmed, and the concomitant increase in reflective functioning, allowing her to anticipate that she was now capable of handling situations that had previously immobilized her and filled her with intolerable and disorganizing anxiety, guilt, and shame. Just prior to my sending this chapter to the editors, the patient stated that she had reached a "critical mass of feeling safer, and that her pulse rate is substantially lower than it has been for 20 years".

Patients so burdened with chronic anxiety, guilt, and shame typically do not show the extent of therapeutic improvement demonstrated by this patient, particularly without psychotropic medication. Despite the long-standing dominance of these dysphoric affect states, she displayed good academic functioning and high professional achievement, indicating that a number of autonomous ego functions had not been substantially compromised. The patient's description of herself as a child who was a spirited playmate is suggestive of good psychic hardiness. Moreover, an elementary school teacher had told her mother that the patient was a natural leader.

From early years, the patient's maternal grandfather was a particularly beloved person. There were many memories of happy childhood weekends and summers spent on her grandparents' farm. Many happy experiences with her older brothers were also fondly remembered. Growing up she tagged along with them, and they protected and supported her. She had a deep and satisfying relationship with her brother A. The patient claimed that losing him led to her to "waking up to what was really important in life". It is likely that these relationships and experiences added to her potential trust, and positive internalizations, and were additional contributing factors that played some role in the substantial improvement she has been able to achieve.

More directly relevant to her capacity for improvement were the facts that she did not meet diagnostic criteria for borderline personality, and demonstrated a number of ego strengths, including impulse control, anxiety tolerance, and sublimatory capacities. She has not been a difficult patient in the sense that the analyst did not experience psychically painful (extraordinary) countertransference (Freedman, Lasky & Webster, 2009) reactions with her. She has not brought disruptive and controlling projective identifications into the interaction, and has not shown generalized aggression-infused, split-off introjects. The analysis is ongoing, and the substantial success of the work and increase in the patient's self-esteem and bolstered ego strength enhance the possibility of exploring the darker residue from the past more fully, that could potentially lead to a swing into the transference, and potentially become a disruptive factor in the countertransference.

Thus far, this patient has not challenged the frame, and once she came to feel and believe the therapeutic space was safe, she participated in a successful therapeutic alliance. That is, she consistently attempts to say what is on her mind, listens to what she herself says, listens to the analyst's comments and questions, and reflects on and attempts to integrate both.

Relation of the abbreviated case summary to annihilation anxieties

The case description includes many examples of annihilation anxieties that reflect typical forms of anxiety experienced and reported by this patient. She summarized the dilemma of her childhood as *"feeling overwhelmed and trapped with no place to go, like running into a wall, trying to escape and realizing there was no exit. And the frightening part was that it didn't stop."* Central to feeling trapped was the secret about the sexual experience, which she could share with no one out of fear that it would destroy the family and eventuate in her mother killing her. When the father incest was remembered, a further strand of guilt emerged, the idea that she had injured him physically. The evidence for this was her memory that, following his ejaculation, her father's penis became limp and smaller, i.e., injured. The wish to harm his penis had come into the analysis prior to her remembering the incest, and she reported a substantial initial increase in her guilt feelings as memories of the sexual details progressively emerged.

With regard to her mother, the patient felt she would never get the love and recognition that she needed. The patient's material revealed examples of each of Freud's (1926) famous four dangers: loss of the object, loss of love, genital harm and superego reproach, as well as most of the six annihilation dimensions described earlier. The details of the patient's material demonstrate how her experience of the four dangers regularly triggered annihilation concerns. Thus, the patient's experience of the mother's emotional abandonment and withholding of love *goes beyond Freud's description of loss of the object and of love, and triggers feelings of disappearing and of nothingness.* In addition, her concerns over genital harm also were infused with annihilation implications: *"I felt the genital penetration as a burning sensation that was like an infected shot. Like father had infected and poisoned me."* And lastly, the superego reproach, which had to do with her feelings of guilt and the assumption of responsibility for the incest, resulted in her feeling *blocked and overwhelmed, lest she reveal the terrible secret which would lead to the destruction of the family and her own death/retribution by the mother,* as already mentioned.

Regarding the traumatic memory of being dried off by her father after her bath, the patient described an experience of watching what was happening from the ceiling, like it was happening to someone else. This dissociative defence is frequently found in situations experienced as traumatic, and that involve annihilation anxieties.

Other dissociative phenomena were reflected in the presence of three "part-selves" about which the patient became aware beginning at the ages of five to seven, following the initiation of the sexual episodes. She described herself as being divided into the Foetus, the Witness, and the Monster Girl/Lollie Hothead. She experienced these three part-selves as helping her throughout her childhood and continued to be part of her experience of herself as split. "They made me feel safe; my secret protectors, my allies."

The patient described the foetus as so large it was blocking my path toward going forward, to going anywhere. It was a needy, infantile part of me. The Witness girl kept control for me, locked everything away, stayed quiet. She was like a parent, helping me by telling me the right thing to do. Lollie was very bad. But she's fun, and hope—she's me, the secret me. Then, I felt like I didn't have a together self. (What was that experience like?) Just getting by. It was so much work. I never really felt satisfied. I was never really together; had only a vague idea of who I was. Instead there was extreme tension in my emotional life, and I felt very cut-off from my mother. I'm coming to see how all this was modeled on my relationship with mother in an important way. It was a daily sense of pain with her. (In these frustrating, ongoing experiences with mother, and the secret stuff with father, the girls helped you get by—even though the price of them helping you was that they contributed to your not feeling together. What is your sense of self like now?) Now the basic experience of relating to another person has changed. Before I met you I was holding on, but any pressure made things feel very chaotic—too much to deal with. That's how it was with my earlier therapist. Somehow here it's been different. I have built up a sense of self working with you. By pushing the girls away I have space. When we were all together it was too noisy, too much trouble. It was like I was in a bunker and there was no room for them, and the time came when I didn't need them anymore, so I cast them out.

These part-selves were experienced by the patient as contributing to her sense of power and agency when she sorely needed it; they served as a foil against the massive experiences of helplessness, terror and entrapment. So they were more like imaginary companion/ part selves than the inner saboteurs of Fairbairn, and are more indicative of ego strength than ego weakness, more suggestive of adaptive than maladaptive defence. Feelings of being Overwhelmed, Trapped, Disorganized, and Destroyed were an integral part of the patient's therapeutic narrative.

The presenting symptoms described earlier—such as chronic dread and fear, intense shame, severe narcissistic trauma by the mother, chronic sexual invasion by the father, pervasive guilt feelings, and the presence of dissociated part-selves—are regularly found in conjunction with annihilation anxieties. Focusing on and exploring manifestations and close derivatives of annihilation anxieties was therapeutically useful in getting to the key underlying fantasies and in working through the specific anxieties involved. The patient acknowledged the value of these ways of describing some of her experiences:

> When I feel someone is controlling me, it can lead to feelings of losing myself, I get lost. (More?) I don't count. I'm forgotten. I feel that I'm not even here. I disappear and it's very frightening.

We thus came to see how these intolerable feelings led to dissociation, including the feeling that she could disappear. In addition to the helplessness, she experienced the disappearing as her revenge, and this calmed her anger. "If I'm not here then it can't happen" [i.e., further sexual assault].

The earlier-described sensation of falling off a cliff into nothingness, following memories of the incest trauma, illustrates the proposition that annihilation anxieties constitute trauma markers.

The falling sensation morphs into a dissociative escape defence from the incestuous memories, and then there is a recruitment of positive memories of playing with her brothers at her grandfather's farm. In the working through, the patient came to see the recalling of the dead girls dream, molesting the boy, the memory of the Swami seduction, and, later, the carnival dream, as key stepping stones to uncovering and elucidating the traumatic history.

Transference aspects

The earliest transference theme related to questions of safety and trust. That is, whether I needed her to satisfy me (as each of her parents had, in their own way), or whether I could help her without "needing her". The first underlying, specific concern was whether I could respond to her need to be understood as she was, without requiring, as her mother had, that she meet my needs for recognition and affirmation. The other particular concern, after the memories of her sexual relationship with her father had surfaced, was whether I would require from her the sexual surrender insisted upon by him. Her own vulnerability in this regard was underscored by her experience with the Swami's sexual advances. When he approached her, she was shocked, but quickly reverted to a passive mode, and silently acquiesced to his requests. For her entire adult life she had felt threatened when confronted with seductive behaviours by men.

In the therapeutic situation I was able to establish a friendly but professional tone, which allowed the patient to experience me as physically non-threatening. A remaining concern was that she would lose control of herself, as she had with the little boy reported earlier.

The early hours were filled with concerns over the boyfriend's mental condition. She later revealed that my helping her understand his behaviour increased her hope that I could help her understand herself. My ongoing interest in the unfolding story about her childhood unhappiness with her mother's exploitive way of relating to her, together with the so far unclarified strong negative feelings and fantasies towards her father gradually led to feelings of safety in the room, and a burgeoning belief that she could explore with me the mystery of what might have happened with her father when she was a child. Her conscious involvement with the details of the mother mistreatment likely had served as a *trauma screen* against remembering the father incest.

The patient's greatest fear in the transference was that I would cast her out. The various fantasized reasons were because she was not improving fast enough, that I did not like her, that she looked attractive, or did not look attractive enough. She additionally feared I would send her away if she were playful, or even worse, if she were flirtatious. I decided not to pick up on any signs of flirtatiousness or sexual innuendos, a stance regularly taken by many psychotherapists with victims of childhood (and former-analyst) sexual abuse. Her fear that I would cast her out played a role in the patient making an effort to control any such tendencies. I believe it will be possible to analyse this issue later in the analysis. The key genetic (historical) connection with the fear of being cast out was that she wanted to cast out her father, because of his sexual conduct. She also expressed fear that I would become envious or disapproving of her accomplishments outside therapy, that I would become tired of her complaining, or that I would move away, or die. One instance of her fearing she had disappointed me was followed by a fantasy of the two of us hugging, kissing, and making love.

From the time of the dead girls dream, the material unfolded in fits and starts, but progressively. I regularly summarized the patient's associations and memories, our cumulative understanding of the dynamic and historical picture and pointed out gaps in the evolving story, taking care not to get ahead of her with speculations concerning what might have transpired. While these are routine analytic functions, I saw them as especially important in a patient with the degree of dissociation in the history, and who was sensitive to sexual seduction, as pointed out. Recently, the patient stated: "The space you have created here has helped me to define myself and to grow stronger."

When I asked her permission to use material from her analysis in a professional publication, she agreed after thinking about it, and stated that one reason she thought I had "chosen" her was because of the progress she had made, but denied any further thoughts about it. Since a major complaint against the parents was that they had used her for their own purposes, the patient may subsequently take up further feelings about my request and her agreement.

In closing, I would like to make two additional points. The first is, my impression from reading the literature is that many analysts deal with descriptions of being overwhelmed, trapped etc., as some kind of end-point or bedrock, and do not pursue such issues further. In this chapter I have illustrated the clinical value of recognizing annihilation anxiety dimensions and working with them. The second point is to include the reactions of the patient presented here to my highlighting her relevant experiences in terms of annihilation anxiety dimensions and sub-dimensions.

> Today, you brought to my attention that what I had been talking about reflected a sense of being trapped. That way of putting it made it more real to me and focused more specifically the basic issue. It led to an aha! feeling. Your use of that term and, earlier, the terms "overwhelmed" and "invaded", and later your repeating the words "overwhelmed", "invaded" and "trapped" that I had used, made me feel really understood, like bells were going off, like you really got my meaning. If you said it was difficult, or something general like that, I don't think it would have had the same effect. When you said, "It's like you are trapped," it triggered an emotional response. It's like it organized the feeling, and I felt a connection, and that I was not alone with a unique experience.

The evocative quality of these annihilation terms is likely based on the fact that they were included as dimensions and sub-dimensions due to their having turned up in the psychoanalytic literature repeatedly. They reflect clinical generalizations and clinical observations that have surplus meaning, which is often related to survival concerns. Rather than treating such terms as end points, which halts psychoanalytic exploration and inquiry, these terms can constitute a jumping-off point, an opening of the window to deeper reaches of the mind. This patient further associated with "trapped" a feeling of being cornered, controlled, and unable to move. At another time, feeling trapped evoked an image of falling into the abyss.

The mutative importance of the transference was reflected in the patient's linking of the analyst's way of working and his choice of words with her capacity to organize her thoughts and feelings. We have similarly found in the therapy sessions of a torture victim

(Freedman, Hurvich & Ward, 2009) a significant correlation between the relative quality and intensity of the transference and meaningful changes in the patient's annihilation dimensions. This suggests a potentially central role played by transference in treating patients suffering from annihilation anxieties. In this sense, the manifestations of annihilation anxieties can be seen as a component in the psychoanalytic/psychotherapeutic clinical process.

Note

1. I would like to thank Richard Lasky, Norbert Freedman, Andrew B. Druck, Jo Lang, and Samera Nasereddin for their input.

CHAPTER FIVE

Breakdown and recovery in the analysis of a young woman

Aaron Thaler[1]

Breakdown phenomena and related symptoms are common features in psychoanalytic treatment dealing with severe disturbances of continuity and ego-integration. The first part of this paper traces ideas about breakdown and recovery mainly through review of Winnicott's work in this area. The second part describes a period of breakdown that occurred during an advanced stage in the analysis of a very courageous young woman, Ms R. This period, which Ms R came to refer to as "my breakdown", involved two years of reliving continuous, almost unbearable anxiety, disorientation, and pain which seemed to have been carried from her early childhood. The description focuses especially on a series of transference dreams produced over the course of one year that reflect Ms R's working through these powerful early anxieties on the way to important growth, symbolization, and recovery.

Although it is outside the scope of this paper, readers may look into illuminating papers by Clare Winnicott (1980) and Judith Mitrani (1998) who also applied Winnicott's ideas to examples of breakdown phenomena arising in the course of psychoanalytic treatment.

Breakdown phenomena and symptoms

In his papers, "Fear of breakdown" (1974) and "The psychology of madness" (1965b), Winnicott explored the meaning of breakdown as it commonly refers to a breakdown of defence organization, but also in a deeper sense, as a "breakdown of the establishment of the unit self" (1974, p. 103). In these papers and many others, Winnicott described the ego of early childhood as un-integrated and always on the edge of "unthinkable anxieties" (1965b, p. 127) or "primitive agonies" (1974, p. 104), such as falling to pieces, falling forever, loss of orientation, loss of relation between psyche and soma, loss of a sense of real, and a loss of capacity to relate to objects. In Winnicott's view, these primitive agonies are experienced in reaction to failures of environmental provision at the point of the infant's "absolute dependence" (p. 104) on the mother. At this stage, there is no possibility of defence against environmental failures because such failures cannot be predicted or encompassed within the immature capacity of the ego to account for events. "The ego organizes defences against breakdown of the ego-organization … but the ego cannot organize against environmental failure in so far as dependence is a living fact" (1974, p. 103). Unthinkable anxiety occurs in reaction to environmental failure in the instant before defences can be established, and this reaction effectively cuts across the line of continuity of being. Such a reaction constitutes an actual breakdown, "a reversal of the individual's maturational process" (p. 103).

Winnicott observed that fear of breakdown reflects a particular kind of unconscious memory derived from an individual's original experience of breakdown, "the unthinkable state of affairs that underlies the defense organization" (1974, p. 103). That is, "[C]linical fear of breakdown is the fear of a breakdown that has already been experienced. It is a fear of the original agony which caused the defence organization which the patient displays as an illness syndrome" (p. 104).

Similarly, fear of death and preoccupation with death often reflect a breakdown that happened early in life, an overwhelming agony and break in the continuity of being that amounted to near total disaster. "Death, looked at in this way as something that happened to the patient but which the patient was not mature enough to experience, has the meaning of annihilation" (Winnicott, 1974, p. 106).

Winnicott referred to this annihilation as a "phenomenal death" (p. 106).

The original agony remains unconscious, however, in the special sense that, again, ego-integration was not sufficient to encompass what happened, and at such an early stage intellectual capacity was not sufficiently developed to organize experience as retrievable memory. This leads to the peculiar fact that something that happened in the past has not yet been experienced in a way that can be remembered as past. The individual is caught in a conflict between the fear of breakdown and the need to reach the original agony around which defences were organized. He or she "must go on fearing to find what is being compulsively looked for in the future" (Winnicott, 1974, p. 105), and "must therefore flee from it, flirt with it, and to some extent be always preoccupied with the threat of it" (Winnicott, 1965, p. 122).

Clinically, we find direct fears of breakdown, madness, and death as well as many derivative symptoms. There may be preoccupations with suicide or active suicidal impulses, fears of imminent loss of control and falling apart, as well as powerful longings to actually collapse. There is often a sense of futility and hopelessness, nothing to look forward to, only morbid expectations that bad things will happen. We hear of feeling doomed to failure, poverty, isolation, that fate is antagonistic, that suffering and death are inevitable. There are fears that loved ones will die or that one will die with no one there. I have heard several patients express similar versions of one young man's associations to the idea of believing in himself and applying himself to realizing his goals. He said as a simple matter of fact, "I never thought about a career, family, because I never thought I'd live that long."

Breakdown and recovery in relation to True and False Self

These ideas about the early breakdown of ego-organization are closely related to Winnicott's ideas about True and False Self (1960b). The True Self exists at the start as "the summation of sensori-motor aliveness" (p. 149), and as a potential that comes alive given "good enough" (p. 145) environmental provision in the earliest stages of object relations. The environmental mother "holding" (p. 145) the un-integrated infant, both physically and figuratively, makes sense of and implements the spontaneous impulses and sensory hallucinations revealed in the infant's gestures and sensori-motor patterns. For example, the mother might respond to a gesture by presenting the breast at just the right moment "just there where the infant is ready to create it" (Winnicott, 1951, p. 239) allowing the infant the illusion of creating the breast. In this manner, the mother's adaptation repeatedly "meets the infantile omnipotence" (Winnicott, 1960b, p. 145) expressed in the infant's gesture and makes it real, giving cohesion and continuity to various elements of spontaneity and aliveness.

Given this good-enough provision, the infant does not have to confront external reality all at once but, rather, "comes to believe in [an environment] which does not clash with ... omnipotence" (p. 146), and which allows the illusion of spontaneous "creating and controlling" (p. 146). Through transitional processes, the infant begins to relate to that which is both a spontaneous impulse or hallucination and also the external object. These transitional experiences forge a loving bond with the object while becoming the foundation for symbol formation and expanding relations with external reality. The True Self "comes to be able to react to a stimulus without trauma because the stimulus has a counterpart in the individual's inner, psychic reality" (p. 149). These processes allow the gradual recognition of illusion and the "fact of playing and imagining" (p. 146), which eventually lead to relinquishing omnipotence. They enable the infant to begin as existing rather than reacting, being truly alive and initiating relations with the world.

As a corollary to this, the good-enough environment is "that which enables [the individual] not to have to meet the unpredictable until able to allow for environmental failures" (Winnicott, 1967, p. 199). Rather than unpredictability and primitive anxieties leading to breaks in personal continuity, the reliable support (auxiliary-ego) of the mother assists the infant in coping with the danger of mounting anxieties and fosters experiences of recovery:

> The first ego organization comes from the experience of threats of annihilation which do not lead to annihilation and from which, repeatedly, there is recovery. Out of such experiences confidence in recovery begins to be something which leads to an ego and to an ego capacity for coping with frustration ... good

enough environmental provision in the earliest phase enables the infant to begin to exist, to have experience, to build a personal ego, to ride instincts, and to meet with all the difficulties inherent in life. All this feels real to the infant who becomes able to have a self that can eventually even afford to sacrifice spontaneity, even to die (Winnicott, 1956, p. 304).

Kohut (1977) similarly described cycles of anxiety and recovery in relation to a maternal self-object as the central factor leading to the development of a core self:

> [The] child's anxiety, his drive needs, and his rage ... have brought about empathic resonances within the maternal self-object .... The relevant feeling states—either the child's own or those of the self-object in which he participates, in the order in which they are experienced by the self/self-object unit, are: mounting anxiety (self); followed by stabilized mild anxiety—a "signal" not panic (self-object); followed by calmness, absence of anxiety (self-object). Ultimately, the psychological disintegration products that the child had begun to experience disappear (the rudimentary self is reestablished) ... (p. 86).

Repeated instances of this cycle allow integrative processes to expand and form the core of a "secure feeling of being a unit in space, a continuum in time, and a center for the initiation of action and the reception of impressions" (p. 156). The sequence of change from anxiety to calmness (feeling understood and calmed), is made possible by the baby's merger with the mother as she experiences an "empathic signal" in response to the baby's anxiety and then returns to calmness (Kohut, 1984, p. 83).

Here, the good-enough environmental mother/analyst is able to identify with and make sense of the infant's distress and to have confidence in the processes of caring for the infant's needs as well as the infant's own capacities for recovery. In my experience, serious failures of environmental provision reconstructed in analyses most often seem to involve a parent's own anxieties interfering with their ability to make sense of their child's anxieties and needs and to have confidence in their capacity for recovery. It seems that this is a particular point at which expectations that bad things will happen (parents' anxiety) are often actualized via projection and transmitted from parent to child.

In Kohut's (1984) view, these problems involve the mother being prone to "empathic flooding" (p. 82) and panic rather than a mature capacity to experience empathic resonance as a signal. This primitive anxiety in the mother may lead to the child's experiencing "uncurbed spreading of anxiety" (p. 83) or walling off against the "overly intense and thus traumatic empathic echo" (p. 83). Alternatively, the mother may wall herself off from the child in order to avoid experiencing the child's anxiety.

In Winnicott's (1960b) view, breaks in continuity of being occur when the mother fails to make sense of the infant's gesture and, instead, "substitutes her own gesture which is to be given sense by the compliance of the infant" (p. 145). A recurring pattern of such disruption leads to overwhelming "unthinkable" anxiety, fragmentation, and various ego-distortions including premature ego-development and False Self defences. These defences involve a dissociation in which the True Self is withdrawn into a walled-off inner reality, hidden and protected by a caretaker-self existing in reaction to the outer world with limited spontaneity and aliveness. This may include elements of closing off and refusing to take things in and/or developing relationships based on compliance. Both alternatives are forms of defensive self—holding in which the outward part of the self is drawn into a merger with, and exists mainly as, a derivative of the pattern of mothering.

Defending the True Self leads to extreme guardedness, de-animation and de-vitalization, as well as resulting feelings of hopelessness, futility, and unreality. The individual lives but is reactive, withdrawn, and often depersonalized. Rather than transitional processes leading to finding the external object and to symbol formation, there is a frozen merger with archaic self-objects, limited symbolization and sense of process, and a tendency towards repetitive, compulsive attempts to gain mastery over catastrophic anxiety, loss, and isolation.

Bach (1985, 1994) has described disruptions of continuity and integrative processes extensively and in great detail in relation to severe problems in emotional self-regulation and building up self and object-constancy. The foundations of continuity, aliveness, and agency are disrupted in children who are not adequately held in the mind and memory of caretakers (Bach, 2006). These disruptions of continuity involve states of traumatic isolation and gaps or voids in the fabric of consciousness that comprise moments of psychic "death of the self" (Bach, 2008, p. 785).

Both Winnicott and Kohut described recurrent disruptions of continuity leading to severe problems in tension-regulation and psychosomatic integration. Both authors referred to a particular ego-distortion involving active intensification of affect leading to states of panic and chaos. In Winnicott's (1963a) view, this is a form of active disintegration or "organized awfulness" as a defence against the dangers of un-integration in the absence of environmental support [breakdown]. At all costs, the genuine part of the self remains walled-off against the noxious environment, and the individual may even choose suicide to prevent the ultimate danger, which is the annihilation of the True Self.

I believe these views of the disruption of early continuity and integration are particularly helpful in clarifying the nature of early breakdown in relation to defensive de-animation, de-vitalization, and ultimately the sense of isolation, inner deadness, and non-existence. The fear of annihilation and the sense of having no life to look forward to reflect the isolating and deadening consequences of early breakdown and the defences organized around vulnerability to a recurrence of such a catastrophe. Many individuals carrying an early breakdown seem to expect and fear annihilation most basically because they have not yet been able to be really alive.

Introjected reliability and regression to dependence

Winnicott pointed out that defences are always organized around anxiety, and defensive reactions to unthinkable anxieties and breakdown tend to be organized at the level of invulnerability. In his paper, "The concept of clinical regression as compared with defense organisation" (1967), Winnicott further explored the nature of breakdown in psychoanalytic treatment as "an expression of the healthy elements in [the patient's] personality", seen in the possibility of becoming vulnerable and breaking down "into some new environmental provision that offers reliable care" (p. 197).

Usually, direct fear of breakdown does not emerge as an immediate factor in analysis until after substantial progress has led to greater ego-strength and confidence in the analyst's reliability. The individual is increasingly able to "build a structure on the accumulation of introjected reliability" of the analyst (p. 196). Being in analysis a long time leads to a capacity to move from invulnerability into a gradual process of regression to dependence on the analyst. From this point, the capacity to have an illness, to be "able to suffer, to go on suffering, to be aware of suffering" (Winnicott, 1965b, p. 128) is a sign of health. When dependence becomes the main feature in the transference, inevitable experiences of the analyst's failures and mistakes lead more directly to the appearance of breakdown phenomena.

Reliving

"Cure only comes if the patient can reach the anxiety around which defenses were organized ... [i.e.] to reach the original state of breakdown" (Winnicott, 1965b, p. 126). There is no real resolution unless "the bottom of the trough has been reached, unless the thing feared has been experienced" (Winnicott, 1974, p. 92). The individual can only get as close to an experience of the original agony as new ego-strength and ego-support in the transference can make possible (Winnicott, 1965b, p. 128). To experience breakdown involves a large-scale release of defences and, at great risk, becoming highly dependent and vulnerable. Winnicott referred to a point in analysis where there is a major shift in the centre of operations of the personality from the False Self to the True Self (1960b). From this point, true vulnerability and dependence allow for an experience of something near the original disaster.

The patient needs to "remember" the original breakdown that occurred early in life, but this cannot be recalled as memory. "The original agony cannot get into the past tense unless the ego can first gather it into its own present time experience and into omnipotent control now (assuming the auxiliary ego-support function of the mother [analyst])" (Winnicott, 1974, p. 91). This can only happen through reliving some part of the original agony and madness "in the transference, in reaction to the analyst's failures and mistakes ... gradually, the patient gathers the original failure of the environment into the area of his or her omnipotence" (1974, p. 91). The "patient now hates the analyst for the failure that originally came as an environmental factor, outside the infant's area of omnipotent control but that is now staged in the transference. So in the end we succeed by failing—failing the patient's way" (Winnicott, 1963a, p. 238).

Under these conditions, reliving some part of the early agony "can be dealt with ... in doses that are not excessive, and the patient can account for each failure by the analyst as counter-transference" (Winnicott, 1974, p. 91). Dependence on the reliability of the analyst/mother and the "experience of omnipotence which belongs to the state of dependence" (p. 91) allow the original madness to become a manageable experience. The patient is "able to tolerate and cope with anxieties which were unthinkable in their original setting" (Winnicott, 1965, p. 127). From here, recovery processes begin spontaneously in the natural start-up of maturational processes.

Ms R's analysis leading to breakdown and recovery

What follows is a summary of the course of analysis leading up to Ms R's breakdown in her 14th year of analysis and a more detailed description of the breakdown period that lasted for about two years. Ms R, who terminated analysis a year ago, is now 46 years old, married, and has two children (fraternal twin girls). She is of South-East Asian descent, is highly sensitive and intelligent, and works in a very challenging area of research, which she finds truly satisfying.

Ms R came to analysis at the age of 25 with several debilitating problems. She especially showed a disturbance in her sense of her own reality and identity. She said in a childlike, desperate manner that she was realizing more and more that her mother was controlling and rejecting, but she was anguished over a sense that she couldn't judge anything because her own thoughts and feelings did not seem real. She said that she felt continuously exposed, that she was worthless, ridiculous, and bizarre, that she was not deep and sincere. She said she would never be able to have relationships or to love anyone enough. She also said that she couldn't tell if she did anything because it was what she wanted or what someone else wanted. Ms R said, "If I can't be something for someone else, there's nothing there."

Ms R's daily life had a nightmarish quality dominated by frequent crises involving desperate attempts to feel connected with people she idealized, especially men who "seemed confident" when they were indifferent, critical, or cruel, followed by inevitable disappointments that sent her lurching into violent feelings of humiliation and helpless rage. Ms R talked about often feeling deeply depressed and crying for entire days in despair, wishing for someone or something to make her feel better. She complained of panic attacks, insomnia, and extreme tension all over her body. She frequently had diarrhoea and stomach aches that made her double over in pain, and regularly had severe colds with bronchitis that lasted for months. She abused alcohol and smoked a pack of cigarettes per day despite having asthma for which she had been hospitalized several times.

Ms R grew up with her father, a successful businessman and her mother who had a brief career as a movie actress. Ms R was born in Hong Kong where her parents had lived for many years. The family moved to London during Ms R's elementary school and middle school years and settled in New York where she completed secondary school and college. Throughout this time, her father was generally remote and often travelled on business for long periods.

Ms R's mother is alcoholic, dependent on tranquillizers, and has had at least two episodes of psychotic breakdown. It became evident in the course of treatment that Ms R's mother dominated, controlled, and used Ms R like an extension to satisfy her own needs, showing absolute disregard for Ms R's autonomy and, quite often, an apparent wish to eradicate her autonomy.

Ms R remembered her mother always demanding to be the centre of attention. She would tell boastful stories in which everything she did or had was wonderful and superior, talk in minute detail about her vagina and her bowel functions, cry, engage in screaming tantrums or silent rages in order to dominate the scene. She was routinely naked when at home and called attention to her body in various ways like performing a seductive dance while fluffing her pubic hair or regularly bending over to expose her anus and genitals near Ms R's face. She taunted Ms R with sexualized references to her exclusive relationship with Ms R's father, their special time together, and the special treats they would share. When Ms R's father was at home, her mother's only interest was in being with him and excluding Ms R. When Ms R's father was not at home, her mother would regularly take her to the parents' bed and "cuddle" with her which meant holding her in a smothering, crushing, sexualized embrace. Ms R remembered, with tears and extreme anxiety, feeling her legs pinned between her mother's legs and in contact with her mother's genitals and feeling that she should stay very still while her mother used her like a rag doll to soothe her own anxieties.

When Ms R asked for attention, affection, or comfort, her mother would ridicule her, calling her "greedy" and "crazy". When Ms R was involved in independent activities, her mother would burst in, demanding attention, sometimes naked and screaming at her. At times, her mother would get her attention by merely approaching and silently fixing Ms R with her eyes.

Ms R remembered that, during the summer when she was six years old and her father was away, her mother looked into her eyes and said "Your eyes are bleeding". Ms R looked in the mirror and did not see blood but felt confused about what was real. Over several days, Ms R's mother brought her from doctor to doctor with the same complaint until one unimaginably terrifying night when Ms R remained alone with her acutely decompensating mother before going out to get help the next day. Her mother was hospitalized for an unknown period.

Ms R recalled that her stuffed animals seemed alive and that some seemed scary and evil. She developed a nightly ritual of lining up her possessions and making plans to leave home in case of an emergency. She also began having recurrent dreams of tidal waves that sucked her and her mother into the ocean that continued throughout most of her life.

This and much more of Ms R's history emerged in the early part of her treatment in fragments that were embedded in her intense accounts of events and their impact on her. As in her dreams of tidal waves, she seemed exhilarated and awe-struck, while also terrified of being sucked in and swept away. She said that sessions were extremely painful and overwhelming and that she was afraid she would "wind up crazy".

I was able to get a sense of Ms R's early transference feelings through the manifest content of her dreams. For example, Ms R dreamed that she was in a small pool that was partially connected to the ocean. She could feel some pull from the ocean, but holding onto a ladder in the pool prevented her being swallowed up by the current. In another dream, Ms R was helplessly locked in the back of a taxicab speeding down Broadway driven by a maniac to her certain death.

Two important trends began to emerge early in the analysis. Firstly, as I learned about Ms R's traumatic past and fragile self-organization, I was especially struck by the absence of subjective aliveness behind her outward symptoms. Despite the intensity of her crises and reactions to events, Ms R seemed so powerfully constricted and hidden that I felt I could easily be induced to overlook her feelings or even forget about her. At times, I believed that Ms R was almost completely cued to my expectations and hiding her needs as she must have done in relation to her mother. Given her powerful de-animation and de-vitalization and lack of a sense of her own reality and agency, I mainly felt that Ms R needed a very predictable, quietly receptive atmosphere in which she could be free to regulate the distance between us and define the nature of our relationship without my getting in the way of her finding her own voice and subjective reality.

In contrast, and despite these defences, Ms R eagerly took on the treatment as her own, actively initiating and becoming engaged in her own process. She seemed to know instinctively that this was what she wanted and needed in order to feel some safety and to gradually find her way to experience, tolerate, and integrate her very substantially dissociated emotional life. From this early period, a strong, facilitating mirror-transference seemed to develop. Ms R seemed to sense my appreciation and confidence in her autonomy and ownership of her analysis as she consistently showed great courage in her willingness to move into increasingly difficult aspects of her experience.

Ms R had a series of dreams of de-animated objects such as a mannequin that seemed perfect, and this initiated an ongoing theme in the analysis involving her agonizing wishes to feel more spontaneous and alive and her need to keep herself contained and de-animated. Ms R said:

> Saying anything positive about myself feels like boasting .... I'm always apologizing, toning things down .... I also get a funny feeling looking in mirrors ... I start to feel it's vain ... I think of my mother ... laughing at me .... I remember, if I felt good about anything, she would rip it to shreds .... I always had to be contained .... It's like now, I don't want my boyfriend to think I'm doing something independent ....

Ms R spoke of having mood swings and feeling terribly exposed as she worked with feelings of being ridiculed and terrorized and with fears of expressing herself more spontaneously. Yet this work seemed to lead her to an increasing sense of her own aliveness and reality. Ms R's growing stability and confidence enabled her to move out of her parents' home despite fears of total isolation and to begin a relationship with a man who was emotionally distant but not sadistic like her previous boyfriends.

At times, Ms R's progress would lead to the sudden emergence of previously warded-off, profoundly disturbing aspects of her experience such as her feelings of terror and humiliation in reaction to her mother's overt sexual behaviour. Ms R appreciated more and more the extent to which she had bought into her mother's reality and denied her own experience of this kind of abuse. She also allowed herself to begin to recognize how fears of being close came up in all her relationships. Shortly afterwards, Ms R said:

> I dreamed that I was in bed with a child that was disturbed ... he had the potential to be a serial killer. He woke up and I was holding him very tight, trying to keep him subdued. I couldn't tell if he was struggling, but then I had the experience of being the child and being suffocated. It was like the feeling when I was carried to my mother's bed and held tight ... . I couldn't pull my feet out from between her legs, I couldn't turn around."

At the time, Ms R could only say that talking more about the experience of being brought into bed with her mother "would kill" her. Clearly, having greater connection with her own anger and her own reality felt equivalent to becoming a serial killer with the potential to destroy her entire world with her mother.

During the sixth year of treatment, and despite extreme anxiety, Ms R was able to begin a challenging graduate school programme and a relationship with a man who was emotionally responsive, whom she would later marry. Also, an important milestone in the evolution of the transference occurred when Ms R said:

> I've been in treatment for six years and I've never asked anything about you ... . It's been a conscious decision that you don't have any problems or even a life out of this room ... . It's been so

> necessary, incredibly to have someone be like that ... . I was never more than an extension of my mother ... . Things were twisted, and I didn't have a figure like that to believe in ... . When you're born and in the early years, that person is the centre of everything, and gradually you separate and see they're a person ... . I didn't have the initial safe feeling ... . Being in treatment is the longest and most stable commitment I've had ... that translates into my being able to maintain relationships in the future with predictability and stability that didn't exist in my life before.

In the period that followed, I felt increasingly comfortable being more active, without feeling that I might undermine Ms R's growing sense of her own reality, agency, and self-regulation. An atmosphere of strong positive transference grew and included our being increasingly able to talk openly about each other. At the same time, Ms R began to articulate a developing negative transference theme involving her feeling that I could know something terrible and shameful about her, including things that she did not know about herself, that I was superior to her and interested only in a distant, abstract way, that I wanted to infiltrate and overcome her defences, and fix her by exposing, judging, and correcting the awful faults that I found in her.

Along with these developments, Ms R's treatment also seemed to enter a phase of more substantial therapeutic regression, as she spoke more freely and openly about her paralyzing self-consciousness and feelings of inadequacy, and of how she had diminished their significance in the past. She said:

> I feel all the time I'm about to be attacked ... . I've been realizing how I'm so easily offended ... . I assume someone is trying to make me feel bad ... . The waitress says: "You always order the same thing," so I think she's saying I'm not adventurous. Andy says: "You're adventurous because you're with me," so I feel he's taking away my sense of self. I'm missing the normal, healthy sense of confidence and entitlement ... . I'm realizing that in my mind, my mother is physically big ... she flaunts herself ... but I don't want to be exposed ... . I envy her freedom ... I contain, minimize, tone everything down ... . She's calculating and aggressive with her body.

As Ms R's treatment progressed, there was an increasing contrast between her regression in the analysis, where the content of sessions involved opening up more primitive and affective material, and her life outside analysis that continued to improve and become more solid. She spoke about generally "taking problems more in stride" in her daily life.

Ms R's regression seemed to deepen as she talked about feelings of anxiety, anger, and devastating isolation. She said:

> … I remember my mother controlled me, made me a part of her craziness … times when she was taking Valium and coming undone … . I was very much alone … . I don't remember ever feeling secure or connected … . It's a new experience for me to be connected with people in my life … . I've always felt tremendous mistrust.

Ms R recalled her experience of being held like a rag doll in order to soothe her mother's anxieties, and said:

> I'm surviving … but I talk about this stuff and I feel wrecked … it takes a few days until I feel more in control … my mother's weird obsession with her vagina … she over-stimulated me … . What do I think about it, do with it? … how weird it is that I know exactly what her vagina looks like! … She had one hundred per cent control … I wasn't allowed to exhibit anything except complete compliance … that's why I walked around feeling like a shadow … not really there … in awe of the incredible power she possessed … and it made her feel satisfied … to be overtly sexual, have me stimulated, aware of sexual things.

Ms R also brought up more openly her negative feelings about herself. She said:

> The image I have of myself is so distorted … the idea that my body is weird … and my face in the mirror looks like a Picasso … all I see are imperfections … . When I look at photos I'm stunned … there's nothing wrong … I have a great body … . Her sexuality blotted out mine … erased my chances of feeling feminine … . I can't look objectively at the whole

picture ... I see random pieces ... defects, irregular parts stitched together .... I only feel better, more objective about myself now when I try to do the things I want to do.

I talked to Ms R about her feeling like parts and that her mother saw and treated her like a part or a thing, and about her feeling more real and like a whole person when she spontaneously did the things she wanted to do.

> Ms R felt panic and a need to make sure her mother was not angry. She said: Talking about what she did sexually is another way of exerting independence, it's so frightening. I know she's angry, and I have to make her feel better ... talking about this whacked out, weird sexual shit is taking away my defences ... it makes me feel naked ... it impacts me for the rest of the day .... There's something scary and sinister about the way she used me .... What kind of monster gets something out of that? So predatory, telling me "You came out of my vagina, out of my thing" .... telling me I owe her my life, she's done so much for me .... It always made me feel so gross .... I have a ball of anger in my stomach, and I have to keep swallowing it down .... I feel like I could kill her ... but if I fight back, I'm isolating myself more and more ... I feel the distance growing ... and it feels like permanent damage ... nothing can retract it.

During sessions, Ms R cried for extended periods and said that she felt terribly vulnerable and panicky. She said that she thought about death much of the time, that good things in her life seemed very precarious, and that she had always thought about herself dying at an early age. She said that sessions left her wiped out and vulnerable, and stayed with her for days.

Over the following weeks, I sensed that Ms R was more openly longing for something from me. During the final session of one week, she had a mild panic attack with tachycardia. She said:

> It feels like a wave, like my heart is doing a flip .... It feels like I'm going to die, then it goes away .... I want reassurance, but I'm embarrassed. But it's good that I told you. I want you to tell

me it'll be all right, but I don't want to need anything … . I feel I'm supposed to have everything together.

Ms R called the next day and arranged to come in. Throughout the session she felt "on the edge" of panic. She said:

> "I'm exhausted dealing with everything myself … . I don't trust … even in our sessions, I have to be taking care of myself … . It's so awful to have to acknowledge the pain that I feel … . It amazes me that it's so scary to let things flow … . I think about dying a lot … . I think you're right here is the fear that I've been walking around with forever … . I felt so uncomfortable when you said you would want to speak with me if I needed it … . I feel I don't exist for you outside sessions … but then I felt I don't want to feel connected … go away … . I feel tremendously exposed and ashamed about needing something … . I don't see myself connecting with other people … I only connect with what other people want … it's not a full circle … . I feel very unimportant … and I feel suspicious … the rug is going to be pulled out from under me … but when someone shows interest … warm feelings … that really scares me … who knows what can happen … it's too close … .

Ms R's treatment continued to move through these important new areas, and by the 13th year of treatment, she was married and pregnant with twins, and she functioned at a high level in a challenging profession. Following the birth of her daughters, Ms R seemed to be a highly attuned mother, and she felt extremely satisfied by her capacity for reliability and nurturing.

Two problems emerged, however, that were sometimes a focus of analysis during this period. First, following the birth of her children, Ms R struggled with a sense of needing help from her mother, and she was drawn back into a somewhat dependent relationship that involved a regressive loss of the boundaries she had established in their relationship. It seemed that, in some degree, Ms R's new role as a mother had revivified her own childhood needs which brought with it confusion between her wishes to be a mother with children and her wishes to be a child with a mother.

A second problem emerged with Ms R's reaction to the strength and independent action of her children as toddlers with increasing autonomy. She was surprised by the strength of their self-assertion, and Ms R was somewhat confused over how to gauge when she needed to step in and set limits and when she needed to allow more autonomous activity.

These challenges, along with the loss of her full-time professional life and frequent disruptions in the schedule of analysis, seemed to put an increasing strain on Ms R's sense of identity and stability. In retrospect, my sense of this strain on Ms R and of something unfocused and less accessible in the transference were all difficult to address at this point. I believe all of these elements amounted to a break in the continuity of Ms R's ongoing process and connection with me which probably comprised some form of enactment related to a transference experience of being overwhelmed, helpless, and abandoned by the analyst.

Breakdown and recovery

After having been in analysis for 14 years, when her children were 15 months old, Ms R suddenly began to break down. She arrived at a session saying that she had been feeling "fuzzy" in her vision and "dizzy" even while sitting still, and had been unable to shake off these sensations. She had begun to feel anxiety "like panic" which seemed unusually intense and continuous. Over the next few weeks, increasing vertigo and terror seemed to take over Ms R's life. Her entire consciousness was continuously affected by sensations of dizziness and disorientation, her visual field always moving and giving her the sensation of herself moving even as she was stationary. She could not read or look in any direction without seeing movement. She could not move without feeling dizzy and losing her sense of balance.

Ms R arrived for a subsequent session with more severe vertigo. She had become so dizzy on the way to the session that she had to sit on the pavement for several minutes before she could move on. She said:

> I'm feeling panic … trapped inside it and there's no relief … . It's so intense … my heart pounding … a feeling of madness taking over … thinking I'm dying … something very bad is happening. There's anxiety like a live wire … feeling I can't get

enough air into my lungs … . It feels like I've been attacked, invaded.

As we talked about this experience, Ms R began to refer spontaneously to these symptoms as "my breakdown". It was unclear at the time, however, what had been the immediate cause of her symptoms. It seemed plausible that there had been an infection that disturbed her vestibular function and acted as an immediate precipitant. There were efforts to explore all physical causes of the vertigo, and several physicians were consulted, but there was no apparent resolution. Ms R also met with a psychiatrist and began taking an anti-depressant that provided some relief from her anxiety. While I encouraged and supported these efforts, I also told her that I believed she had moved into reliving some kind of overwhelming disorientation, pain, and anxiety reflecting something similar that had happened when she was very young.

Shortly afterwards, Ms R said she had woken up in a panic from a dream in which she and her husband were trapped in a taxi driven by a serial killer who was going to take them somewhere and dispose of their bodies. Ms R had grabbed the driver and was pinching him, scratching his face, trying to gouge out his eyes, and eventually "made the cab roll over". Although we were unable at the time to do much with the dream, it provided a clearer sense for me that Ms R's breakdown involved an active process that had powerful transference implications.

In the following session, Ms R said:

> I wake up trembling … my first sensation is anxiety. I'm very sick, going crazy, want to go to a hospital … . I'm feeling no one can help me … but I am letting everyone know and they're responding. I'm letting things come out … even anger … I don't feel so much that I have to justify it … . I'm open about what I'm going through … not doing everything perfectly … I'm melting down, I feel like I need to be in bed and have people take care of me … .

Ms R also said:

> I think about how much this is tension and anxiety I've always carried around … . I'm so tense … I feel I have to get up and

> do all these things ... . Even though we have a baby-sitter coming in the morning, I'm trying to do everything to get the children ready ... make their lunch ... but all the stuff I used to do has been short circuited ... the dizziness. I feel terribly imprisoned ... the depression, anxiety, panic takes over ... then there's no room for anything else ... just a feeling of dying ... it's a matter of survival. I see that I was ready for this break to happen ... these sessions are a lifeline.

As we talked about her past containment and de-vitalization and reviewed a lot of earlier periods in her analysis, Ms R was able to appreciate how she had gradually developed the strength that led to her capacity to let this breakdown happen and to relive these experiences now. We understood with increasing clarity that Ms R was allowing herself to be more alive and to have her feelings "spill out" or "break out". We were also able to relate this new spontaneity to Ms R's experience with her children and their "breaking out" with growing autonomy and independent action. Ms R talked about how difficult it was to have two girls acting up with little concern or self-control, and she had a sense of remembering feeling that she had been always on the edge of falling apart when she was very young.

It seemed to me that this aspect of Ms R's experience with her children had revivified her own early experience of being dominated and controlled and unable to hold onto her own reality and autonomy in relation to her mother. It also seemed that her breakdown now reflected what Winnicott referred to as a large-scale release of defences and a shift in the centre of operations of the personality, relinquishing the False Self and exposing the True Self.

Ms R said:

> There's something wrong with me ... . I feel so revved up ... and there's no let down ... spasms of terror ... oh my god, it's unbelievable ... the level of fear ... grinding my teeth ... a feeling of falling apart ... losing my mind ... . But I can see that it's the collapse of this big structure ... being perfect ... keep the floors immaculate ... cook dinners ... get everyone presents ... take care of the children ... it's not sustainable ... that's what happened with work too. The extreme anxiety stimulated all

> these stress hormones … . Now I want to get back to a normal cycle … it's a process … I have to say no … I can't make too many commitments.

Somewhat later, Ms R said:

> I see how much I was caught up in all of the hustling and bustling, trying to be perfect … anticipating everyone's needs … bring all these special foods to our rustic vacation … running and running and who cares … . I'm not stressing over the string bean puree and stuffing the chicken … things that were very important don't seem to matter. I just can't do it all, but then who am I?

As Ms R talked about a sense of emptiness and fears of isolation in giving up her former containment and efforts to please everyone, her vertigo and anxiety seemed to be very gradually decreasing. She said:

> I feel afraid of falling to pieces … on the verge of that most of the time … . I remember feeling this way a lot when I was really young … . It's a very lonely feeling, that something is terribly wrong with me and no one will be able to help me. Now I'm inching back into my life … but I don't know what that means … it feels like everything is different … I feel childlike in a lot of ways … I feel so dependent on our sessions … and such sadness … terrible pressure in my chest … . I'm in a lot of pain … it feels so physical … almost unbearable … I never would have believed that anxiety could be this bad.

After about ten months of working in analysis in this way, Ms R came in with the first in a series of transference dreams that reflected a coherent process of working through her early anxieties. What was immediately notable in these dreams was the clear representation of my embodied presence that had been more muted and indirect in the past. I present these dreams and associations mainly without intervening material because this seems to capture the way the dreams functioned as nodal transference representations moving the process forward in a powerful way.

Throughout much of what follows, Ms R was still experiencing intense anxiety, vertigo, sadness, and pain, often crying through sessions, and just managing to get through. Yet, as these dreams advanced, she reported gradual improvement of her symptoms until completing work on the eighth dream when she had essentially recovered and was free of symptoms.

Dream one—December

Ms R: I got an invitation from my first boyfriend to a performance .... I was excited, nervous, I felt like I wasn't dressed right, but I had a really nice, periwinkle blue scarf ... the invitation had no telephone number ... I was clutching it in my hand ... on the way I dropped the scarf and it got all muddy, and when I got there the place was closed .... I looked at the invitation and it said "I'll be there every day except Friday ...". It felt like such a lost opportunity .... I realize it's about the session, you said you might be able to reschedule to Friday and I could let you know about my schedule, but I didn't call you.

AT: Were you afraid to ask?

Ms R: I felt uncomfortable ... even talking about it is problematic .... I'm the person who's afraid to make phone calls, afraid of feelings .... My boyfriend could be supportive, could see the problems with my mother .... He thought I was special .... The invitation was like your card in the beginning when you'd write the session time .... I've been having feelings about you, at times I have a realization: I don't have to be so anxious because I have you ... but it's only momentary .... I compartmentalize it ... it feels really emotional to talk about it ....

AT: It seems like you feel maybe you can rely on me, but it doesn't really feel safe, as if I gave you my card with no telephone number. How can you call me to reschedule on Friday if it seems that I didn't want to make room for you, don't want to be called?

Dream two—Three weeks later

Ms R: My parents' apartment was gone, they got rid of it ... I couldn't believe it ... the terror ... I'd never be able to go back there again ... everything dark inside ... wind blowing through the

empty rooms. I feel a pit of fear in my stomach, the things I've held onto, I realize they're not real, what am I going to hold onto? I was realizing there never was anything there … . I was showing you "Look where I grew up, there's nothing there" … the apartment was always so austere, somehow you had already been there, it felt good to show you … . I feel there's something terribly wrong with me … so if I ride it out it'll get better? My whole way of viewing my world has shifted … I'm really relying on you … I know I can't do it alone … it's way too intense … everything was warped growing up … ideas about what happiness was supposed to be … being connected and having relationships is happiness.
AT: I think the apartment is like your mother's mind, like a cold, dark, empty place with no people, no relationships.
Ms R: It feels like a sickness … I feel it physically … . I'm trying to figure out what this thing is and get to know it and be with it … so sad, pain like an open wound in my chest … . I'm aware that what I'm feeling so intensely now I've been grappling with my whole life … it's clear I've always been signing away my life … . I feel a shift, feel disillusioned, I'm not idealizing my friends.

Dream three—January

Ms R: I'm telling Andy that I'm going for a session … I'm going to sleep in your office so I won't miss it … . There was a glass table in the middle of the floor … I broke it … I was trying to make room for my sleeping bag on the floor when I shifted the table and the whole thing fell apart … I'm so sorry … trying to put it back together … it's weird … how do I integrate my relationship with you into my life … there was something nice about it … . You've been saying I'm afraid of breaking something … what you think of me … going to expose something … .
AT: Breaking some barrier between us.
Ms R: I was really embarrassed … a very intense feeling … transparent … something about it represents a possible comfort level … like this could be a safe place … . I have a lot of moments when I feel alone and I think but I'm not alone, yet there's the discomfort … fear of being close … it frightens me … it always feels difficult taking in positive things …

AT: Like you're afraid you might miss a session because you partly do want to stay away. Something is happening between us, the glass is breaking, and you are making some room for yourself here, but it still feels dangerous.

Ms R: I want to feel taken care of and safe with you, but I'm afraid of relaxing into that, the trust ... being able to rely on you so much this year ... it means so much ... a stepping stone ... needing to talk at different times ... not compartmentalizing.

Dream four—March

Ms R: The couch was really high up and I had trouble getting up on it ... there was a throw folded up in a square ... I was lying on it and it got all messed up and I was trying to straighten it ... all this anxiety ... . I was telling you something in a lot of detail ... something about self-realization and you said, "You got that from a book, that's not really you." I was trying to say "Yeah, but it really is how I feel," and I was trying to put this throw back up on the couch, but it was really high and I couldn't reach it. It's my discomfort, not wanting to leave any traces of myself ... I always have to be aware ... . I thought about your sensing yesterday that I could be angry at you for not being able to fix it ... all this bad feeling, waves of sadness ... physical pain ... . Fuck, I'm trying so hard to get through it, doing everything I can, reaching out to friends ... ultimately it's me that has to go through this ... . I need relief and I can't seem to find it.

AT: And instead of helping, I'm saying you're not doing it right. I'm seeing you as full of problems and defects the way your parents see you.

Ms R: I'm plagiarizing my own life ... . I'm thinking about the dream with the scarf that I dropped ... and blankets, comforting, I like blankets, my grandmother had throws all around ... I remember when I visited I'd put them over me and go to sleep ... my mother has a nice throw but no one is allowed to use it ... getting into bed last night ... I couldn't feel snuggly and relaxed ... I felt agitated. When I asked you if it's going to be this bad forever and you said it won't, I believed you ... . When I'm feeling really bad I repeat that to myself, but it's hard to believe when I feel so bad … . But it's so important whether I really believe you … . My whole life I felt that they saw these problems in me because I was shitty … . I didn't have that feeling that we're all struggling and trying to get through … having compassion … . My parents don't see anyone but themselves … it's almost like they feel contaminated by other people … . I mourn that I didn't have anything, I was so alone.

In the following session, Ms R used the throw in my office for the first time and continued to use it through the rest of her analysis. She immediately found it very soothing and seemed to physically relax, to move more freely on the couch, and to experience substantial relief from the intense ongoing anxiety.

Dream five—May

Ms R: We had a session and it ended … I had a key for this building … . In the lobby there was a big chair … with a straight back … solid … . There was some kind of event going on … viewing of a film … . I really wanted to be there to see the film, but I was worried about running into you … . I felt intense anxiety … trying to leave without having you see me … I'd have to explain being there … . We were talking last time about being open, vulnerable … . My worry I could do something, reveal something and you wouldn't like me any more … that containment … . I try so hard to please everyone … anticipate their needs … it's not enough to just be myself … but with this breakdown, I know I don't have to do everything alone … . Over the years of analysis … my whole perspective on what's important has changed … that's disorienting … the feeling of vulnerability … facing the bottom dropping out, and I have to put the pieces together in a different way … this is a dream about a boundary that I don't want to cross … I'm not supposed to see you outside … . I have anxiety at the end of sessions when we face each other … I want to contain things.
AT: Having a key could mean that you feel you belong, but you have to justify it.

Ms R: I'm aware of how I always keep my house key separate from my work key .... I think about how I used to line things up in my closet .... I like to know where things are .... The chair was throne-like .... I feel contained now .... I invest so much in controlling everything.

AT: It's hard for you to really feel that you might belong, that you matter, and that you are important to me.

Dream six—June

Ms R: Something I did led to the death of a lot of people and I kept it a secret .... Then I was going to tell you I had committed this horrific act ... take the risk ... because I couldn't live with the secret .... I'd blown up a building or something ... scary .... You can't go back .... You've done this terrible thing ... so afraid of what would happen, change how you'd perceive me .... But I couldn't live a lie any more ... it was too burdensome .... Last night I felt so guilty ... I really didn't feel like being with the children .... They're getting stronger ... their "breaking out" hurts me sometimes ... looking back I think sometimes the early time with them was a hard time in my life ... the complete dependency .... The first time I had an episode of vertigo, I felt there's no one else here to take care of things .... Having to meet the needs of two infants was very intense ... I know it's something about the absolute dependence ... about how my own needs weren't met .... I think I'm still waiting to get into what I need ... it was hard for me to be so selfless when the girls were infants ... to pour so much of myself into them ... what did I get from my mother? But I know whatever the pain is ... I'm going to go through it ... when I struggle with sadness I'm glad to know we're going to have a session .... We all have losses but can share it ... I see my mother is so cut off .... I was always preoccupied with fear of terrible things happening that you don't recover from .... It's some form of healing that happens over time ... it's a part of life ... it's so reassuring to know there are people around me who can do that .... I feel such sadness in my chest ... my parents didn't give me these really important life skills ... it's hard to work all this out at my age ... I see how all of this has made it hard for me to be alive, being depressed for so long without really knowing it. The sadness is so intense it feels like a sickness, a chemical thing in my brain … . It hurts to be alive … a deep physical pain … but it's definitely gotten better … but then I can also feel I'm never going to get over this … . I think when you go on vacation it's disorienting … that session time … it's a strange feeling, whoa … last summer I had a lot of anxiety.

Dream seven—October

Ms R: We were having our session on the beach, it was kind of similar to a tidal wave dream … . I was so freaked out about it not being in the office … an open environment … out of context … . I had a towel on the sand and the tide was coming up and getting everything wet and you were helping me move it … it was a feeling of being freaked out … I'm not supposed to be with you on the beach … . Talking yesterday about my feeling that you're not going to like me and my relying on you makes me feel kind of freaked out … afraid to be close … when you say we are working this out … that freaks me out and I don't know how much I can get into it … . I see my fear of being connected … saying me and you together … I've never really had that connection … even though I rely on you. I'm still afraid … . With Andy it's also a fear of dependency … but my love for him and the children infuses me with such a feeling of being alive … I see the other places where that doesn't happen … . I think of my parents … they're like dead people … . In the dream I didn't notice the water but you did … you moved the blanket so it wouldn't get wet.

AT: What used to be so terrifying about the tidal waves is now right here in me and in your feelings, and allowing yourself to be so vulnerable.

Dream eight—November

Ms R: I went to the new gynaecologist … her office was crazy … she looked like a witch … the office was weird … I told her I want to have another child but I'm depressed … the nurse brought me over to be examined … it was not normal … . They had me sit on some thing that was supposed to stimulate my vagina and should be able to read the aura of my vagina … . I didn't know if I was supposed to be stimulated … then she said, "You can't have a baby … you're too depressed … come back another time." I'm depressed … I have two children, but my life is not my own … . I've grown up being told there's something wrong with me … . I'm just now getting to understand so many things about the girls … . I worry that you're going to think I'm not a good mom … I've been trying to give them things that I thought I wanted … like having a parent that's excited about doing things … . I see it's not about the things I want to give them but the things they're excited about … . I think about how magical things seemed at times, how idealized my parents were … but I was always so alone entertaining myself … it's like the Wizard of Oz … but waking the girls up is magical … . I had to sit on that thing that measured the aura of my vagina … . My sexuality is all tied up with my mother's nudity and the giantness of her vagina … she eclipsed me … I remember seeing the videos of women giving birth, and coming in and saying to you, "But the vaginas are so huge …". The baby crowning … it reminds me of the largeness of my mother's vagina … . I never knew what she wanted … was I supposed to touch it? It was so awful and upsetting and freaky … . I've never been able to erase those images … seeing the childbirth videos, I thought there's no way that could be me … . The nurse sat me down on this machine … it was a kind of vibrating machine like a concave bowl, like a plunger type thing … when I was in labour, both girls had to be suctioned … I pushed for nearly two hours … I was really scared I'd need a C-section … .

At this point and for many sessions to come, we were able to talk about Ms R's feelings about her vagina and about herself as inadequate, passive, concave, and depressed, while feeling that her mother was always larger than life, equipped with a grown up sexuality and a huge powerful vagina, like the image in the childbirth video of what seemed like a huge vagina with a baby's head coming out. We could also talk about her experience of me as a witch-like doctor who could detect and judge her as small, inadequate, and defective. But here, especially, as her own creativity and aliveness were reflected in the process of dreaming and symbolization, we were able to see clearly that her experience of being marked and damaged by her mother was not a permanent fact but a psychological structure, a product of her own conflicts and adaptations, with a meaning that could be understood in terms of her childhood self, with an immature child's body and sexuality, being confronted with her mother's powerful adult body and sexuality. Since she had always been seen and treated as a thing rather than a human being, and undoubtedly her mother also felt herself to be a thing, these concrete differences had assumed the central meaning of their relationship. Ms R was able to see that she had accepted this limited psychic reality as equivalent to her entire reality. After working on this eighth dream for several sessions, Ms R noted that her anxiety and other symptoms were basically gone. She could sense they were there in the background, and she worried they could return, but there was no recurrence.

The intense dreaming of this period came to a close, and Ms R became more actively engaged in several areas in her life outside analysis. Being with her felt very different after this period of breaking down. She spoke and moved freely in a way that was spontaneous and alive, and she spoke movingly about feeling that she had been "reborn". As we talked about these changes, both Ms R and I expressed a great deal of mutual gratitude.

Over the following four years of analysis, Ms R had several significant stressors and feared at times that extreme anxiety, disorientation, and pain would return. Echoes of the same feelings emerged at times, along with deepening experiences of dependency, which led to further consolidation of autonomy and agency. A long termination phase also involved a similar cycle of these feelings worked through at even deeper levels of meaning, but there was no recurrence of symptoms near previous levels, and there was a secure sense of breakdown belonging in the past.

Discussion

Through what appears to have been the reliving of an early breakdown, Ms R was able to bring this experience into the here and now of the transference, to tolerate and work through something close to unthinkable anxiety, disorientation, sadness, and pain, and to move forward with new strength and aliveness. One can readily hypothesize that the degree of autonomic dysregulation involved in Ms R's unbearable anxiety, disorientation, and sense of disintegration reflected a similar, early breakdown at the level of basic, sensori-motor organization and a failure of the kind of environmental provision and mutual regulation that begin in the infant-caretaker dyad.

It seems that Ms R's breaking out of her powerful defensive containment and de-animation, and moving into connection with her own agency and reality, necessarily brought her through this early breakdown and her early relationship with her mother. This process turned her world upside down as she had originally been helplessly engulfed and whirled around in an all-encompassing tidal wave/merger experience with her mother, an experience in which Ms R had almost been lost forever. As she risked another near-annihilation in leaving a fixed orientation towards serving the needs and expectations of her mother, she was eventually able to stabilize and find a new orientation to her own reality and agency.

One important element of this process involved Ms R's also building up and becoming oriented to an internal representation of a reliable environmental mother/analyst as a part of her finding a way back to her own early dependency and rudimentary omnipotence. As a child, Ms R was shocked into premature awareness by failures of environmental provision, and she developed the various defences that have been outlined above. Rather than using a typical transitional object at night to soothe anxieties and help her go to sleep, she developed a compulsive alertness to the possibility of the unpredictable and reassured herself by ritually lining up her possessions in case of emergency. In the course of analysis, Ms R was increasingly able to risk using the transference experience of a reliable analyst as a basis for relaxing defences, regression to dependence, coming increasingly to know her own spontaneous aliveness, and eventually reliving an early breakdown.

Following nearly a year of reliving almost unbearable terror and pain, Ms R began to dream in a new way. In retrospect, it appears that her dreams gave representational form to several important transference developments occurring at that time involving the spontaneous start-up of maturational processes and recovery from illness. First, images of the abandoning boyfriend/analyst, the analyst who said she is not real, and the witch-like gynaecologist/analyst who said her femininity is deficient and defective, symbolized complex traumatic elements in terms of Ms R's subjective reality experience of being failed by her analyst. By "staging" within the transference these traumatic elements that originally came from outside, Ms R was able to bring these experiences within her own control and newly found area of omnipotence. Working through these threats of annihilation which, within the matrix of transference, did not lead to annihilation, strengthened Ms R's growing subjective reality.

Another important process reflected in these dreams was Ms R's movement into transitional areas of spontaneous "creating and controlling" while also finding, on her own terms, a growing experience of libidinal connection with the analyst. It seems that feeling more real and alive naturally carried Ms R into increasing connection with the object. Her dream about breaking the glass table seemed to represent something like the dissolution of a glass barrier that some people experience between themselves and the world. Ms R was breaking out more into the open and was able to risk being connected and vulnerable. Dream images of the analyst as trustworthy companion, witness, and confidant reflected new experiences of genuine connection and the growth of an internal object. The images of a scarf and throw and towel are also interesting representations of transitional object qualities such as soothing, comforting, and protecting which reflect Ms Rs growing feelings of connection.

A third aspect of therapeutic process reflected in these dreams is Ms R's growing feeling that she exists and is held in the mind and memory of her analyst. Images of the analyst's lobby, office, and couch seem to represent a growing transference experience of moving out of isolation into believing that she has a real place in the analyst's mind and heart. In dream six, she told her analyst that she had "committed this horrific act". She was terrified that it would change how I "perceive" her, but she could not tolerate feeling isolated any longer. Her associations to the dream reflect her poignant realization of the basic, life-sustaining effects of being held in the mind of another person. To paraphrase Ms R: although terrible things may happen, recovery is possible because we can share our authentic experience. Knowing that we truly have a place in the mind of another and can share our problems allows healing to occur over time.

Overall, this sequence of multi-layered, richly textured creative symbolization presents a clear example of spontaneously unfolding maturational processes. The dreams seem to reveal complex, interrelated integrative processes simultaneously knitting together out of various elements of experience the continuity and cohesion of the self and of the internal object.

Lastly, it seems important to address concerns about regression and breakdown being potentially anti-therapeutic. In my experience, regression is not a response to the analyst's technique or an outcome that we can choose to foster. Kohut has made it clear that patients' healthy compensatory structures and adaptations should be respected and do not require analysis (1984). We may be satisfied to live through analyses that proceed along standard lines without meeting a regression.

Meanwhile, various kinds of regression occur regularly in and out of analysis. Many patients move into a regression to dependence as a natural development of their own therapeutic process, which includes letting go of defences against unpredictability in response to the reliability found in the analytic setting, i.e. the analyst's behaviour. Patients in this kind of regression become real sufferers who, for some time, are truly ill. Surprisingly, I have found that patients in this kind of regression are generally stable in their lives outside analysis (in making decisions, meeting obligations, caring for the needs of others) in spite of their terrible suffering.

We can only see where a patient may seem to need a regression to dependence, and be as ready as possible to "meet" this if and when it happens. If we decide to work in this way, we should be committed to see the patient through to whatever depth needs to be reached. If we enter into the patient's reality and follow the patient's process, the patient may develop increasing confidence in the analyst's capacity to understand and deal reliably with dependency and, eventually, even experiences of chaos. Confidence in the patient and a belief that the necessary truths lie in the patient's own reality and urge to health can enable the analyst to wait for the depth and fullness of the transference to evolve.

Ultimately, the regressed patient is highly vulnerable and at great risk. There is a real challenge to the analyst's commitment and capacities to follow the patient into areas of dependency and disintegration, to hold the less integrated patient through time, and to make regression a good-enough, productive experience. This may require the analyst to achieve some personal growth. Many of our patients can help us do this and teach us how to meet their needs in the therapeutic process. I am especially grateful to Ms R for having taught me a lot about following the patient's own process of coming alive.

Note

1. I am very grateful to Jocelyn Scher, Sheldon Bach, Kate Oram, Patricia Doyle, and the members of the IPTAR Study Group on Winnicott for their helpful comments while I was preparing this paper. I am also grateful to the Linda Neuwirth Memorial Section at IPTAR for selecting this paper for their 2010 award.

CHAPTER SIX

On shame in narcissistic states of consciousness: clinical illustration

Mary Libbey[1]

> *Language in its most specific function in analysis, as interpretation, is a creative act similar to that in poetry, where language is found for phenomena, contexts, connections, experiences not previously known and speakable. New phenomena and new experience are made available as a result of reorganization of material according to hitherto unknown principles, contexts, and connections.*
>
> —Hans Loewald,
> On the Therapeutic Action of Psychoanalysis (1960)

This paper will focus on the phenomenology of narcissistic states of consciousness and aspects of the analyst's contribution to the therapeutic action of psychoanalytic treatment with patients manifesting such difficulties. After briefly reviewing the literature that I found most helpful and influential in my understanding of these states, I will present a patient with an unusual ability to vividly describe this mental terrain. I will then summarize four phases of the nine years of treatment to date, a treatment that has been productive and therapeutic, and one that has also taken place on two levels—the conscious verbal exchanges between us, and the unconscious, non-verbal, interactions in the transference-countertransference matrix. I will describe the issues and experiences that the patient presented along with what went on in my mind as he talked—my own personal feelings and thoughts. I will then present what, in retrospect, I now understand about what went on between us while we were talking about other things. My purpose is twofold: to add to our knowledge of these states and the transitions between them with the aid of my patient's illuminating self reflections, and to illustrate how narcissistic transference-countertransference configurations, at both conscious and unconscious levels, can contribute to a positive treatment outcome for these patients.

Narcissistic states of consciousness

My appreciation of narcissistic states comes largely from the work of Sheldon Bach (1985, 1994, 2006). Bach wrote about the experience of persons with narcissistic states of consciousness as having either a predominately heightened state of self-consciousness, with awareness stemming from the vantage point of his or her objective self, or alternately, a predominantly heightened subjective sense of being, with a seeming lack of self-consciousness, awareness originating from his or her subjective self. All people have both ways of being, which alternate more or less smoothly, and the two states have as many idiosyncratic variations as there are people. But in the person who suffers narcissistic states, one or the other prevail, and whichever prevails, the other is hard to access. A transition from one state to another cannot be made automatically, nor at will or without great effort, and the two states cannot be experienced simultaneously. Waking life is consumed with a continuous effort to stay safe in one state or another, or in painful transitioning from one state to another when required by external circumstances. Bach (2006) uses the terms *transitional phenomena* and *lack of reflexivity* to refer to the difficulty in moving between self states. My understanding of narcissistic states and the transitions between them has been further enhanced by Broucek's writings on shame (1982, 1991). He wrote also about the difficulty with transitions, and discussed it as a function of the lack of a continuous core sense of self. Just like Bach, Broucek wrote that a continuous sense of self entails the ability to move flexibly, even smoothly, among perspectives and realities (internal, external, subjective, objective, one's own, another's). Difficulty moving smoothly from one state of mind to another has its origins in the child's early experiences of the mother as stranger. A rupture in one's sense of self entails the experience of a breach with a significant object, be it conscious or unconscious, internal or external. The associated affect is shame. Broucek's continuous sense of self is similar to the ability to accept the paradox, a concept of Winnicott's (1971). Fonagy has tackled the inability to move beyond a fixed perspective, calling it the *psychic equivalence state* (Fonagy & Target, 1996; Fonagy, 2000; Allen, Fonagy & Bateman, 2008). Many earlier authors have written about difficulty with transitions as stemming from the child's earliest experiences of mother. For example, Mahler and McDevitt (1982) wrote about such difficulties for those individuals who could not manage the early separation from the mother, and Broucek wrote about such difficulty as a function of the child's early experiences of mother as stranger (1991).

For the patient who experiences narcissistic states, the terms *transition* and *reflexivity* connote a mental process related to shifts in perspective, but do not convey the disorientation and multiple intense affects that are part of it. It is quite a state, in and of itself, just as difficult to move into and out of as other narcissistic states. It is a transitional state of shame, a state of *narcissistic disequilibrium*. It is sudden, shocking, and disruptive. It can be brief or protracted. It is extremely painful and greatly avoided. While the underlying threatening affect is shame, the conscious affect may or may not include shame, along with component affects such as terror (Libbey, 2007; Hurvich, 1989), envy (Lansky, 1997), rage (Kohut, 1972), indignation, entitlement, vindictiveness, and vengefulness (LaFarge, 2006). It entails an internal experience, whether conscious or unconscious, of a breach with the object and a fall from the self.

Case illustration: Dev

Background and history

Dev is married, in his mid 30 s, a professor of English literature at a large university. He came to treatment for "writer's block", the extent of which was serious. His Ph.D. dissertation had been completely stalled for months. He was facing deadlines, which threatened him with taking an additional year to graduate. In his daily efforts to write he would sit for hours in a state of anxiety, unable to begin, and eventually give up. The son of immigrants from South Asia, he has a brother, five years older. The brother was born in the parents' country of origin and he speaks their native tongue. Dev was born after the family had been in the United States for one year, and they taught him only English. He has talked little about his father, whom he describes as a depressed, retired academic, who takes off on his own in his car for days at a time, a bit of a nowhere man. He describes his mother, a retired bank teller, as "weird", someone who speaks in vague abstractions, is superficial and concerned with manners, and who for a long time has been involved in meditation and spiritual ideas in a retreat with a guru, where she also does a lot of volunteer work scrubbing floors and bathrooms. He criticizes his parents in many ways, but also believes they love him and have sacrificed a lot for him. But he despairs of any "real" relationship with them. "All you've got is an absence of emotional relationships—we are here, we don't feel it, but we can see it."

Indeed, Dev announced early and often that the most significant thing about his history was the absence of any connection with his mother at birth:

> My mother was in a twilight zone when I was born. I was born in the twilight zone.
>
> My mother decided two things before I was born—that she would only speak to me in English and that she would not breast feed me. She sacrificed a relationship with me so that I could become a successful American. She made a decision that she wasn't going to have anything to do with me.

His parents and his older brother spoke their native language to each other throughout his childhood, leaving him out. "There was always a whirl of confusion around me growing up." He has maintained throughout the treatment that he does not have a mother tongue, and this, along with the other inevitabilities of immigrant culture, is central to his problems.

Here is Dev, early on in treatment, describing his experience of a lack of self and the development of his barren internal world:

Let's imagine in some amount, 10%, 5%, 25%, that I was somehow nothing to my mother, and nothing to my brother and father. And let's just imagine someone who's nothing and feels himself to be nothing, and he's kind of out in the world, and he figures out that he needs to learn how to speak, and wants to, and wants a sense of himself because he needs it and wants it, but he can't access any internal resources to figure out what he wants to say about who he is, because no one has told him who he is. No one told him anything. So he's a blank walking around in the world. So because he can't figure out an internal way, he starts to piece things together from the outside world. Everyone has to do this to some degree. Language is not internal. So he figures out who he is through external representations. He figures out other people, finding little pieces that seem right, little pieces that correspond to what he does want to think about himself. What results is a way of speaking and being that feels like an amalgam, a *bricolage*—that's French—a putting something together through various parts, making something out of disparate items—the pop culture, mother, father, brother—that he thinks are interesting, and he's pretty good at it. There's some sensibility, but its hard to feel the sense that there is anything internally holding it together. It doesn't feel very secure. So as he grows up he fits in pretty well, because it always comes from the outside. It doesn't seem weird.

And then he goes to therapy. The therapist says what do you really feel? All he has access to are words, allusions to TV shows, philosophy, movies. They seem related, but all are external. It's not organically created in any way. When it comes to talking about himself, it doesn't feel inaccurate, but it never seems accurate either. It's not one-to-one. You can't really have that when you've always looked outside for who you are. Everything I say are metaphors. The things I say are not trustworthy.

What does feel authentic is feeling emptiness. But that's a very scary feeling too. One feeling I could pinpoint is fear. It's really scary. It's also really embarrassing. It's hard. When someone says "How do you feel?" they're curious. My wife says, "What do you want for dinner?" It's logical to say, "This is what I want, this is who I am." It's embarrassing to say "I don't know", because I've built myself on being knowledgeable.

It seems incredibly unattractive to answer to my wife: "Nothing. A person who feels nothing wants nothing." I can only imagine she would say, "That's a very unattractive person." In the beginning of King Lear—I fucking love King Lear—he's dividing the land. Goneril and Regan say the right things. His favourite, Cordelia, says, "Nothing". He says, "Nothing comes of nothing. That's unacceptable." She keeps saying, "I have nothing to say," and she gets banished.

Dev described his mind as an empty space: "Thoughts and ideas come and go in a space of overall lack." He said that he was a prisoner in his mind, and that he had no ability to speak from within. He said he was always extremely anxious and self-conscious around others, and he never knew what to say. "I am never *not* self-conscious around other people." He also described what seemed to be two highly formed, circumscribed self states, one a high-pitched self consciousness, and one a blissfully unaware non-existence. While the anxious state took up "14 out of 16 waking hours of a day", he told me that moving in and out of either of these states was extremely difficult.

Thus Dev began treatment with what I understood to be experiences of deflated narcissism-self-consciousness, excessive humility, eagerness to please, and rigid self states. In his sincere, respectful manner, he told me how his mind worked. He was able to describe his mental topography well. Uniquely, his reported thoughts rarely included events or people. He was clever and well-spoken, and had interesting associations to characters and vignettes from movies and novels, which created the impression overall that he was more in and of the world than he felt. Frequently, when to my mind I had said nothing in particular, but had seemingly got it right by him, he would burst out with excitement: "Exactly!" or "Right!" or "Wow, that was really profound", or "Wait, I need to think about what you said for a few minutes". I did not know why he got excited at these times, and he had trouble answering when I asked about it. In hindsight, along with my view that what he said was a façade of being interested, I believe he *was* excited about being responded to in terms of his internal world. It was a pleasure to work with him, and I imagined that my positive feelings were picked up by him. All of this had additional meanings only later ascertained.

Phase one: discrete self-states

I recommended psychoanalysis to Dev because he was so verbal about his "empty mind" (which did not seem empty at all), able increasingly to elaborate on his experience of intense shame states, was perceptive about me, and had a verbalized positive transference. When proposing psychoanalysis I told him he was good at, and seemed to get something from, talking about and trying to understand himself. His response was startling:

> Oh no! Someone else who thinks I'm good at things! This is terrible! I'm not good! You'll never be able to understand me if you don't realize that I feel terrible all the time. My confident self is fake. I never feel confident, articulate, or assured. My confident self is a façade!

This was the first of the many ways Dev taught me that while presenting a façade of being confident and well-spoken, he was completely unable *not* to be involved in painfully watching himself. He said his self-objectification was like a plaster cast that he was trapped in. It separated him from others, and he wanted desperately to get out of it. I thought of the movie *The Diving Bell and the Butterfly* and he told me about the movie *Johnny Got His Gun*. In both movies the main character is locked inside himself, one completely paralysed, and the other with no limbs or senses. Neither could communicate with anyone.

In the early years of treatment, Dev claimed that he only experienced himself as existing in states, what turned out to be three states, which I will call: a state of heightened objective self awareness; a state of "absolute subjectivity", similar to Bach's (1985) subjective sense of self and Broucek's (1982) subjective self awareness; and a protracted transitional state between these two marked by intense feelings of shame.

State of Heightened Objective Self-Awareness: This first state was his most common one, that of extreme self-consciousness. Dev said that *whenever* he was around other people, *anyone*—his wife, his daughter, his students—he felt acute self-consciousness. He said he heard his calm authoritative voice as an alien voice coming from the outside, while inside he felt terrible. Usually he planned ahead of time how to get a presentation of himself right, so that his complete inability to be natural and spontaneous would not show.

> I do not know how to greet my dog. My wife does it so spontaneously. I can't stand it. I walk in the front door and I try to do it the way she does it. I act all excited and hug and pet Penelope, while my wife is standing there watching me—but even when she's not—so the dog will think I am happy to see her. I am happy to see her, but my expressions seem awkward and odd, so I don't think she will know it.

Even when alone, he described a mental conundrum as to how to proceed:

> After how many seconds would a normal person turn on the water in the shower, does my hand look normal turning it on? How would a normal person crack an egg? How would they look walking from the refrigerator to the counter with the eggs? Would they wait or just go ahead?

Thus, his self-consciousness occurred not only around other people for whom he put on a normal façade, but also with an outsider inside him who watched him and who discussed with him how to make himself function like a normal person who did have a self.

State of Absolute Subjectivity: Dev's second self state was a subjective state of believing that he did not really exist. No one was real. He insisted that he absolutely believed this. "We could all be part of someone else's dream." "You could be some strange computer. Good at some things, terrible at others." He was able to relax into these beliefs when alone. He felt timeless, non-existent, at one with the universe. This state was his home base. He was able to lapse into this only when he was alone, either in bed having just awakened in the morning, or when surfing the web—looking at politics, porn, not thinking, "floating around in a world of peaceful, calm nothingness". He loved this state, and spent as much time in it as he could.

Dev described how he reluctantly managed to get out of this state when he had to face the world. He described how he intentionally walked himself to the kitchen table, sat down, and made a list of the things he had to do that day. This list included "take a shower, get dressed, make breakfast, eat breakfast, clean kitchen, dump garbage, go to dry cleaners," etc. He insisted that without this ritual he would not be able to do anything. He would remain in a state of chaos not knowing what to do first.

State of Transition—A State of Shame: The third state is what Dev and I have come to call "the transitional state" and "the blast furnace". This third self state, an extreme version of his self-consciousness, did not exist before treatment but, after a year or so, involuntarily came about at the beginning of every session, as he transitioned from being alone to being with me. It was an affect flooding, but as it was happening I saw no visible evidence of it. Sometimes, he would put his head in his hands, but only sometimes. He was always silent. Sometimes he broke the silence with a brief "uh …" as if he wanted to speak, but could not get the words out. He did not want me to help him out of it. At some point, he would take a big breath and say "I'm thinking three things …" and then proceeded in his helpful manner, almost as if he was speaking about someone else. "I sound calm and lucid, but what I'm feeling is just horrible—it is like sticking my head into a blast furnace of shame and embarrassment." It would last on average five minutes. More recently he has said that when he gets through it, it reduces down to 50% or 25% shame, more like self consciousness, for the rest of the session.

With vivid imagery he described his feelings while traversing the gap from being alone to being with me. "It is like being hit by a Mack truck," or being in a place where "words are thrown up and blown together like shards in a washing machine". "It feels like I am running my head into a wall at 60 miles an hour." "It is shattering. It feels like my mind will blow apart." Sometimes he scrunched his face up into paroxysms of pain, or say "God!" in hushed self disgust. Sometimes he felt like he was going to vomit or developed a headache (see Libbey, 2007, on annihilating shame; and Hurvich, 1987, on annihilation anxiety).

While Dev said the *words* that he felt terrible and anxious every waking minute and suicidal every day, in the absence of accompanying visible or audible affect (he said all this in a not-terrible, not-anxious way) I found myself more absorbed in the content and its clarity than in touch with his pain. I was fascinated. For reasons I could not understand at the time, I did not question his lack of apparent affect. It was a lecture about a topic of extreme interest to me and I was not going to miss a thing. I did not hesitate to talk with him, as talking was easy for both of us. For example, I might mention the possibility that he felt shame about being glad to be back after a weekend; or angry about something in our previous session, in effect inviting him to reflect with me on his feeling. He would contemplate what I was saying, earnestly, but then at some point say, in the most rational manner, maybe with a touch of annoyance: "You sound so calm while you are talking about how terrible I feel." And then increasingly, "I *hate* it when you ask me questions! It makes me feel like what I have said isn't adequate." I would then feel that sudden awareness that an analyst feels upon the realization that one's comments are completely out of touch with the patient. I would pull up short, try to shift and ask him to tell me about that, or try to make sense of what just happened between us. This upset him even more. He did not want to figure things out. He wanted recognition.

After he told me enough times that asking him to join me in figuring something out was disruptive to him, I at least knew not to contemplate this out loud, much less ask him questions, but rather to apologize and/or empathize with being forgetful or not getting it. I realized that I had been joining his objectifying self state, going along with his calm rationality in his descriptions of his agony. I began talking differently, simply telling him what I heard him saying, less with certainty than comprehension, for example, "Perhaps, you are saying ..." or "I think I hear you saying ..." anything other than queries or requests for reflections from him. These were brief, unambiguous comments, in ordinary language in which I simply strove to *recognize* what he was trying to communicate about himself (see Allen et al., 2008, p. 116). He voiced gratitude and excitement about my "truth telling", my "smartness", which in turn made me *feel* smart, interested, and alive, and encouraged me to continue both with the framework of thinking about narcissism spelled out by Bach (1985) as well as the technical measures best delineated most recently by Fonagy (Allen et al., 2008).

I think the enthusiasm I felt for this treatment from its inception, for one thing, reflected an unconscious communication from Dev. In hindsight, I believe he was trying to keep me gratified, loved, alive, interested in him. In this sense, he needed *me* to feel, to hold and contain *his* alive feeling self, so that he did not have to own it until he became able, at which time he could identify with me. He could not access his own immediately alive self, and became angry if I attributed any such feelings to him. Rather, he induced and saw me as an honest, emotionally present, and exquisitely verbal person, whom he admired and wanted to be like. I could never be too alive or too real for him. Errors of mine in recognition were okay. He was very forgiving. But if I conveyed to him that he had the talents or feelings that he attributed to me, much less that I wanted to hear them from him, in other words that someone was alive and at home in *him*, he became very upset:

> You don't seem to be getting that there is no "you" there when you say, for example, "Are you saying you feel ...?" or "I feel like you are saying ..." or "What the hell are you talking about?" You want me to be more straightforward. The impulse that drives me to be abstract is shot down by you. When you say, "You feel ..." you are speaking in a language that is not about me. I never feel one way; I don't know what the fuck I feel. I feel I'm always in the gap between many feelings, between one or more selves, and there's a nothingness in that gap. I feel a nothingness, a blankness, an in-between, splitting apart, in the cracks between things. That doesn't seem like a feeling. That seems like a lack. There's always something lost in what's bothering me in going along with that fiction of yours that I go along with that there's an "I". Why don't you talk about sitting next to an atomic bomb?

I told him that "I listened for the words in his gaps while he listened to the gaps in my words." In other words, I tried to find words to articulate the feelings I heard hints of in his diffuse states while he was trying to create and find in me a person who feels, a person centered in their emotional self, with whom he could identify. Very gradually, he did give voice to his identification process with me. Eventually he told me that he wanted to be like me. He told me he was imitating me with his students, and that he had become very popular as a result. How? He said, "I talk Mary Libbey talk. I tell them that I understand all their scared, bad feelings about papers, interviews, etc., and that I have felt the same way. It's easy." At this stage of the treatment he made use of the treatment as imitation. Later, he began reporting that he talks to me in his head all the time. Recently, he reports that I talk back to him in his mind, and often he begins sessions telling me about these conversations.

Phase two: from shame to idealization and hatred

Increasingly in what I will call a second phase, around the fourth year of treatment, Dev began using the word *authenticity* for what he so admired in me and for what he wanted for himself. He began to talk less about nothingness and more and more about wanting to have a self, wanting to be real, wanting a voice with which to speak authentically with feeling to others. During this time his own striving for authenticity with me came to revolve around his conviction that he felt most real when he was in his transition state of severe shame, which had come about in treatment. It became, and remains, how he begins every session:

> At the centre of me is this self-consciousness and shame. If you are going to say something, the next thing is you're going to have to get down and feel the full force of it. You're going to have to turn up the dial, that's the only way you are going to feel centered, and oriented enough. That makes me pissed off that I can't say what I have to say without feeling that. The Herculean effort is to convince myself that I am going to survive it.

His idealization of my manner of speaking continued, as did its positive effect on me. While I still believed his was an unconscious effort to create a feeling in me of being loved and enlivened, I think he was also preparing me to take what was coming—his envy and hatred of what he saw as my authenticity as well as overconfidence.

He began to envy and hate me for many things in addition to my ease of speaking. He became less calm and charming, and before I quite realized it he was constantly expressing anger. He became angry about sessions I had to cancel, angry that he had to ask to reschedule, angry at himself that it was difficult to ask for anything, angry that I made him feel like a "weirdo" for not just telling me what was on his mind, and angry at me that all of this was so "easy" for me. He was angry that he was doing the work alone, that I was not supportive, that I did not understand that his mother was not at fault for how absent she was, that she was innocent in the face of the immigrant experience, which was simply a fact of life for immigrants, a fact that I should acknowledge, but in my confident American self was clueless about. "How could someone so smart about some things be so stupid about other things?" He was angry because he saw me as blaming his mother for being intentionally the way she was, angry that psychoanalytic authors are overwhelmingly white and do not take into consideration other cultures.

> In short, I'm full of rage about a lot of things. We have both put a lot into this. You should know more about the immigrant experience, which my mother had no choice about. There are books out there.

He would then abruptly alternate, and rail against his mother who spoke to him in such poor, broken English that when he was young he thought she had a speech defect. "I don't have a mother tongue! Broken English as a second language—that's my mother tongue!" He expressed anger that he never felt emotionally safe around her, angry that he had to accommodate her, "Talking to her is like grabbing at ghosts—there's really nothing there," then angry that he could not tell the difference between not wanting to overwhelm her and not wanting to overwhelm me.

At my end, I actually felt that his getting angry directly at me was a good thing. I felt like a proud mother—not that he was childlike (which he never was, too grown up in fact was more like it)—but a mother whose child feels safe enough to attack her. I also felt that he was more desperate to be understood than destructively angry. And I continued to feel the countertransference pleasure in his finding me so admirable, honest, and down to earth. In hindsight, I think he was unconsciously aware that these were the qualities he could eventually hate me for. This all allowed me to continue to let him continue to enliven me, to admire me, to envy and hate me, and eventually to identify with me. But I also began making interpretations, partly to tell myself I was actually working in addition to enjoying these sessions, but mainly because it was now easier to put things together about him. Putting things together had become easier because his anger at me now alternated regularly with anger at his mother, and at himself, and the reasons for his anger towards each of us were similar.

At one point when he was responding positively and excitedly— a little too excitedly—to something I said, I told him I thought he got excited when I got something, because he believed that I, like his mother, was too culturally impaired to understand him—his mother too lost in her immigrant experience, and I too lost in my presumptuous American experience, a derisive comment he made a lot about me. I had not called attention to his own excitement for some time, as he had told me early on that it was not real, that it was part of his façade. He responded: "I get *so* excited. I remember everything you say. Like the first time you used the word *manage*," which I don't remember. "You said I *manage* people. It was such a big deal!" It was a big deal to him to have someone responsive to his motivated self. It was a big deal to me that he was owning more particular feelings previously inextricable from the shame which had overpowered them.

I have had additional thoughts about the meanings of Dev's anger at me, which has persisted to the present. Was it inevitable? Why did he not feel shame about it, like he did about other feelings that came along? One could say that his interspersing attacks on me with reassurances, gratitude, and flattery were evidence of conflict about it, and in that sense it was simply the true expression of natural aggression. But he never sounded in conflict about it, and his anger never seemed like pure aggression either. It seemed like there was something different going on. Additionally, rather than feeling defensive, which I am fully capable of, I usually felt admiring about his ability to criticize me. I often took his criticisms literally and tried to accommodate them. My feelings seemed more like the feelings a parent would have about their child's anger—less threatened, more glad for the child's assertion and what it means for their developing ego. I do think Dev's anger was primitive. I think it was born of envy and was expressed as hate. Envy entails hating the object for having what one does not have oneself, like the child who hates the parent for their power and his dependency on them, or the boy who hates girls he is attracted to but feels he is not good enough for. While Dev projected many (of his own) positive traits onto me, he also projected negative traits—smugness, self-satisfaction, superficiality, thick-headedness, "smart in some areas, stupid in others". He envied, emulated, and hated me for all of them. Hating me seemed liberating to him. "I hate this. I hate talking to you. That must mean I hate you. I do. I hate you." He came to be able to hate me instead of feeling he had no choice but to accommodate me. I think in this sense he "used the object", me, in the service of destroying the object, again and again, while the object survived, in the service of separation (Winnicott).

Phase three: from idealization and hatred to a sense of self—a first child is born

By the fifth year of treatment, Dev had become convinced that "mother, language, culture, and shame" were the puzzle pieces to understanding his inability to feel a sense of "centeredness", or "realness". How they came together, he stated calmly, we had not yet figured out. That he thought these issues could inevitably come together signalled the fact that we were already working much more interpretively together. Beyond this, his reference to the two of us as *"we"* had a dual effect on me that was becoming more frequent. The first part of this dual effect was the by now suspicious familiar feeling of gratification. The second was a feeling of being startled. He had, unannounced, relayed a qualitative change in his experience of himself. This time it was a feeling of togetherness, as in "we are a we". Such communications increased from this time on.

During this time his own striving for "authenticity" with me came to revolve around his growing willingness to acknowledge that *he did feel real*, but only in his acutely anxious shame states that occurred only in treatment and when writing. Nevertheless it was something else that he had never said before, when he swore that all of his "feelings came and went in a space of overall lack". Again at this comment, made as if it was old news, I was quite startled.

In the fall of the fifth year of treatment his first child was born. A month later he reported the first dream he had ever reported in the treatment, another qualitative change:

> I had a dream last night. Michele and I had another baby in quick succession. It was like, we were talking. We had sex, and we thought the breast feeding would act as a contraceptive, and that didn't happen, and we were immediately having this other baby. And I felt extremely self-conscious. This was weird. Not supposed to happen. It was a little dangerous having another baby so close to the first one. We were rushing around. Michele was still going to work. She couldn't take off more time. The baby was massively deformed, really fat, and not moving. His head was huge. Instead of normal, eyes, nose, mouth, ears, he was just a big Mr Pumpkin Head. The nose was smashed into his face. There were little holes where the nose should be.

> The ears were little scars on the side of his face. I don't remember the eyes. Everything was out of whack. We had this incredibly deformed child. It was a weird emotional state around it. It was: "We gotta love this baby. If we don't, no one else will. I can deal with this. We can and we will. We are OK with it." We were not as pleased as we were with Irene. It was not really what we wanted. We didn't feel 100% like we did with Irene. But the overall sense was that this is not totally traumatic, but not great. We already didn't love this baby as much as we did Irene.

In discussing the dream, he said:

The deformed baby was me. I was the second child. I was not as attractive as my brother, but basically accepted. The family still functioned. But it is horrific to think of myself as this massively deformed child. So gross. Michele's younger brother was born deformed, without one arm, with one hand, and the other arm very deformed, caused by a drug his mother was prescribed. He's five years younger than Michele which is how much younger that I am than my brother. (He went on to describe how Michele's brother has done OK in life, giving her parents a lot of credit for it.)

Like him, I was taken with the five year difference that had shown up in his dream. It reminded me that this was his fifth year of treatment and that he had been mentioning recently that he had experiences of being real for the first time in his life. He agreed that he does feel very "malformed" and "abnormal", like that baby, but that he can stand it.

> The rebirth of my deformed ugly self, and I can stand it. It's a rebirth but it's terrible. I do feel there's a centre I have, but it's very horrible. It's disappointing. OK. Five years out. I do feel empowered and centered, but also horrible. It's not what I had hoped. I'm unbelievably better than where I thought I'd be after five years. But I didn't feel I'd be wrestling with such horrible feelings, but I also didn't imagine I could do it and it would be OK.

His intense shame states and his anger remained, as other feelings emerged. He increasingly spoke of *wants* and *needs* from me, feelings he had not given voice to before. He told me that he does not like being alone with his intense feelings. He wants other people to "mirror" them, or "resemble them themselves". He then shifted his attention to me, asking with some desperation in his voice for mirroring from me:

> These sessions are a big deal to me. I want them to be a big deal to you. I want you to be focused on every minute. I can't stand these feelings if you take them for granted.

Shortly after the above session he spoke offhandedly about having more than one way of being, and wanting to be able to move among them more easily. Had I set him up for this with my own ways of constructing his dilemmas as having to do with a lack of reflexivity? I really do not think I could have said the following the way he did:

D: I teach sometimes forcefully and thoughtfully and sometimes off the top of my head. What is hard is when I feel I have to be one way or the other. I can't think back and forth then. When I get arrhythmic I am no longer responding to where I am at, myself. I'm facing my mother, and I have to make traumatic choices. I have to deal with her, be present. The concept of floating in and out is no good. I have to make radicalized decisions. She's some force that splits me in two, in a way that makes it seem the two can't be at the same time.
ML: There has always been a press from her.
D: Yes, and it's so inappropriate to the situations I find myself in now. I'm trying to make choices between things as if she's there, but they're inappropriate. Any choice seems so radical, big, permanent, absolute.
ML: Things could be only one way with her. Change, and she wouldn't know you.
D: But now in my mind it has changed. What you just said used to be how my mind works. Now it's not the way it works. There were actually two people, me and my mother. Unlike her, I can think about different ways of being.

In this phase of the treatment, I felt like Dev's sense of self was coalescing before my eyes. I marvelled at his expressions of anger and need, his musings about moving more smoothly among self states when teaching, his awareness of his separateness and about his differences from his mother. I had never been involved in a treatment that *so closely* resembled the literature about the effective treatment of narcissism. Dev was describing his gradual release from his mother's internal grip on him. I felt like I was learning from him how to do it for myself too.

Phase four: finding an authentic voice—a second child is born

In my experience of the treatment, a new phase began with Dev's increasingly comparing and contrasting "concrete experiences" with "living in abstractions". Living in abstractions was something he had not altogether minded, as it was what he was used to—what he grew up doing with his family. He said "being concrete" was when he had "real feelings" and gave voice to them. His "being concrete" has come about more frequently as his daughter Irene has grown, and he has developed a relationship with her.

In one session early in this fourth phase, Dev spoke about a moment with his now four-year-old daughter Irene that he described as "moving", that he referred to as a "concrete experience".

> It was this experience of feeling like other people, rather than not like other people. How do I feel about Irene? Then I lose it. That move to the least bit more concrete. Everything falls apart when I try to make that move. I have flashes of Irene, my Mom, myself writing. But it's unstable. My mind gets split in two.

Later on in that session, I told him that I thought that both his concrete self and his abstract self were real parts of him. I reminded him that he had told me he feels proud of his teaching and good about being a popular professor, just like he feels moved being with Irene. I told him his "abstract" self was no longer an alien self, but really him. He said he was very relieved to hear this. He said, "It is when I try to put the two parts of myself together that the second part is unable to speak, *but it's not total.*"

In another session he got very involved in complaining that he was a blob. "There is a blob inside me that is like the monster emerging out of a dumpster in the movie *Mulholland Drive*. In the movie, it comes out, then goes away and never comes back again, and it was nothing." I felt something new with him, impatience, like this was a phony complaint-like whining. I told him that I thought that the blob self was *not* nothing, but part of him—the emotional part—as much a part of him as his speaking self is. He replied with an unequivocal yes, but then added: "But I feel there is a huge gap between them."

By now, Dev was no longer talking about his nothingness. Now he declared that his shame states at the beginnings of sessions were about telling the "truth". He still told stories to make points, but they were not from movies or books, they were from his current life. For example, he told a story of a fight with his wife, and obviously felt and named his anger.

Now he welcomes shame in sessions because it helps him to feel a "sense of self". He had shifted to referring to shame as a "relief", a "constant", "centering", and "grounding". Unannounced, this was another shift in his experience of himself.

> If I can talk through this shame, I'll feel more in touch, more in touch with my own language, more in touch with my relationships, more in touch with the other emotions I have.
>
> I'm floating around in a million pieces. Shame binds everything together making it whole. I like wholeness. Shame becomes the foundation for my sense of self. Stop having big ideas. Just focus on yourself. I become small. That can be centering. There's real stuff in the world around me. It's belittling but a relief too. I can see everything clearly. Increasingly I feel like I am being educated in shame.
>
> I'm starting to be true to myself, and Dr Libbey helped me to do that. I feel the benefits of feeling what I feel, and communicating it to you. I know that knowing what I feel doesn't just happen. It starts with feeling humiliated, then a little bit focused, then there is a real stage where I feel a lot of humiliation, but also centered. I say to myself, "Dr Libbey is not going to support you. She doesn't give support. She gives the truth. OK, Dev, you get to do what you think best."

More recently, Dev recalled his original goal in seeking treatment. At that time he wanted an ability to communicate, to be free of his blockage in written expression. He wanted what he now calls "an authentic voice with people as well as in writing".

D: In the beginning of analysis, I started to write the book. That was always much more pressure than my suicidal thoughts. What I felt was the problem with communication. Analysis has always been this place of a desperate attempt to communicate. Now I can write things. And it's not bullshit. *The things I say are true. I'm less concerned with whether or not people get it anymore. I've gotten this practice with you in saying things that are true.*

I think the reason I don't understand why language feels different to me now is your fault, because you don't understand my experience of language. So I have to find my own language on my own. I don't understand it yet. I had always thought language was made up—that words only exist in relation to each other. Separate from that they had no meaning.

ML: Is that a postmodern idea?

D: Yes. Although that's a much broader category. I used to believe that no words or ideas had any meaning except the meaning they had to the reader. Now I don't believe that any more. *Now I know that people are real and their language is real. People have actual histories, actual emotions.*

I felt startled, even astounded. He was debunking the postmodern critical theory he teaches and writes about. Even more exciting was that he was doing it because he believes individual human beings, himself included, are each actual, real, whole people, not people who change as the reader or listener changes. I remembered his idea early in the treatment that we could all be part of someone else's dream; we change as the dream changes. By now, Dev was using the terms "language", "talking about emotions", and "having a voice" interchangeably:

> There's a whole realm of real emotional life that is very real, powerful, robust, that doesn't have anything to do with language. But language is a part of it. There's something about language that makes you feel on top of things. Without it you won't. So it's not just an experience of emotion, but something about feeling on top of it. Language makes you feel competent about feelings. If you have that experience of competency there's a feedback loop. Emotions make a person's voice more real; voice makes emotions more real. I think a lot about

this. I think a lot about writing. I think, "Dr Libbey's writing doesn't seemed learned. But it is. It's crafted in a way she doesn't know about. How wonderful." It's like, "I don't think about this stuff at all." I want to write like you talk and write. A kind of lived matter-of-fact-ness. A non-obnoxious take-it-or-leave-it-ness.

In the closing of this ninth year of treatment, four years after their first child, Dev and Michele had their second child. Unlike with the first child, he found himself *excited*. He was brimming with "confidence as a parent, and still a person, who is still him". The baby could not breast feed initially, and his wife wanted to give up the effort. He declared to her: "No! This baby will not get less than the first baby! This baby must have every opportunity the first one had."

He took charge and gave his wife round-the-clock assistance, fed and took care of the older child and his wife as well, while his wife pumped milk. He took care of storing the milk, warming it, delivering it to his wife to give to the baby. All the while Michele helped the baby get the hang of breast feeding. It was an exhausting marathon. For two weeks they did not go out or see anyone. In the course of it he gave affect and voice to his immediate feelings, as they were happening:

> She is the second born and she deserves every chance just like our first child! This will work! I can make this work! *I feel invested, empowered, compelled, and a sense of moving forward. Breast-feeding is the truest thing for both Michele and me!*

In this comment he says similar—albeit more enthusiastic—words to the words he used in the Mr Pumpkin Head dream. In that dream, just after the birth of his first child, he said:

> We gotta love this baby. If we don't, no one else will. I can deal with this. We can and we will. We are OK with it.

In this session he reiterated that he was a deprived second born child who was not breast fed, and that this would not happen to their second born, Marion. But this was no time for dwelling in the past. It was time for abandon:

> *I feel abandon! I feel free! I feel ecstatic! I feel ecstatic abandon!* The breast feeding is still not working. I have lost my keys on the way here. I don't know who is going to pick up Irene. We don't have anything for dinner. But I feel confident! I can figure this out! And I feel confident in Marion! I need you to tell me that you feel confident too that this will work. I need to know you believe in me.

It was easy to tell him that I believed in him. First of all, he was *asking* me. I realized he had really never asked me a direct question. Secondly, it had been exhilarating to hear his involvement, emotionally and practically, in his family, and to see the range of his reach. I told him this was how I saw him. Late in that session he told me that feeling understood by me made him feel strong. When normal breast feeding took off, Dev described carrying his newborn and talking to her:

> D: This is the only way she'll get to hear my voice and know me. I talk at my job so other people don't have to, because I care about them, and I don't want to put a trip on them. I talk to others in order to acknowledge how difficult it is. But talking to you is me being myself. Then always elsewhere I have a retrospective sense of being myself. I still don't understand how it all fits together. Language is a part, but only a part. I still don't think you understand what I mean about language.
> ML: I think I do understand 75% of what language means to you. I think that when I understand 100% of it, your treatment will be done.
> D: That's funny. I have also been trying to imagine how I'll know when I'm ready to stop. I think the opposite! I understand 75% of what you say about feelings and I even agree. I have had the thought that when I understand 100% of it the way you do, I'll be done.

It is interesting that Dev's own transformations into a "centered self" occurred at the times of the births of his daughters. There was much background work leading up to these experiences of course. But the circumstances of his own birth were blows to him. He felt he was abandoned by his family. Remembering this, it is not hard to see Dev's own children's births as momentous. He loaded them up with meaning—identifying with the first as himself, in some way feeling born again himself, albeit as a pumpkin head. His second child represented all the dangers of being born a second child, all the dangers of being neglected compared to the first, but also all the opportunities to get it right this time. This child would not be a burden! He would sink into the joys and responsibilities of parenthood! His self was born again and then again when each child was born, as he was emerging and re-emerging in the treatment relationship.

Dev has continued to talk about how he too feels he is changing. He has talked, for the first time, about sexual fantasies. How might he seduce his students? What kind of Lothario would he be? The wise, knowledgeable professor? Which student would he pick? What would he say? Would he ask her to go for coffee, or would he just demand it? He reminds me that he loves his wife and is very attracted to her, and has absolutely no intention of acting on these fantasies. When I told him I thought he was perhaps having the adolescent fantasies now that he could not have when he was an adolescent, again, he said he had the same thought. He has described the experience of being real in the relationship with Michele. She also feels more real. They talk to each other and take each other's feelings into consideration. It makes them both a little nervous because it is so new. I find myself sitting back with the feeling that he is on his own now. Thoughts about his terminating come to my mind involuntarily, and I feel sadness for my loss and happy for him.

Concluding remarks

This paper has focused on the psychoanalytic treatment of a patient who presented with painful, unyielding narcissistic states of consciousness, especially pronounced during transitions between the polarities of subjective and objective awareness. I have attempted to illustrate how the analyst's ongoing contemplation of this patient's experience of narcissistic states was central to the treatment.

Generalizing from this case illustration, the narcissistic patient's ongoing sense of self, fragilely tied to the other, may be viewed as threatened in the inevitable transitions that occur, planned and unplanned across the frame, as well as by transitions in perspective that occur, such as shifts from the vantage point of the patient's subjective awareness to awareness from a vantage point of objective awareness. Because patients prone to narcissistic states lack reflexivity, these shifts do not occur automatically, smoothly, nor without some amount of effort and self-consciousness. Rather, any transition has some degree of abruptness and rupture for the patient, like something has just happened that must be withstood, like being faced with a "blast furnace". The patient's reaction is immediate and has multiple components—shock, self-consciousness and shame over believing the breach is due to his or her own inadequacy, fear of not being able to make the transition along with the analyst and losing the tie, as well as a feeling of impending annihilation that comes with losing the tie. Efforts to recover, such as compliance, umbrage, or rage, may follow. Recognizing shame in one's patient, the analyst may have to acknowledge his or her own empathic failure. Or an apology may be warranted. Or the analyst may want to speak about what he or she had in mind, altogether different from what the patient has imagined.

Psychoanalysts have traditionally assumed that transitions between emotional experience and objective self-reflection will occur seamlessly in response to interpretation, and may tend not to notice the self-consciousness that some patients feel in transitions— for example, when the analyst shifts from the patient's manifest content to a comment about the patient's transference, or a comment on unconscious motivation, or from the session proper to its abrupt end. We may unwittingly bypass the patient's self-consciousness at these times, assuming these feelings are routine—simply part and parcel of being in analysis (Appelbaum & Stein, 2009). Often analysts will make a comment at these junctures that results in greater shame in the patient, for example, speculating about the patient's feelings about loss or loss of control. Openness, awareness, and attention to feelings along the spectrum of narcissistic vulnerability—the shame spectrum—such as chagrin, self-consciousness, embarrassment, humiliation, and mortification—are relieving to patients. Inattention to these feelings, especially in relation to the analyst, may leave these painful affects intact and unintegrated.

Recognition and attention to shame became a crucial aspect of Dev's treatment. From his earliest years, Dev did not experience the recognition of his affects by others. His feelings were not acknowledged, mirrored, or named. A global, undifferentiated shame state became the repository and default position for all the feelings he could not distinguish or organize. The subject of shame in our work together, was, fortuitously, regularly initiated by Dev, and I also took it up with him regularly and consistently. Very gradually I attempted to tease out other affects that came and went, or were hidden in the wings of his shame. In this process, his undifferentiated affect of shame began to share the emotional stage with many forms of anger, at many objects, past and present. Anger eventually made room for excitement, and with it a resurgence of sexual feelings. He also experienced, expressed, and lived out love and caring, both in the treatment, and at home with his wife and children. All these feelings, ever increasingly elaborated and developed, enabled him ultimately to declare that indeed he was "an actual person, with actual feelings, and an actual history".

From an intrapsychic perspective, as spelled out in the clinical section of this paper, Dev's growth occurred through multiple processes of internalization. Threatening affects, opinions, and characteristics of his own were projected onto similar enough characteristics of mine, where they could be held for safekeeping. These projective identifications took unique shapes, as he attached what he could not experience himself to real enough traits of mine. Many of his projections were positive, and not hard for me to contain. Many of them were negative and I considered them. I could always see well enough what he was saying about me. As he became ready, Dev allowed himself to re-own these characteristics—first through imitation, then identification, which took the form of conversations in his mind between internalized objects, him and me, and ultimately, integration, evidenced by a steadily developing capacity for tolerance of both his shame and of other differentiated affects, as well as an ever growing capacity for self-reflection.

From a more interactional and intersubjective perspective, in the unconscious enacted dimension of the treatment (Katz 1998, 2002, and this volume), similarities in our characters led Dev and me to take root in each other's minds. Our narcissistic issues were similar, which resulted in mutual unconscious identifications and idealizations. Consciously, we both aim to please, and do it well. Unconsciously, we were both good at adoring, and we both wanted to be adored. We were both second-borns, prone to deflated rather than inflated narcissism in order to accommodate parents, who already had their hands full, and in order to find our place in relation to older siblings, who had already taken the big shot role in the family. We both had mothers who were loving and sacrificial, but who were not able verbally to mirror our intentional beings, and tried, rather, to shape us to models of their own. Both our fathers, while also fundamentally loving, were more isolated, more involved in their own interests. We were both consciously aware of our own personal experiences of shame, and we both became interested in it as a subject for intellectual study long before the relationship between us began. Dev told me only recently that his master's thesis, which he wrote well before he came to treatment with me, was on shame in the work of Henry James, and that a major shame author he used was Francis Broucek! I believe that, implicitly—that is, unconsciously and without notice on either of our parts—we recognized and appreciated in each other the experiences we shared. These mutual identifications *and mutual idealizations* were part of the internalization process for this patient in this psychoanalysis. What I consciously accurately experienced as Dev's strengths and potential for change, I experienced *unconsciously* as qualities I identified with and admired. And he did the same.

Dev and I were also different in important ways. In a good patient-analyst match, the patient finds an analyst whom he or she unconsciously senses is enough like his or her old objects so that early issues can be repeated, but different enough from his or her early objects so that something new can happen. Dev was an intellectual who had no access to his emotional self, much less words for it. My mind, on the other hand, is a world of emotions and imagery. Applying imagery and words to emotions and ideas is my strong suit. Sometimes I feel self-conscious about not being an intellectual. Each of us had what the other personally wanted. He once said to me: "You idealize intellectuals. You don't know you are smart enough on your own." Dev could describe his world of abstract ideas—how ideas lined up, sized up, circled around and informed each other, as well as the lack of emotion in which he lived. I went to his chilly places with him, resonated with, and provided emotional meaning to them. I gave words to emotions and experiences that I imagined led him to such internal places, might have kept him there, and what might lay still hidden within them. Together, for the first time, we both found, as Loewald said, new language for experiences not previously known or felt.

Note

1. The author wishes to thank Judith Hanlon, Gil Katz, and Seymour Moscovitz for their helpful editorial comments.

CHAPTER SEVEN

Anonymity: blank screen or black hole

Carolyn Ellman[1]

In this paper I would like to continue some of the work that has been highlighted by Kohut (1971), Bach (2006), and Ellman (1998), namely, the conditions that make for trust and containment in the analytic space. While these authors have written in great detail about how one can enter the world of the patient in order to further their sense of "owning" the treatment, I do not think enough emphasis has been put on the difficulties that ensue when the analyst is seen as entering a space that can seem rigid and cold and shame-inducing. This can happen particularly *at some point* in the treatment when the patient enters into a three-person system and wishes suddenly to know more about the therapist (Aron, 2006; Benjamin, 2004). When the analyst at that point cannot in some way become more real to the patient (sometimes by answering direct questions) a deep narcissistic wound and rupture may occur. I think this issue is particularly complicated at this time in our history since clinicians tend to (at least on paper) divide up into those that feel they can answer questions and loosen the frame and those that do not (mainly because of a political pull to align with either a Freudian or Relational position). Therefore, I would like to explore (*on paper*) what it is for a Freudian analyst to sometimes disclose personal information.

Some elements of analytic practice are essential to making a safe environment—such as respecting the patient's boundaries and maintaining a stance of abstinence that allows the patient's fantasies to evolve without feeling endangered. However, the issue of what the patient can know about us and how it affects the transference and analytic relationship seems more confusing because it may change over time (for many patients). Anonymity often protects the patient's space from too much intrusion but it also protects the analyst from revealing too many things about themselves, which would make *them* feel exposed in a way that would undermine their ability to work effectively as an analyst. But what has struck me as particularly interesting over the years is that certain things that a patient learns about the analyst (even if the patient has not been told them directly) can actually lead to more transference, more fantasies, and more productive work. The blank screen does not necessarily produce more fantasies; however, what it *does do*, is help to provide a consistent frame in which the therapist (and patient) remain focused on the patient (with minimal intrusion).

In doing clinical work I believe there should always be some state of discovery and I believe this is true when suddenly a patient wants to know where we are going on vacation, why we are cancelling sessions for a doctor's appointment, or who has died (if we suddenly cancel to go to a funeral), etc. If we immediately react that these things have nothing to do with the patient and all that is important is their fantasy about what we are doing, we may actually stop the field of inquiry and close off the possibility that maybe the patient may *need* to know something that we are doing that actually has an effect on them. A patient may actually feel for a long time they do not want to know anything about us and suddenly it comes into their mind as a certain "curiosity" that something is going on in the therapist's life that interests them. How do we create an atmosphere so that the patient does not feel that there are certain questions they are not supposed to ask (because that is "how therapist's work")? I believe this can leave them in some terrible place of isolation with a person who has suddenly made them feel they have overstepped their boundaries and gone into some forbidden space. It is important that we do not cut off something about the patient's curiosity that lessens their ability to use the analyst as a "new object".

I agree with many of the statements that Stone (1961) wrote a long time ago, which, for some reason, have only now been put into practice by many Relational analysts and contemporary Freudians, namely, that not revealing some feelings and not being more present at certain *crucial* points in the treatment, can actually destroy what up to that point had been an excellent treatment. Stone points out the extreme inconsistency of the "anonymity" issue since in his day even the strictest Freudians practised in their homes (which clearly revealed a great deal about them). Since their patients were often from their Institutes, many personal things (hobbies, children, places that they were going on vacation, and much more) were known to many colleagues and patients. Stone pointed out that for him the essential line of distinction was between the transference-countertransference complex in its primitive sense and the irreducible requirements of a real adult human relationship which he felt were crucial for the work to continue.

Many analysts report that, even when the analysand knows a great deal about their "real" life, the primitive transference will still emerge. Sometimes it only starts to emerge after something happens that makes the patient feel they "know" the analyst more and feel a deeper sense of trust.

The original thinking about anonymity clearly started with Freud's thoughts about "abstinence" (1912a, 1912b, 1915) and the need to help new therapists not to believe the patients' fantasies that were projected on to them as if they were real. It was true particularly in the sexual transference that the patient was looking for a gratification that would be highly destructive if it were acted out. The analyst was cautioned to be detached, a blank screen, like a surgeon, and to try and be outside the experience as much as possible so that they would not respond to these fantasies. Freud was trying to help analysts deal with their countertransference. He was clearly trying to set up what Shafer (1983b) would call an "atmosphere of safety". The concept of "abstinence" seems clearly an essential part of making the situation "safe to express everything that one feels". I believe this is also true of the notion of the analyst trying to be non-judgmental about the patient's material or—as Anna Freud (1936) said—equidistant between id-ego and superego. The concept of anonymity, however, seems to have grown out of "the blank screen" concept that projections occur more readily if one does not know too much about the person. It was thought that this would help "free-association" and prevent the analyst from intruding himself or herself too much into the treatment. As with everything else in psychoanalysis, it seems that every statement is true for some people and not for others (and at some points in the treatment and not at others!).

Lipton (1977) pointed out that Freud's behavioural recommendations were never intended to characterize a position of neutrality governing the analyst's entire approach to analytic treatment, including the personal relationship, which develops between analyst and patient, which necessarily, by definition, is individual, idiosyncratic, not susceptible to prescription and codification, and must be defined by its purpose to allow the continuation of the analysis and not by a rigid, behavioural–oriented, immediately-judged standard. Lipton pointed out that all Freud's recommendations were for beginner analysts—to help them control their behaviours and not interfere with the emergence of the patient's unconscious. When teaching candidates, everything is simplified and the complexity of being somewhat natural with patients is actually disturbing to new students. It does take a lot of experience to recognize when disclosing something is of value to the therapeutic process, when one should offer an opinion, and what "being human" actually means to each analyst. It seems so much easier to fit into the stereotype that analysts never answer questions about their lives, should not go to events which patients are going to attend, and should try to keep their "real life" as far away from the analytic setting as possible.

I think the issues around anonymity in a dynamic sense come up when there is a break in continuity or empathy. For example, as much as the therapist tries, disruptions occur—some things are imposed from without. Analysts do have to cancel sessions for various reasons (vacations, sickness, death of a family member, doctor's appointments, etc.). I would even include weekends and the bill at the end of the month as part of this issue. These are the places that the analyst's life actually intrudes on the patient's sense of safety and they are often the places where the analyst is also confused about what they are "doing to the patient". The amount of time and energy I spent worrying about redecorating my office was strangely misplaced. Of course, ideally the analyst explores what it means to the patient to have disruptions but the patient may or may not be able to access feelings about anything related to the analyst's life—especially if the patient feels that they are not allowed to ask anything about it and are afraid to know.

But just like the "primal scene", the patient/child must feel that they are free to fantasize about what is going on with the parental couple. The child of course does and does not want to know about their parent's sex life but the sexual life of the couple is a fruitful and powerful source of desire and striving in the child's fantasy life. The child/patient can be easily overwhelmed if the analyst intrudes upon them but some "permeable barrier" must be there so that the patient does not feel so shut out of the analyst's life. With certain patients the "frustrating, non-gratifying object" may prove to be the perfect source for Oedipal fantasies and yet at some point in the treatment a shift may occur where the patient wants and needs to know more and one has to be sensitive to these shifts. Does the patient really understand why we do not answer questions about our vacations, cancellations, etc., or have we introduced something into the treatment that is a forbidden area of inquiry? Is it easier not to answer because we are confused ourselves about how much we do or do not want to reveal? Why are patients so compliant about not asking questions? Patients seem to accept these rules about not asking questions as if it is simply "part of therapy". Thus, most treatments proceed with very little intrusion into the therapist's life. Patients rarely ask questions but when they do, it often signals a new stage in the treatment and one needs to be sensitive to the implications of this and not handle it in a "stereotyped" manner. Many interesting examples in the literature discuss where change occurs when something inadvertently is revealed. Clearly, I am talking about treatments in which the focus on the interpersonal relationship is not considered the main or only agent of change.

What the patient knows about you and does not know can change over time and I have been struck over and over again how often the patient does not tell you something they have heard. Do we play some part in that as if we are not supposed to talk about ourselves either or reveal too much in our clothes, our office, etc.? Unlike the patient in the paper by Adler and Bachant (1996) for whom they argue it would have been very destructive if a therapist told his patient he was adopting a baby, some patients have been inspired to fix up their own homes by my doing mine. Does it destroy the treatment when the female therapist gets pregnant and the patient has to deal for months with their painful feelings of envy, exclusion, and loss?

But, the fine line of keeping a safe place where the patient's rights and dignity are respected has to be constantly thought through. The analyst has to examine and re-examine what and why they are doing or not doing things that may affect their patient. To me, the extreme nature of this problem is with the dying analyst. It is an extreme example of some idea that the analyst's life is their own and should not be imposed on their patient. How many patients have been left terribly bereft and angered when they have asked their analyst if the analyst were very ill. Having treated a dying patient (who was a therapist), I know it was very difficult for her to face her own death by talking to her patients about it. But sometimes, hiding behind the idea that silence about one's illness is better for the patient, the analyst robs the patient of the chance to have a human response. It often prevents both of them from working through their grief about the loss.

Some patients for complicated reasons related to very early pathological object ties, have no interest in finding out anything about you until some point in the treatment when they start coming out of a narcissistic withdrawal into a more developed form of object love (Bach, 2006; Benjamin, 2004). It is interesting how often they can actually be angry then that you have not told them more things about yourself as if you have been the one who has been so distant and unavailable for so long. It is still a slippery slope about what they want to know (and what you want to tell them and feel is for their benefit to know). One may have to be a self-object for a long time until the patient can allow complicated objects into their representational world. Greenberg (1986) points out that "the silence and anonymity which constitute unmodified classical technique enable the patient to include the analyst in his internal object world, while a more active or self-revealing posture establishes the analyst as a new object" (p. 97). For him neutrality is an optimal tension between the patient's experiences of us as an old or a new object. This point is very much like Loewald's (1960)—we are both setting up a condition that is optimal for the patient to regress and experience us in the transference while at the same time providing a new object relationship (see also Grunes, 1998).

Since I truly believe in a psychic space in which the patient dictates what and how they use it, the non-intrusiveness of the therapist is very important (especially I believe in keeping the frame in a very careful way—starting on time, ending on time, giving the bills at a certain time, letting patients know way ahead about vacations, etc.). Even when I have told patients very clearly that it does not bother me at all to tell them where I am going on vacation, very few patients ask. That has convinced me even more that they are very happy to have the traditional standard of neutrality and anonymity because it makes them feel safe. But, it can also keep them distant and I have come to see that the blank screen is not necessarily a place for projection. It can become a black hole that leads to further and further self-absorption.

The problem is not in terms of the level of fantasy that is involved; the problem is how overwhelming it is for the patient at any particular time in treatment to have to think about the analyst's life and whether the therapist can handle such an intrusion. The therapist may have to possibly stay with a patient's fantasies about them that can be quite disturbing since some of them may be true and some of them might be difficult to hear and respond to in a neutral way.

Many of my examples come from supervisees who, because they were younger therapists, felt they were caught off guard when they were asked about personal material and had to deal with the patient's questions. In two cases, I actually encouraged the supervisee to reveal information since it was either obvious to the patient what the answer was and, in the other case, the supervisee had to disrupt the treatment to be away with her mother who was ill and it would have been very confusing for the patient to understand what was happening without being extremely upset. I think it was the working through of these revelations that was the most important part of the self-disclosure. (I wonder if this is not the big difference between a Freudian and Interpersonal position on this topic).

A powerful example happened with a lesbian therapist with a lesbian patient, who had not sought out someone who was lesbian, but it had been an assignment at some clinic where the therapist was in training. In spite of this communality, there was very little else that they had in common and the therapist was doing an excellent job dealing with an extremely militant sexually acting out woman who could be very threatening to many people in her life and work. Apparently, the year before the supervisee started supervision with me, the patient had asked the therapist if she was gay as she was telling a story about a gay bar out of state and leaned forward and said assertively, "I'm sorry, are you gay or straight?" The therapist just kept an exploratory stance and wondered why this was asked, and the patient said she only wanted to know if she had to explain all the details about the bar scene. The therapist just explored what it would mean if she were gay or if she were not and the patient, recognizing that the therapist was not going to answer, just kept talking about her experiences. The therapist at that time was glad that she had not disclosed very much since she felt it allowed the patient to talk more about her bi-sexual experiences in addition to her experiences with women and gave her the freedom to explore more of her sexuality. The patient was happy not to deal with who the therapist "really was" and yet as much as she was getting out of the treatment, as the time got closer and closer to the patient terminating (due to some new work assignment), it seemed she really could not talk about the relationship with the therapist (in fact she was quite contemptuous of the therapist's attempts to engage her on that level!). As luck would have it they ran into each other at the Gay Pride Parade. This time the patient said directly "Now I know you are gay" and the therapist, still trying to keep an exploratory stance, said, "I might be. What are your thoughts about it?" In supervision, we discussed how this was starting to feel like a game that was more alienating than helpful and actually made it seem as if the therapist was ashamed of her sexual orientation. So the next time it came up, the therapist finally said, "Yes, I am gay." Of course, the patient had an immediate response of "I knew it all along" and the therapist felt exposed and not sure where to go with it. What followed I think is the more important issue and the hardest and most difficult part of such a sudden disclosure. Suddenly, the patient was flooded by feelings about the therapist but they were not of the kind that made the *therapist feel safe*. They were more like: "Oh, so you are sick and base like me and what kind of kinky sex do you like?" And, "Do you frequent such and such bar—an S&M bar?" The attacks were personal and frightening. They did not stop for a long time. The therapist was afraid to go to some places she normally went to and now felt totally intruded upon and exposed. She felt the patient was now in her life and the patient was using it not only to project her own self-hate onto the therapist but also to defend against feelings of love for the therapist that were now more in the room. My job was to help the therapist to get back to a neutral position where she could help the patient see why she was so overwhelmed and how the patient had kept herself from being loving towards the therapist for years (just as she kept herself from loving her partner in life). The patient was now using this not as a way to share but as a way to torture, etc. What came into the room was much more the way the patient was in real life than anything that had transpired before. In the end the patient left, having worked through some feelings that you rarely see except in an analysis. I think the therapist also wound up feeling much less ashamed of her own homosexuality and more integrated in her feelings of owning who she was (since not only was she not ultimately degraded but there was a working through of mutual respect as the therapist helped the patient see the wall that had kept her from loving someone). Contrary to what most people think about these disclosures, the patient did not keep asking the therapist more and more questions but went back to doing the work of treatment. The therapist was also convinced that she and her patient had needed time before they could deal with this issue and that it would not have been productive if it had come out early in the treatment when this patient had very little trust and little ability to self-reflect.

Before I get to my own case examples, I will go to one more supervisee who actually wrote a paper on how she dealt with the death of her mother and its impact on her patient. Sometimes these situations come up because the therapist is caught unaware (such as the patient seeing the therapist at the gay pride parade) and/or the therapist has to take time off and it is not an ordinary vacation (such as for an operation or for a family member who is ill). In the case of my supervisee, her mother was very ill and she felt she had to fly overseas to be with her (since it was not clear how long her mother would live). She could not really tell her patients how long she would be away since the situation was unclear. So she decided (with my encouragement) to tell her patients the truth and perhaps set up a way to have e-mail while she was abroad. She called when her mother died to let her patient know. When she came back, of course the patient was happy to have her back (since he was going through a very difficult transition himself) and he could not express anger about her being away (since of course he knew what had happened and at first acted sympathetic). The difficulty was getting back to the fantasies about what this meant to the patient. The patient was happy to push the whole thing underground and so was the therapist. She was relieved that the patient had survived her being away and wanted to get back to the "work". I pointed out to her that he may have been afraid "she would die" or that there may have been feelings aroused about his own mother dying. The patient proceeded to have many instances of acting out loss until the therapist was able to get back to what it meant to think about "a mother dying"; how frightened he had been that she would not come back the same; how dependent he was on her as if "she were his mother" etc. Knowing what the therapist was going through had a profound effect on him. Would it have been the same if the therapist had just said, "For unfortunate reasons, I will have to be away for several weeks and I will call you when we can resume sessions?" There is no doubt there would have been fantasies. The analyst is sick. The analyst is having a death in the family, etc. But the bottom line is that these fantasies are often somewhat deadening and stereotyped. "She will not tell me anyway." "It's her life. So why should I care? I am just furious about being abandoned." Is the abandonment just about the time away or something about imposing such a loss on the patient without understanding their need sometimes to be taken into some small part of the therapist's life? For some patients this is something they truly value.

In the situation with my patients, I feel that I did not have to tell the patients that my mother died. I was not out that long. I was not being pressured by the patients to know who died and they would have been content to know there was a death in the family and go back to the work of analysis. In fact, I have had to cancel other times to go to a funeral of a colleague and it seemed easy enough to tell them that since it seemed rather routine and other than saying, "I hope it wasn't anyone you were very close to," again they wanted to spend time on themselves and not me. So, even though I did have to cancel some sessions suddenly to run to the hospital (which indicated something out of the ordinary was happening), it was not a long illness and I was able to handle most of it without being out that long. It is true that at the time, I had just read a great many articles by Antonio Ferro (who is a Bionian with an interesting theory about the analytic field). In one of the articles (Ferro, 2005), he wrote about the analyst's depression and he makes a point that if the analyst is depressed (even if they are unaware of it), they may not be able to contain the patient's projections of depressed and unhappy affects and they have to find a way to deal with that in order to be there for the patient. Several of my colleagues found this quite difficult to believe since many people go through depressions and do not think it affects their patients. Quite the contrary, many times they believe that it actually helps to work to forget one's problems as one submerges oneself in someone else's world. But, at the time I did wonder: "Could I really hide from my patients that my mother died (not just a casual acquaintance)?" I thought it was better that they know in case they felt something was going on that they could not make sense of and believed it was in them and not me (sort of a reversed projective identification). So, when some people said, "I assume it wasn't anyone that close since you are back at work," I said, "Actually, my mother died but she was very old and it wasn't unexpected." Some people were actually more in touch with the impact than I was, because they said, "Losing a mother is a big thing, no matter what." Needless to say, many patients did not ask anything and if they did not, I did not impose it on them and we went back to our work. I did not see any evidence with those patients that they were picking up something different in me. I did ask the patients whom I told what it meant to them and then we moved on (or so I thought). The problem was very complicated: 1. I did not know myself what it meant to me and would not know for a long time what a large impact it would have; 2. After telling them, I really did not want to talk about it any more and found it hard when some people started fantasizing how I was very lucky to have her so long and how special that relationship must have been (since the relationship was so much more complicated than that); 3. I did not realize that it made me seem vulnerable in a way that I could not process. I was very good at seeing it in my supervisees but not in myself. I had a hard time seeing this as making me vulnerable (even though it clearly was affecting my patients). I think one of the problems was that I could not process it myself. For example, it is two years later and I am just now really finding out the profound effect it had on one of my patients. This patient is so sensitive to changes in other people and picks up affects and internalizes them so that I felt she really had to know what was happening. She was one of the people I had to cancel to run to the hospital. (She actually has some classical hysterical features in which she does actually take on others' moods in a somewhat dramatic way). I knew right away that I had made a mistake. She seemed very agitated and suddenly felt that I was very vulnerable and that maybe she had to take care of me now. She had some strong feelings that I was not omnipotent (as she had thought) and that maybe she brought death to those around (she had had an unusually large number of deaths of people in her life for such a young person). I knew that her grandmother had died when the patient was five and it had had a profound effect on her mother, which was also one of the reasons that I wanted to tell her because I wanted to prove that, unlike her mother, I was still functioning and fine. What I did not know is that her mother actually never got over the grandmother's death and as more and more of the history came out I started to realize how terrified the patient was of losing me (more in mind than in body). The patient's mother blamed herself for the grandmother's death (since the grandmother had asked to go to the hospital for chest pains and the mother said she would take her the next day). The grandmother actually wound up calling something comparable to 911 in another country and on the way to the hospital the driver had a car accident and the grandmother died. The mother became an extremely driven, overworked person and from the ages of five to ten the patient cannot remember anything about being with her mother. The patient became extremely phobic and afraid to leave the house. Neither one of us had any idea what it meant to tell her my mother died. She could process some of it and I was in tremendous denial about its impact on me. I do not think this was helpful to this patient: it was too early in the treatment, and even though it clearly brought out interesting material, it undermined the analytic sense of safety. For some other patients, the impact was more or less minor. For one patient who asked, it had a positive effect since it brought up deep feelings about losing her father that had really been cut off for years. She burst into tears and started talking about how she had been kept away from her dying father by her mother who did not want to "burden the children". The patient had lived for years acting in a somewhat childlike way, not feeling she could take care of herself or others and had not really even been allowed to mourn. This had a very positive effect since she felt I trusted her to handle this and she started a process of dealing more directly with her husband and giving more space in her life to her friends and family. She spent very little time worrying about me but rather started taking on issues that had been frozen since the father's death. It is also important that this patient had been in treatment for many years and we were at a different point in the treatment. So, with each person I told, I have tried to understand the meaning to them of my having a mother that long and the feelings for many of them when thoughts of losing a mother came up (both losing their mothers and possibly me). On some level, I realized they did not want to think of me even having a mother since that brings up some image of me as a child and not the powerful person that they desperately need to rely on. The trouble in all these self-revelations is judging where the patient is in their life. The patient who lost her grandmother was not in any place to deal with the trauma of her early rupture with her mother. We are just mending the terror that brought up. This would be an "analyst-induced enactment" (Ellman, 1998), since this problem was put on the patient to deal with. Some patients who still have their mothers were not as affected and went on to material that was important to them (such as the patient's loss of her father). Another patient who never could deal with his own mother's death and avoided dealing with her will, etc. had a complex reaction to hearing my mother died. His first response was quite manic. He wanted to rush over, order food, and take care of me. He then missed sessions for weeks until we could sort through his guilt and confusion about his own mother and his confusion about whether and why he felt he had to take care of me. It ultimately was quite positive since for years he had vacillated between being overly concerned about his mother and then distancing himself so much as if he never had a mother. As long as the therapist gets back into their role and sees what something means to the patient a great deal of good can come from it. But, you have to be very clear about your own ability to think through the very complex transference and countertransference reasons that have led you to reveal something. Sometimes therapists do not want to explore the reactions to their disclosure. I think there are dangers in revealing something and also dangers when one takes a very stereotyped "therapist" stance since a narcissistic wound can occur that takes years for the patient to stop feeling "you're not part of them". However, if the therapist is skilled, some honesty in important moments of "rupture" can bring out powerful transference material and the "fact" that has been revealed then becomes a tool for very profound transformations and deepening the treatment. It is clear that one cannot always control when these "ruptures" occur, but it is important for us to keep studying at what point in the therapeutic relationship some self-disclosure can facilitate the transference and when it is actually not helpful but something quite destructive to the patient's sense of well-being. It also should be noted that my position is not that the disclosure is the "curative" factor. Rather it is seen as something that can at times clear the air for the patient to feel respected and taken into account and in so doing a space opens up "within them" that leads to more of their unconscious fantasies and trust. Something about the disclosure makes the patient feel the analyst's reliability on a deeper level.

So much depends on timing. In the beginning of treatment (for most patients), they need to know you are in their world, in love with finding out what they are all about. This is particularly true of narcissistic patients (Bach, 1977). This state may continue for most of the treatment with such patients. Just as with the child and the parent, too much emphasis on the analyst/parent would be very disruptive. Vacations, cancellations, unforeseen events at the beginning of treatment are hardly helpful events that lead to interesting insights. In fact, I would argue that these events could be extremely disruptive to treatment (because they emphasize the analyst as being outside one's inner world). As with the child, a space needs to be created for an illusory (and simultaneously real) relationship. For some patients the lack of self-disclosure allows for a safe containing function to develop; for other patients the lack of knowing about the analyst allows them to project into the analyst various parts of the self (including destructive parts). But even the mother who has to contain the infant's projections also has to give the infant the feeling that she is really with it in some way. This can be done by interpretations, but also something about the analyst's presence often is needed to hold onto (a smile, a comment at the end of the session, etc.). Sometimes patients' questions are a moment of connection that allows for some needed contact in what is mostly a frustrating situation. Often a question is the signal that a new phase is being initiated between the pair (Ellman, 1998). A colleague who had a patient who could not forgive herself for the death of a patient of hers finally revealed over a very long time of getting no results that she too had had something like that happen. It was only at that point that the patient could finally forgive herself since the shame she had felt in front of her omnipotent, powerful therapist never let up no matter how "perfect" the analyst's interpretations were. The colleague (a very thoughtful analyst) did not observe over time that this revelation in any way hampered the treatment. As far as she could see, it only allowed for a further understanding of some of the patient's severe masochistic issues and omnipotent, sadistic-masochistic fantasies. However, it took a very long time before the analyst felt she had worked through her own pain and felt safe enough to deal with this. She was also open to questions from the patient as to why this came up at that time.

In the final analysis, most patients feel that their space is something very special where their needs and feelings are primary and should not be intruded on. A patient asking something about the analyst (such as, did the analyst see a certain movie?) are not the facts that are dangerous to the patient. And as Chused (1992) points out "if questions (and the lack of questions) are never mentioned and the only derivative is a lessening of questions, the issue of secrets may go unexamined" and the patient may believe that the analyst has many things to hide (p. 178). The patient is more afraid of finding out something about the analyst's feelings, and vulnerabilities. Fears of one's destructiveness towards one's inner objects make the patient terrified of finding the therapist's weaknesses which would confirm their ability to destroy her or feeling unbearable envy towards something she just did. The interesting thing about the analyst's real life is that trying to treat the patient's interest and questions with respect is actually an essential element of allowing the patient the safety to actually regress. I think it is related to what Wolson (2006) would call the analyst's relational unconscious that fosters love in the relationship and what Bach (2006) and Ellman (1998) would describe as the essential elements for analytic trust. A patient can only fully re-experience and work through their relationships with their transference objects within a carefully titrated experience of being in the presence of the analyst as a thoughtful, available object who is not experienced as hostile and withholding but acts in ways that further openness and growth (Jacobs, 1999b).

Note

1. The author would like to thank Alexandra Woods, Marley Oakes, and Steven Ellman for their helpful comments on this paper.

CHAPTER EIGHT

Ferenczi's concepts of identification with the aggressor and play as foundational processes in the analytic relationship

Jay Frankel

I understand clinical psychoanalysis as a process of symbolizing experiences that have thus far been too imbued with fear or anxiety to allow them to be thought about. Symbolizing these experiences allows them to be held in mind, considered, tested against ongoing reality, placed into some realistic and workable perspective, and integrated into the personality. As this happens, new patterns of thinking, feeling, and perceiving can emerge. Given the right conditions, symbolization is a natural activity of the ego. Thus, the clinical challenge of psychoanalysis is to create conditions that allow the symbolization of excluded experience to occur.

Such conditions, designed to invite the patient's experience into the analytic space in a vivid way, include a situation that does not impinge very much on the patient's experience and that offers an unusual degree of freedom of expression of thoughts and feelings by the patient, and an analyst who can be felt to be essentially benign, dependable, and emotionally resonant.

But given that anxiety prevented symbolization in the first place, the most basic condition the patient requires, and from which the other conditions are inextricable, is a feeling of safety (cf. Sandler,

1960)—a proposition about which I believe there is widespread agreement among analysts.

However, the central role of a sense of safety was not always understood. Analysts' explicit appreciation for its importance only began in the middle of the 1920s, when Ferenczi came to grasp more fully the impact of trauma on his patients, in terms of their subsequent expectations of lack of safety from other people and their self-protective adaptations to these expectations. The later phases of his "experiments in technique", from the late 1920s on, were a search for a way to provide enough safety in the analytic relationship so that the treatment would not simply reproduce a feeling of trauma as the patient remembered his earlier traumatic experiences, but rather would enable the patient to let go of his rigidly defensive anticipation of trauma and enter into an analytic process in a more open, free, and productive way.

I note in passing that some patients have a more securely internalized good and strong object and thus are more likely to carry a sense of safety within themselves; those who do not are likely to have a greater need for the situation to provide this and for the analyst to adapt his technique in order to do so.

Two of Ferenczi's clinical concepts, developed during this period, define the therapeutic dialectic of danger and safety and have been important in the development of my own thinking about the analytic relationship: identification with the aggressor—a term Ferenczi introduced and used in a different and broader way than Anna Freud later did—and play.

Prelude: active technique

Ferenczi's technical experiments began earlier, with his "active technique". From about the mid-1910s to the middle of the 1920s, working within a pre-structural model in which drive pressure alone was understood to provide the necessary impetus for the essential therapeutic processes of free association and transference, he addressed treatments that had become "stuck" by imposing a high degree of abstinence and frustration on his patients. Essentially, he tried to prevent the patient's siphoning off libido into other channels, thus forcing it to come into the patient's transference and associations. Ferenczi had not yet begun to think in terms of safety—an idea that would become more theoretically workable as he began to appreciate the pathogenic effects of trauma and as psychoanalysis moved more generally, in the mid-1920s (Freud, 1923, 1926), towards an ego psychology where anxiety came to be seen as the determining factor in shaping the outcome of intrapsychic conflict.

After the middle of that decade, despite never giving up the idea that the capacity to renounce pleasure was key to both psychological development and analytic cure, Ferenczi gave up active technique, for several reasons. Two that are relevant to our present concerns are that abstinence makes logical sense only where pathology arises from libidinal conflict, not when it reflects ego deficit, and that in any given case apparent libidinal conflict may mask narcissistic pathology that is actually based on ego deficit (the reverse is also true); and that in cases where the transference is largely narcissistic, the tie to the analyst may be too weak to withstand the deprivations of active technique, and the treatment will fail (Glover, 1924).

Today, certainly, an appreciation of the ubiquity of narcissistic difficulties, even in patients whose suffering largely reflects conflict-based pathology, only adds to our understanding that analysts must respect the potential influence of narcissistic factors in every treatment. My reading of Ferenczi is that by the late 1920s he had become more respectful of how much people cling to both reassuring wishes and to (mis)perceived sources of security—how difficult it generally is to renounce the pleasure principle and thus how pervasive narcissistic pathology is.

A third reason Ferenczi abandoned the active method is that the prohibitions the analyst imposes on the patient in active technique can become a vehicle for the analyst's unconscious expression of sadism towards the patient (Ferenczi, 1928; Glover, 1924). Additionally, this sadism can become a source of masochistic gratification for the patient, and thus a source of both increased guilt and resistance to cure.

Finally, Ferenczi also became increasingly aware that trauma lay behind much psychopathology—as noted above—and thus how the authoritative analytic stance and deprivation of active technique could reawaken traumatic experience for some patients. In his "mutual analysis" period of the early 1930s, Ferenczi (1932) learned both how unconscious the analyst's sadism and aggression can be, and how traumatizing to the patient.

Providing safety: relaxation technique and mutual analysis

In the second half of the 1920s, as Ferenczi came to appreciate both the problems with active technique and the various impacts of trauma, his efforts to reinvigorate stuck treatments—his experiments in technique—turned successively in two new directions: "relaxation technique" (which he also called "neocatharsis"—see Ferenczi, 1929, 1930, 1931) and "mutual analysis" (Ferenczi, 1932, 1933). Both were efforts to avoid what he had come to see as the ease with which not only active technique but even the standard analytic treatment of the time could traumatize patients. Thus, these new methods were attempts to address the expectation of danger that his traumatized patients brought to analytic treatment, and to provide a degree of safety that would allow frightening, warded-off aspects of the patient's experience to emerge in treatment in a way that could be tolerated and worked through.

Relaxation technique—essentially the opposite of active technique—was based on nurturance and indulgence. Mutual analysis was Ferenczi's later effort to address problems he had discovered when treating traumatized patients with relaxation technique, especially the inexorable influence of the analyst's unconscious negative countertransference, regardless of technique, and what Ferenczi saw as the inherent destructive potential of the analyst's authority *per se*. This final phase of Ferenczi's technical experiments centered on the analyst's self-disclosure and open self-exploration with the patient. The crucial discovery that turned Ferenczi towards mutual analysis was what he called "identification with the aggressor": a pervasively destructive, persistent residue of trauma, centering on the victim's hypersensitivity to, and automatic defensive compliance with, the aggressor, and subsequently with people in general. Ferenczi found that this response also manifested itself in analytic treatment, where the analyst, despite his benign aspects, was seen as dangerous. This will be discussed in more detail below.

My focus in the remainder of this section will be on how both the relaxation and mutuality approaches were designed to manage the potentially traumatizing aspects of the therapeutic relationship and provide the necessary degree of safety. I will address this historically in terms of Ferenczi's and his successors' thinking, as well as my own, including how these two approaches might be balanced and integrated in a way that I think does justice to clinical realities.

The effects of trauma, and relaxation technique

One effect of trauma that Ferenczi discovered was splitting, which included regression (for his trauma theory, see especially Ferenczi, 1932, 1933, and Frankel, 1998). In order to cope with unbearable experiences, people split their personality into several parts: 1. a relatively grown-up part that manages the threatening reality in order to maximize the chance of survival, and that protects and soothes the more vulnerable parts of the personality; this part feels nothing, since feeling would only interfere with its efficiency at its task; 2. the hurt, vulnerable part of the person—the traumatized inner child in whom all feeling and pain from the trauma reside; this part is usually more or less unconscious; and 3. another inner child-self who lives in a daydream of the happiness—either remembered or imagined—of the time before the trauma; this part may also be unconscious.

The understanding that parts of the personality have become frozen in time—that there exists an inner, undeveloped, traumatized child-self—gave Ferenczi a new reason to pursue relaxation technique: the analyst must create an environment of maternal care in which the patient's inner traumatized child-self is shielded from frustration and disappointment, and tenderly nurtured rather than challenged; the rigours of a more depriving treatment become, for the traumatized person, simply a repetition of trauma, including the feeling of having been emotionally abandoned. The offering of tenderness invites this inner child-self to come into the open in the treatment, to work through in this safe, loving environment the traumatic experiences that had been split off, and thus to resume its stunted growth. Ultimately, this will allow the patient to grow stronger, to the point where he can—only then—tolerate the frustrations and disappointments inherent in, and necessary to, analytic cure.

Successors to relaxation technique

Ferenczi's relaxation technique was the precursor of what may be called—perhaps oversimplifying—the re-parenting approaches of British object-relations theorists and of self psychology. Very similar to Ferenczi, British object-relations analysts like Winnicott (1965a, 1971, 1975) and Guntrip (1969, 1971) spoke essentially about the patient's true self having been buried due to parental care that was impinging, not adequately attuned to the child's needs, not "good-enough" (Winnicott, 1960a, 1960b)—essentially due to the parent's own needs asserting priority over her responsiveness to her child's needs: the trauma of having a narcissistic parent. The child's response is to create what Winnicott (1960a, 1960b) called a "false self" through which he interacts with his world on the basis of compliance—similar to Ferenczi's caretaker part of the personality: what Ferenczi referred to when he said that "[T]he misused child changes into a mechanical, obedient automaton" (1933, p. 162). For both Ferenczi and Winnicott, the consequence to the child of not having the necessary protective or facilitating environment is the development of—or in the case of the patient, the inability to let go of—a false and inauthentic experience of oneself and way of participating in the world.

Among his many contributions in this area, Winnicott introduced the concept of transitional phenomena (1953)—the child being allowed, and taking, unchallenged ownership over a part of the real, physical world and feeling it to be his personal creation—a successor to the safety and feeling of possession, and the specialness, of his relationship with his mother, and a bridge to his finding personal meaning and feeling at home in the larger world. The classic example is the young child's so-called security blanket, or a special soft toy, which he endows with a life of its own. The concept of transitional phenomena also includes the idea of transitional space—a state of mind, sometimes associated with certain settings or relationships, that is imbued with a sense of personal freedom, self-expression, and creativity, and which allows the development of personal meaning. In early childhood, this presupposes an environment that to a large extent accommodates to the person and does not require the person to accommodate and comply with it. Winnicott's notion of transitional space can be understood as a further articulation of the therapeutic environment Ferenczi was trying to create with his relaxation technique.

Michael Balint (1968), who had been a patient and student of Ferenczi and later became a colleague of Winnicott, also spoke about the analyst's contribution to creating the kind of environment that is necessary for some patients' treatment—notably, patients suffering from narcissistic disorders or narcissistic states. The analyst must avoid being a "separate, sharply contoured object" and must allow himself essentially to be "used" by the patient—to be perceived and treated in accordance with the patient's pathological object-relational needs, until the patient has come to the point (I think largely related to his having established the safety of the analytic relationship) where he can risk letting go of these pathological and regressive modes of relating. These ideas of Balint's are very much in line with Ferenczi's emphasis, in his relaxation-technique phase, on the analyst indulging and adapting to the patient's needs and with Winnicott's idea about the importance of the analyst being attuned and not impinging, thus allowing the patient to develop the analytic setting as transitional space.

Kohut (1971, 1977, 1984) is another successor to the Ferenczi of relaxation technique. Kohut focused on the needs of the self—people's basic needs for recognition and admiration (which he called mirroring), to idealize, and to feel merged with the caregiver. These needs are rooted in early development but are lifelong, and when they have not been adequately met in childhood they distort the personality in a pathological way. Thus, Kohut, too, saw the analyst—at least with the group of narcissistically disordered patients that Ferenczi, Winnicott, and Balint also focused on—as first and foremost in a re-parenting role, which requires creating an environment that is highly attuned and responsive to the patient's needs and illusions, with relatively little opposition, challenge, interference, or frustration.

Sheldon Bach (1985, 1994, 2006), building on the work of Ferenczi, Winnicott, Balint, and Kohut, proposed that a "merger"—a blurring of boundaries—between the psyches of patient and analyst, along with a deep and abiding sense of the patient's importance to the analyst—essentially feeling as a loving mother would towards the patient—is the intersubjective matrix that permits healing. It fosters the patient's self-regulatory ability by temporarily meshing it into an intersubjective, mutual regulatory system involving both patient and analyst, and it facilitates the development of a stabilizing "evocative constancy"—the sense of being held in the mind of the other in a sustaining way, and the ability to hold the other similarly in mind—and is thus the essential curative factor in the treatment of narcissistic disorders.

The discovery of identification with the aggressor and the shift to mutuality

Returning to Ferenczi's technical experiments, Ferenczi found that his relaxation technique was often unsuccessful at helping his disturbed patients in an enduring way. He discovered this most pointedly with a patient whom he referred to as "RN" in his *Clinical Diary* (1932), who we now know was Elizabeth Severn, an American psychotherapist. Ferenczi really went to extremes in applying his indulgent relaxation technique with her: "[G]radually I gave in to more and more of the patient's wishes, doubled the number of sessions, going to her house instead of forcing her to come to me; I took her with me on my vacation trips and provided sessions even on Sundays" (p. 97). But the treatment bogged down in stalemate. Briefly, despite Ferenczi's extreme exertions, Severn ...

> maintained that she sensed feelings of hate in me, and began saying that her analysis would never make any progress unless I allowed her to analyze those hidden feelings in me. I resisted this for approximately a year, but then I decided to make this sacrifice.... To my enormous surprise, I had to concede that the patient was right in many respects .... Women of her type fill me with terror, and provoke in me the obstinacy and hatred of my childhood years (p. 99).

He concluded that "[M]utual analysis appears to provide the solution .... Curiously, this [his open self-analysis in her presence] had a tranquilizing effect on the patient" (p. 99). She became less demanding, and Ferenczi felt he had become a more engaged and effective analyst.

Ferenczi also experimented with mutual analysis with other patients. Unfortunately, he became ill and died before he got the chance to step back after time had passed, and evaluate this experiment with a cooler and more critical eye—something he had done with his previous technical experiments and that he stated as his intention should he recover from the illness that proved fatal (Balint, 1958). His experiments in mutuality are documented in his *Clinical Diary*, and his tentative conclusions about the analytic relationship and analytic technique are outlined, in brief and muted form, in his "Confusion of tongues" paper (1933).

One discovery that was intimately connected with his decision to attempt mutual analysis was "identification with the aggressor": a pattern Ferenczi identified not only in Severn but in other traumatized patients as well (and in himself) of "an exceedingly refined sensitivity for the wishes, tendencies, whims, sympathies and antipathies of their analyst, even if the analyst is completely unaware of this sensitivity. Instead of contradicting the analyst or accusing him of errors and blindness, the patients identify themselves with him; only in rare moments of an hysteroid excitement, i.e., in an almost unconscious state, can they pluck up enough courage to make a protest; normally they do not allow themselves to criticize us, such a criticism does not even become conscious in them unless we give them special permission or even encouragement to be so bold" (1933, p. 158). It is this defence—developed as an adaptation to childhood trauma and carried over as a tendency in all subsequent interpersonal relationships, including that with the analyst— that required mutual analysis as a solution. Ferenczi felt that the analyst had to be open about his inner experience if the patient was to have the courage of her perceptions about, and reactions to, him, and to defend herself from him when she felt threatened, rather than accommodating and complying as she had learned to do in the original traumatizing situation.

Ferenczi said, "The most important change, produced in the mind of the child by the anxiety-fear-ridden identification with the adult partner, is the *introjection of the guilt feelings of the adult* which makes hitherto harmless play appear as a punishable offence ... he feels enormously confused, in fact, split—innocent and culpable at the same time" (1933, p. 162). Thus, identification with the aggressor involves not simply accommodating what the abuser expects but also colluding with or protecting the abuser by taking the blame for being abused, resulting in feeling oneself to be the bad one.

This description makes clear that identification with the aggressor often takes the form of a complementary identification (Racker, 1968)—identification with the object in the other's mind—rather than the more familiar concordant identification, where someone identifies with and models oneself after the other's self.

Going more deeply into the nature of what he saw as the analyst's misuse of the patient, Ferenczi came to believe that it was generally the analyst's "professional hypocrisy" (1933, p. 159) that pushed the patient towards identifying with the analyst as an aggressor—towards colluding with the analyst's self-protective evasions and "not seeing" the analyst's blunders and other problematic features. This "hypocrisy" (a word that suggests conscious deception rather than unconscious conflict in the analyst, which is sometimes but far from always the case) mirrors the parental "hypocrisy" in the patient's history—the parent's denial of the child's abuse, neglect, or exploitation. It was this *second* event—the parental denial following the original mistreatment—that was the most damaging aspect of trauma and that caused the fracturing of the personality, precisely because it deprived the child of an understanding parent, emotionally abandoning the child (1931, p. 138; 1929; 1932, pp. 115, 164, 202; 1933, pp. 163–164) and leaving him unbearably alone at a time of desperate need and great distress (1932, p. 201).

Clinical observations regarding the very frequent occurrence of identification with the aggressor in people who have not been grossly traumatized (Frankel, 2002a, 2002b) both reinforces the notion that subtle but ubiquitous events such as emotional abandonment (for instance, by disavowed emotional disengagement from, or disguised emotional exploitation of, children) really do function as traumas, and alerts the analyst to the potential operation of identification with the aggressor in many patients, not only in those who have suffered gross trauma. At the very least, this identification takes the form of blindness to aspects of the analyst the analyst would rather the patient did not address, and compulsive, silent compliance with the analyst's sensed but unspoken wishes and preferences.

The idea that feeling left alone can be traumatizing suggests that, to the extent that a patient cannot bear the aloneness that the standard analytic situation imposes—the couch, which eliminates face-to-face communication, and nearby a relatively silent, unexpressive, and opaque analyst—the analyst must openly express his emotional accompaniment in some way. Ferenczi felt that one particular way for the analyst to establish or restore his emotional presence was to acknowledge his own mistakes and countertransference problems that had contributed to mutually generated impasses (1932, 1933).

And because of the patient's traumatizing experiences with parental deception, foremost among the errors the analyst must acknowledge is his avoidance of complete honesty. Ferenczi saw the analyst's acknowledgement of error as an opportunity to help the patient free himself from his compulsory identification and accommodation—from his collusive protection of the analyst by "not noticing" the analyst's lapses and failures. In Ferenczi's words:

> Something had been left unsaid in the relation between physician and patient, something insincere, and its frank discussion freed, so to speak, the tongue-tied patient; the admission of the analyst's error produced confidence in his patient. It would almost seem to be of advantage occasionally to commit blunders in order to admit afterwards the fault to the patient. This advice is, however, quite superfluous; we commit blunders often enough ... (1933, p. 159).

I emphasize here that Ferenczi was talking about two inextricably related clinical phenomena, one involving a problematic interactive development in the analytic relationship—a collusion between patient and analyst that reflects the patient's (often complementary) identification and compliance with the analyst's unspoken and often unconscious wishes—and the other a technical stance of countertransference disclosure designed to undermine that collusion and mitigate the anxiety and mistrust that lie behind it.

Mutuality and contemporary views of interaction and countertransference disclosure

Ferenczi's experiment in mutuality has been seen as a progenitor of the recent interest in the interactive dimension of the analytic relationship, especially among interpersonal and relational analysts. Despite how uncharted these waters were when Ferenczi long ago undertook his experiments with mutual analysis, he was nevertheless aware of many of the complications of the interactive dimension. But I believe that subsequent experience allows for a clearer discussion of these complexities. Current controversy about interaction and analytic expressiveness testifies both to the clinical possibilities it opens up and to its dangers. Because of the possibilities and dangers on this road that Ferenczi first travelled—due to the clinical importance and the complexity of this approach—I want to take a detour to address this clinical issue.

Some contemporary analysts have taken the position that everything that happens in the analytic relationship is co-constructed to a significant degree, and thus, that making sense of the patient's experiences requires some degree of openness by the analyst about his own inner experience. Ferenczi's discovery of the "dialogue of the unconsciouses" (1915) between patient and analyst is an important conceptual basis for a more interactive form of analytic work as a general stance.

However, I see a preference for a more interactive approach across the board as clinically somewhat naïve, for several reasons. First, an interactive, actively exploratory stance by the analyst can impinge upon the quiet atmosphere needed for the patient to develop the analytic setting as a transitional space for himself. Related to this, an exploratory mode tends to hold a patient on an adult level of verbal, consensual reality, and to impede the development of regressive phenomena in general.

Additionally, a self-disclosing *stance* by the analyst, or even the high level of implicit self-disclosure that comes with a very interactive stance, can disturb a patient's self-object transference—the need to idealize or feel perfectly mirrored by or in harmonious merger with the analyst. Some patients may require that such a transference be relatively undisturbed for long periods of time, if treatment is to be authentic and therapeutically effective.

An analyst's self-disclosure can also disturb the patient's development, and awareness, of object-related transferences, as particular elements of the patient's conflicting perceptions and feelings towards the analyst may be stirred up, or stifled, as a result of what the analyst discloses about himself. And when the matrix in which transference perceptions and feelings is characterized by a high degree of interaction between the participants, as well as a focus on the analyst's contribution to the patient's experience, the patient's ownership of his own transference perceptions and feelings may be undermined.

An interpersonal or relational analyst may object to some of these arguments, saying that even when an analyst tries to mask his feelings and reactions, a patient will sense and respond to them; indeed, that the analyst's act of attempting to mask his reactions adds the complication of repeating the parent's (possibly traumatic) denial of her disturbing (even if subtle) behaviour towards the patient as a child—a complication that, at the least, constitutes a roadblock in the patient's effort to understand his inner experience.

I agree that there is no truly neutral stance—no stance that makes the analyst opaque to the patient or avoids his influence on the patient. But my impression is that a less interactive, less disclosing stance may often help minimize, contain, or shelve this influence. Certainly, it does not invite intersubjective factors into the spotlight, but encourages an inward-looking attitude in the patient.

The extent of the analyst's influence, I think, is variable from patient to patient and moment to moment. There are several factors that I believe affect the degree of the analyst's influence. These include: the use of the couch as opposed to a face-to-face interaction that provides many more cues about the analyst's reactions; the extent to which the analyst tries to be neutral in the sense of a non-judgmental openness to all sides of the patient's experience (Chused, 1982), and thus strives to minimize the impact of his own inner reactions; the extent to which the analyst experiences poorly contained conflict regarding the feelings he chooses not to express, and the analyst's capacity for self-discipline in general—difficulties in these areas may undermine this striving; and the extent to which the patient is motivated by narcissistic anxieties that make it especially urgent for him to divine the analyst's feelings and motives.

All these factors affect the degree to which intersubjective rather than intrapsychic events demand attention, or, conversely, the degree to which intersubjective factors may, without denying their existence, take a back seat in the service of allowing inner experience to emerge, develop, and become the focus of exploration. I will have more to say about these ideas when I discuss play, below. Especially when narcissistic anxieties are in eclipse, a patient may be quite capable of focusing inwards and attending to his evolving thoughts and feelings as objects of analytic interest, without very much of a feeling of urgent focus on the analyst's actual feelings and intentions.

In summary, Ferenczi discovered how extensive and influential the intersubjective dimension of the analytic relationship can be, but I think the more radical approach of placing the active, explicit focus of investigation of it at the centre of technique *on a general basis* is naïve.

Interactive stance and diagnosis

But I think that there are situations in which a more interactive stance is vital to the treatment. Certain aspects of clinical experience point to the issue of diagnosis, or at least "diagnosis of the moment" (Frankel, 2006)—specifically, the extent to which narcissistic sensitivity or disequilibrium intrudes on the patient's functioning—as a factor determining whether a more interactive, expressive stance by the analyst is indicated. My thoughts here to some extent follow those of Balint (1968), Kohut (1971, 1977, 1984), Winnicott (1965a, 1965b, 1971, 1975), Killingmo (1989), and Bach (1985, 1994, 2006).

Essentially, patients in states of narcissistic disequilibrium may feel too distressed to attend to, elaborate, and explore their inner experience in a quieter, more abstinent analytic setting, and may require active self-expression by the analyst in order to mitigate their feeling unbearably alone in the sessions (Bach, 2006; Davies, 1994; Frankel, 2002b). And when such patients feel disturbed by what they feel is the analyst's insensitivity, lack of attunement, or other similar error, and thus unable to proceed or even remain in the analysis—and this happens readily, due to these patients' histories of deeply hurtful interpersonal relationships and the often highly developed sensitivity to subtle emotional cues that results from this, which is now directed towards that greatly needed object, the analyst—such patients may need the analyst to actively address these moments of impasse by his openly owning and sometimes even exploring his own disturbing behaviour (Ferenczi, 1933; Benjamin, 2006). Due to their history with environmental failure, patients in narcissistically disturbed states are highly sensitive to others' lapses (Balint, 1968). When it occurs, even on a small scale, their need for reparation—for the analyst to take the initiative and the risk in re-establishing contact—can easily trump interest in their inner lives. Indeed, being asked to focus inwards at such a time may feel to them too isolating, too risky, and unjust. Analysts openly owning their own failures may constitute the reparation patients feel they need at such a moment.

Also, perhaps, only by the analyst offering such acknowledgment can the patient's stabilizing self-object transference (Kohut, 1971, 1977, 1984) to the analyst be restored, and the sense that the analyst is a good, dependable object—badly needed by the patient—be rescued from the threat of being overwhelmed by the bad perceptions and bad feelings triggered by the analyst's error. Many writers, including Balint, Winnicott, Kohut, and Bach, have emphasized that narcissistically disordered patients may feel unable fully and authentically to participate in treatment without the analyst allowing a particular kind of (illusory, even pathological) object relationship the patient feels he needs for the time being.

In all these ways of understanding the dynamics of the analytic relationship, the analyst is more open because the patient feels it as a real necessity, not simply in order to explore the intersubjective field in the absence of the patient feeling that mutual openness and exploration is vitally important.

Analytic self-disclosure, analytic authority, analytic responsibility

There is another consideration that limits analytic self-disclosure, operative probably even in analysts who might deny this is so (e.g., Renik, 1999). I believe that all analysts—even those who try to avoid patients' regressing and to steer clear, as Ferenczi did, of the potential dangers of analytic authority[1]—accept a somewhat parental role, even if they would rather not believe this is so (see Aron's, 1996, discussion of asymmetry within mutuality). (Other analysts might be surprised that anyone would question this.)

Such a role limits what an analyst will decide to say to a patient. The analyst's implicit parental role is linked to our understanding as analysts that there is an inherent heightened vulnerability in a patient placing himself under our care and opening his innermost experience to us, and that this vulnerability awakens regressive states (Ferenczi, 1931), buried, anxiety-laden wishes and early traumatic experiences. Tact and discretion unavoidably guide our clinical decisions. Is a parent being inauthentic when she chooses not to discuss with her child her own entire complicated range of thoughts, feelings, and life experiences, or is she accepting the psychological realities of, and her responsibilities towards, her child?

The effect of narcissistic states on the clinical interaction, and two stances to address the issues raised

This brings us to the issue of diagnosis, which affects the patient's attitude towards his less than ideal perceptions of the analyst—the extent to which the patient cannot tolerate disturbing perceptions and feels that these must be addressed in some way by the analyst.

The patient's ability to function analytically despite perceptions of the analyst that are less than ideal reflects a capacity to play, as I will discuss below, and is intimately related to the questions of diagnosis and technique. Modifications in technique along lines of either relaxation or mutuality (or some combination) are essentially the two modifications used by those who treat patients who are unable to tolerate perceptions of the analyst as less than perfect.

Narcissistic disorders and narcissistically disordered states, which may be thought of as a broad category encompassing the range of so-called deficit pathology, are the result of patterns of childhood trauma—often traumas related to having narcissistic, self-absorbed parents who have difficulty providing attunement or keeping the child in mind as a living presence: both forms of impinging. The results include a high degree of sensitivity to others' feelings and attitudes on a defensive basis, an intolerance of differences from what someone feels he needs, and difficulty regulating negative affect. Thus, analysts, Balint thought, must take care not to disturb—not to draw attention to their differences from the objects these patients feel they need. Further, sensing that their difficulties are the result of environmental failure rather than inner conflict, these patients are primarily oriented to others' failures, departures from perfection, lack of attunement.

This understanding has two very different implications. The first, reflected in the writings of many of those who focus on the treatment of narcissistic disorders, is that if analysts are to avoid retraumatizing such patients by repeating the sins of their parents, they must try to remain attuned, malleable, adaptable, accommodating, affirming—akin to Ferenczi's earlier, relaxation stance. This approach should minimize the stirring up of these patients' sensitivities, make it possible for them to be comfortable enough to participate in treatment in a relatively open way, and help them learn to regulate negative affect.

But the second implication—also reflecting the fear of repeating the parents' sins—stems from the fact that we cannot avoid stirring up these patients' sensitivities, and that the greatest sensitivity of patients in such states may be to others' dishonesty, including subtle evasions, disavowed exploitation, and run-of-the-mill self-delusion. These are all forms of emotional disengagement which, I believe, following Ferenczi, are often the most disturbing traumatic element. Due to these patients' sensitivity and our own inevitable imperfection as analysts, we will inevitably be unmasked by patients in a state of narcissistic disturbance—our commonplace weaknesses, lapses, and elisions experienced by them as assaults, humiliations, profound disappointments. In the transference crises that result—since continuing to participate in treatment after experiencing what feels like such an insult may push these patients to the edge of what they can bear—we are thus forced in the direction of speaking to them openly and sometimes with genuine self-examination about what was going on in us when we "were" so insensitive and thoughtless: an acknowledgement of something that we did that may have felt small to us but very hurtful to them. This was the situation that led to Ferenczi's later, mutuality stance.

For me, these two, often contradictory, positions define the range of the basic analytic stance. They may also be called the "relational dialectic", since they define the conflicting truths which the broad group of relational analysts seeks to accommodate in some fashion. I interpret the first of these, the relaxation or object-relational stance, in a kind of quiet version—affirmation and "holding", in Winnicott's sense of the word, mainly by listening in a quiet but active, empathic way, perhaps with occasional comments that are resonant with what the patient is feeling or at least that do not offer too much challenge or disruption. (Ferenczi, in a lovely but little known 1931 paper called "Child analysis in the analysis of adults", said that with patients in a regressed state, the analyst should gently ask questions, use simple words and sentences appropriate to the age to which the patient has regressed, and never interpret or try to "put anything into" someone in this relatively defenceless state.) This is my "default" stance, because I think it is this quiet, non-intrusive positioning of the analyst that fosters a certain state of mind: a safe, transitional space in which referential activity (Bucci, 1985) and symbolization in the sense of giving form to previously excluded or unarticulated experiences, and in the process finding space to think about them (Freedman, 1997), occur—where attention can be directed inwards without the distraction of girding oneself against a potential external threat; where the mind can loosen up; frightening inner experiences can begin to be thought about; calcified, defensive modes of experience start to become more fluid; connections can be made between contents or levels of consciousness that do not often come into view at the same time; and new experiences of self and other begin to coalesce. These are events that have intrinsic therapeutic value and also provide the experiential material that will allow later interpretations to be really useful. This stance can be thought of as an affirming version of the classical setting, with less inscrutability and fewer interpretations than some analysts would use. Indeed, I think an analyst should be most protective of transitional space, and should generally not interpret if doing so would intrude upon this space.

I emphasize that I do not think an inaccessible or stereotyped stance contributes the necessary sense of the analyst's benign presence, and I do think that some degree of personal expressiveness, within the parameters I have just described, makes an essential contribution to the stance I am recommending. Too much interaction by the analyst, however, can interfere with the productive transitional state of mind in the patient that we hope for.

I think an analyst should stay in this holding stance when it is possible to do so. But depending on the state of his attunement and the patient's level of narcissistic disturbance in the moment—specifically, the patient's ability to regulate negative affect and let go of a defensive hypervigilance—there will be times, more or less often, when the patient will no longer feel safe or steady when the analyst maintains a quiet, holding stance. At these times, the patient needs something else—some more active manifestation of the analyst's presence in a personal way—a simple personal statement about himself, for instance, or an acknowledgement about a fault or error he has made that will re-establish him as a safe and protective object.

I have basically been talking about a stance that applies to the treatment of patients with narcissistic disorders or in narcissistic states. However, everyone has narcissistic vulnerabilities. Hopefully, the analytic setting will help all patients feel safe enough to expose these in their treatments, allowing their basic object-relational difficulties and anxieties to be worked through. Thus, whether the primary diagnosis is narcissistic disorder or something milder, I think the holding stance I have described should be the basic stance. To repeat, the extent to which narcissistic anxieties direct a treatment will determine how often a departure from this stance towards a more active, reparative one, probably involving some degree of open self-disclosure, will be necessary.

From this perspective, some patients—the more neurotic, who generally feel safer, who are more capable of regulating negative affect, and whose distress arises mainly from internal conflict—present an interesting problem: do we shift away from our holding stance when they become upset or when they demand some more active participation from us? I think the answer is that it depends on what a patient can actually tolerate. Patients who can struggle productively despite experiencing great conflict and upset feelings, without feeling isolated and traumatized to the point where they lose the basic sense of safety that allows them to symbolize—or to hold on to what they are currently experiencing in a way that will allow them to symbolize it later—should be allowed to do so without interference from a more interactive analytic stance. This may be true even if the patient asks for more activity by the analyst—that request, or demand, can be an important part of the patient's conflict and should be allowed to come into the transference without being short-circuited by addressing its reality aspects. The determining factor is whether the patient can "hold" the material without losing the basic sense of safety and the capacity to really think.

I want to finish this section with just a few more words about the clinical implications of the identification with the aggressor concept, specifically how it may influence the patient's participation in the treatment and what it means for the analyst's technique. A patient may be reluctant to express anger or may be compliant towards the analyst, as Ferenczi observed. Or the patient may go along with an analyst's way of thinking about something even if he sees things differently—or at least he may be very tentative in openly registering, or even being aware of, his own contradictory perceptions. Or a patient may take blame irrationally when it is the analyst (or someone else)—rather than himself—that he is really angry at. Similarly, a patient may engage in self-examination or self-criticism when he feels he really needs some response from the analyst, or he may analyse his own participation in lieu of "noticing" something the analyst has done—being a so-called "good patient", as if to say, "I did it, not you". Knowledge of the concept of identification with the aggressor should sensitize analysts to clues in patients' associations or behaviour that may indicate that such an identification is operating.

Analysts also need to be aware of the heightened impact they have on patients by virtue of their analytic role. Their inherent position of authority is likely subtly to induce identification and compliance in patients, and may also sensitize patients to the analyst's lapses in attentiveness and engagement, which can become quite disruptive to some patients. Thus, while analysts should not deny the authority they have, they should also not make a point of it.

Play and the structure of the analytic relationship

While identification with the aggressor emphasizes the elements of danger, rigidity, compliance, and the potential for foreclosure of self-knowledge, play as an analytic concept points us to possibilities for greater freedom, deeper and more authentic experience of oneself, expansion of possibilities of perceiving, thinking, and feeling, emotional growth, and revival of areas of development that had been stunted.

Here, I want to flesh out how the concept of play applies more specifically to adult therapy. I want to be clear at the outset that I am not talking about playfulness by the analyst, which I think can serve, depending on the clinical moment, either to facilitate or to interfere with the analytic process. I am talking about play as the underlying structure of analytic therapy.

Play is an inherently compelling activity that exists in "a reality apart", as Steingart (1995; also see Meares, 1995) has called it. It involves the capacity to live in an absorbing, self-created alternate reality with conviction while not denying ordinary reality (Meares, 1995), and to feel this "reality" in earnest, while acknowledging that it is provisional, invented, and "doesn't count". There is no confusion about what is "really" real. Huizinga (1955) used the term "magic circle" for the play reality—a phrase that emphasizes both the specialness of the play reality and the boundary that makes this reality possible. An example of a magic circle is watching (or performing in) a play in the theatre, where we willingly suspend disbelief even as we are never confused about what is really real or when and where this reality ends.

Winnicott (1971) placed play within the larger concept of transitional phenomena: a personal reality that is created and can be maintained only within a protective, non-intrusive, and unchallenging "holding environment" (1960b). This conceptualization emphasizes the fragility of play, consistent with Ferenczi's thinking. Indeed, empirical research on the play of children and non-human animals indicates that a modicum of safety and well-being is an absolute prerequisite for play (e.g., Lewis, 2005; Smith, 2005). Clear boundaries of time and space add to this safety and are necessary to support play (Huizinga, 1955). Winnicott's comment that "children play more easily when the other person is able and free to be playful" (1971, pp. 44–45) underlines the high degree of recognition that is inherent in social play and that, in conjunction with safety, invites more open self-expression.

Analytic therapy, like all important relationships, particularly intimate relationships, becomes a play reality: a compelling and important additional reality that does not negate ordinary reality, that exists within a relatively safe arena clearly defined in time and space—the "magic circle" (Huizinga, 1955)—complete with its own story line, special atmosphere, and experiences of self and relationships with the other that exist only within this magic circle. Beyond this, analytic therapy includes the specific elements of play and offers benefits that are closely tied to the beneficial consequences of play; I will outline all of this shortly.

We can think of analytic therapy as a play process that can range between two different forms, intersubjective and intrapsychic. The natural tendency of the analyst to identify either with the patient's self-state or the patient's internal object (Racker, 1968) creates a process of mutual enactment—an intersubjective kind of play. The mutual enactment may be so subtle that it escapes the conscious notice of both participants, or the patient may be intensely focused on the analyst and press him to fulfil a role, leading to a scenario or game being played out in a very obvious way (though the feeling of playfulness may be missing).

Patients influence the analyst to enact a role, either repetitive or reparative—and the analyst is inevitably drawn into doing so, at least on a subtle level, whether reluctantly or willingly and despite his theoretical stance or conscious intent. But the analyst's personal psychology also inevitably contributes to the form of the enactment (Sandler, 1976). Relational analysts may advise going with the flow of these enactments, to some degree—that therapeutic impact requires this kind of highlighted *interpersonal* actualization of inner dynamics.

But play also occurs in the intrapsychic arena. The patient lies down on the couch and free associates—allows his attention to wander loosely, flexibly, without conscious direction, where thoughts, feelings, and perceptions can arise in surprising ways, be manipulated at will, and combine in new configurations, precisely according to the characteristics of play (as elaborated below), while the analyst feels free to let his attention hover evenly, playing with the patient's associations and behaviour in his own mind, and making interpretive comments when the time seems right.

Here, while the analyst is not a player in the obvious sense, he provides a necessary background—a frame that offers a holding or containing function. Winnicott's (1958) idea of the capacity to be alone in the presence of another can be taken as a model here. Mother provides the sense of safety necessary for the child to become absorbed in his own world; mother is essential but can sometimes be ignored. Here, the analyst is both the holding "environment mother" as well as sometimes being the "object mother" (Winnicott, 1963b), there to attract transferences.

Ferenczi (1931) proposed a somewhat different metaphor: "The analyst's behaviour is thus rather like that of an affectionate mother, who will not go to bed at night until she has talked over with the child all his current troubles, large and small, fears, bad intentions, and scruples of conscious, and has set them at rest" (p. 137). If mother is mentally absorbed in what her child is doing, she may be said to be playing a role in the game, in a way, even if she is not interacting with her child. An analyst who is similarly absorbed in her experience of and with the patient is likewise playing a passive, observing, or witnessing (cf. Frankel, 2001; Poland, 2000) role in a game with asymmetrical roles.

It seems to me that the level of safety the patient feels determines whether the primary arena of play is intersubjective or intrapsychic. When a patient's narcissistic anxiety exceeds tolerable levels, the patient does not feel safe enough to play "alone" in the intrapsychic arena. By narcissistic anxiety I mean the fear of losing the inner sense of benign connection to the other that forms the basis for the experience of stable internal representations of self and other (Bach's, 2006, "evocative constancy")—it is this sense upon which the regulation of negative affect and the basic sense of safety are based. A patient in such a state will not trust that the environment is sufficiently benign or protective and that they will be safe if they take the environment's benevolence for granted and turn their attention inwards, to the workings of their own minds. On the contrary, they feel they must devote a good part of their attention to keeping a close eye on their potentially dangerous environment—the therapist—and to obtaining reassurance of its benevolence. In such a case, the play arena expands to include the intersubjective field. The analyst's relative anonymity and a condition of relative abstinence are felt by the patient only as obstacles to getting what he feels he needs, not as a facilitative dimension of the treatment situation. In such a situation, the analyst will almost certainly need to expand his ideas of what boundaries and what degree of his own personal participation are appropriate, if the potential for play and a productive frame of mind in the patient is to be preserved.

Even an expanded set of boundaries must be clearly defined, however, if real play is to happen. I suggest that an appropriate set of boundaries includes regular session times, clear payment arrangements, the analyst neither interfering in nor getting very personally involved in the patient's life outside sessions, and the patient similarly not being allowed to participate in the analyst's life outside sessions—all boundaries that serve to define a clear basic physical and material structure of analyst-patient interaction, protecting the autonomy of both participants, while not clearly prescribing the more psychological modes of interacting within these physical constraints and protections. One more element of boundaries that is always appropriate and called for, and that also protects the patient's autonomy, is a genuinely neutral attitude by the analyst, following Chused's (1982) definition of neutrality as a non-judgmental willingness to listen and to learn.

As patients' anxieties get worked through in the intersubjective arena, and their inner object-relational disturbances develop towards health, there is likely to be a spontaneous shift towards working in the intrapsychic arena. It often seems as if, given an adequate feeling of security, patients naturally seek out the intrapsychic arena—that as they grow, they sense the unique benefits that can be obtained from playing within the confines of their own mind, within the protected conditions of an analytic frame and the play space it creates. This is another reason I believe that analysts ought to be less than enthusiastic in *seeking out* greater interaction with patients, always leaving room for the patient to move unimpeded towards a relatively classical frame.

I note here that a situation of intrapsychic play by the patient, when genuine, does not imply that the analyst denies, or that the patient is unaware of, the analyst's independent subjectivity—contrary to some critics of the more standard psychoanalytic set-up, from Ferenczi to the relationalists. Play theory helps us see that the standard analytic set-up is a play construction, agreed to by both participants, each of whom plays their role. The patient does not *fully* mistake play reality (for instance, the analyst's silence) for ordinary reality (for instance, that the analyst is bored, angry, etc.), but *chooses* to take the contents of his mind— his *own* fantasy, even when it concerns the analyst—as playthings, rather than using the *analyst's* subjectivity as play material, as happens in intersubjective play.

Play in Ferenczi's thinking

In Ferenczi's 1931 paper, "Child analysis in the analysis of adults", he explicitly likened his patients' regressed states to "play" (p. 132) and "games" (p. 129)—games the analyst must join in if the patient is to be able to remain openly in that state and be able to "reactivate" (p. 131) the fantasies and traumas associated with that state so they may be worked through. These games are essentially altered states in which the patient relives an infantile period in his life: "[T]he freer the process of association actually became, the more naïve (one might say, the more childish) did the patient become in his speech and his other modes of expressing himself"; "the serious realities of childhood were concealed beneath this play" (p. 130). The analyst must respect the fragile boundaries of the "game": his questions to the "child" that emerges from within the adult patient must be "adapted to a *child's* comprehension" (p. 130); he should not introduce "into my questions and answers things of which the child, at that time, could not possibly have known" (p. 130). But while "adult patients ... should be free to behave in analysis like naughty (i.e., uncontrolled) children ... if he drops his role in the game and sets himself to act out infantile reality in terms of adult behaviour, it must be shown to him it is he who is spoiling the game. And we must manage ... to make him confine the kind and extent of his behaviour within the limits of that of a child" (p. 132).

When he wrote this paper, Ferenczi was in the process of explicitly grounding this clinical approach in a theory of traumatic pathogenesis. This is emphasized in the subtitle of "Confusion of tongues between adults and the child" (1933), written soon afterwards. The subtitle is "The language of tenderness and of passion" and refers to "[a] typical way in which incestuous seductions may occur ...: an adult and a child love each other, the child nursing the playful fantasy of taking the role of mother to the adult. This play may assume erotic forms but remains, nevertheless, on the level of tenderness. It is not so, however, with pathological adults .... They mistake the play of children for the desires of a sexually mature person or even allow themselves—irrespective of any consequences—to be carried away" (p. 161). "The playful trespasses of the child are raised to serious reality" (p. 164) only by the parent's treating them as such. This theory of traumatic pathogenesis underlines the importance of the analyst providing a frame that protects the analytic space as the patient's language of tenderness re-emerges.

Implications of empirical research on play for psychotherapy

Consistent with Ferenczi's idea that certain therapeutic processes require a state of play, empirical research on play in animals and children suggests that play fosters development and psychological growth in particular ways that are relevant to psychotherapy (Frankel, 2008). The following section provides a very brief overview, based mainly on this research, of how play is likely to facilitate certain therapeutic processes (see Frankel, 2008, for more detail).

I emphasize at the outset that play—certainly play in a therapeutic context, but in other situations as well, such as play-fighting—often does not appear playful, in the sense of being light and fun (e.g., Sutton-Smith, 1997). The defining element of play, as I understand it, is a separate, safe, special, and deeply felt reality in which certain creative processes naturally occur. Such a space can, and often does, feel dark, intense, earnest, and serious.

Play has a provisional quality: it does not "count" in terms of real-world consequences. For instance, the self-handicapping aspect of play-fighting (e.g., Fagen, 1981; Power, 2000), in which the stronger play-fighter exercises self-restraint, means that, unlike in real aggression, there is low risk of injury. This fosters venturing into unfamiliar territory and testing limits with relative impunity (Bruner, 1976; Gosso et al., 2005): in animals, the testing of the limits of physical capacities and social behaviour; in psychotherapy patients, the testing of limits regarding feelings, fantasies, and emotional and (in the transference) interpersonal capacities. The background of safety and the high degree of recognition inherent in social play welcome visits from unfamiliar, previously defensively excluded aspects of self, allowing patients to get to know their inner fantasy and emotional lives in a clearer and more intimate way.

Research findings confirm that play facilitates the approach to and exploration of areas of experience that might otherwise be too frightening (e.g., Sroufe & Wunsch, 1972). The obvious parallel for therapy is that a therapy structured as play will facilitate the exploration of areas of experience that are imbued with anxiety and that therefore otherwise resist our attempts to reflect productively on them.

Play is characterized by certain qualities: fragmenting, reordering, and lack of completion of behavioural and ideational sequences; mixing and matching elements from different contexts; exaggeration; repetition; non-literality; flexibility; reversing roles and relationships (e.g., Bekoff & Byers, 1998; Burghardt, 2005; Fagen, 1981; Power, 2000). The psychoanalytic set-up fosters these qualities—free association, for instance, facilitates mixing and matching, non-literality, reversals, and exaggerations, in relation to memories, fantasies, perceptions, and so on. Reversals and exaggeration can occur in the transference. A psychoanalytic patient can learn about his emotional reality and interpersonal capabilities almost as a young animal learns about novel and initially frightening objects in its physical environment, and about its own capacities in engaging these objects—by playing with them.

While characteristics of play such as fragmentation, exaggeration, flexibility, non-literality, and mixing elements from different contexts contribute to innovative thinking and creative problem-solving in sessions in regard to one's difficulties in living, research also suggests that play, in turn, fosters the development of a greater *capacity* for innovative, flexible, and effective ways of thinking about personal and interpersonal dilemmas going forward (e.g., Bateson, 2005). Among the research findings that have held up best are those that show that play fosters higher-level cognitive skills related to the ability to symbolize (e.g., Singer, 1995; Smith, 2005).

Finally, while play develops capacities for restraint in place of reacting more reflexively (Bruner, 1976; Fouts, 1997; Fry, 2005), analytic thinking (e.g., Winnicott, 1971), consistent with empirical research (Bruner, 1976; Gosso et al., 2005), suggests that play also helps people gain a stronger sense of themselves as capable of action, influence, spontaneity, and initiative.

The conditions that have been observed by researchers as necessary for play are also relevant for the conditions we should strive to create in psychotherapy. These include: an atmosphere of safety, which relies most basically on a clear frame and firm boundaries; a nondirective, relatively unstructured, and unpressured set-up, without too much input to cope with, which allows an inner directed, intrinsically absorbing play process to emerge and makes room for the patient to pay close attention to the constant, unconscious play of her mind; and what input there is from the playmate—in this case, the analyst's comments and interpretations—being offered as what Vygotsky (1978) called play "pivots": objects that open up play and imagination—a broomstick that becomes a horse, for example—rather than something that formulates and forecloses at the expense of evoking.

Summary

My view of the analytic process centres on creating conditions necessary for a symbolizing and integrating process to resume in areas of thinking and feeling that have become excluded from mental processing due to anxiety. Ferenczi introduced two opposing foundational clinical concepts that bear directly on these conditions, especially the key condition of safety, and that thus define the range of potential for the functioning of analytic process: from traumatizing and foreclosed through expansive, authentic, and creative.

Identification with the aggressor refers to fear-driven compliance with the other in thought, feeling, perception, and behaviour— one becomes what a person implicitly senses the other wants from oneself—and the loss of one's own authentic experience. When identification with the aggressor is active, therapeutic potential is foreclosed. *Play* is the special state of consciousness that develops in a safe and protected environment and that, through its inherent qualities and the high degree of recognition that occurs in a situation of social play such as the analytic relationship, facilitates a genuine, creative analytic process. An important aspect of the analyst's task consists of mitigating identification with the aggressor and promoting the elements of play, in the broadest sense.

Note

1. For instance, by not privileging the analyst's thoughts and reactions as *a priori* more reality-based and/or mature than the patient's; not paternalistically feeling we know what is best for the patient, even if we keep this to ourselves; not subtly displaying an attitude that undermines the patient's trust in his own perceptions and agency; not fostering dependence, regression, idealization, etc., in the patient largely in order to meet the analyst's own unconscious needs.

CHAPTER NINE

Cultivating meaning space: Freudian and neo-Kleinian conceptions of therapeutic action

Neal Vorus

Introduction

This chapter attempts to address the following question: how does change take place in psychoanalysis, from a contemporary Freudian perspective?

One might think that the answer to such a central question would be rather obvious. In fact, it is remarkably complex and difficult, and likely to be answered in different ways depending on whom you ask. Possible answers include: "making the unconscious conscious"; "learning to self-reflect"; "integrating split-off aspects of personality"; "achieving personalization of self"; "internalizing a good object"; etc. One explanation of the proliferation of these ideas is that it simply reflects the range of pathology that one meets in clinical practice; different patients need different cures. No doubt there is truth to this; it would be remarkably reductionist, and counter to honest clinical experience, to assume that everyone uses treatment in the same way in order to achieve the same results.

However, there is a second factor that this chapter aims to address, and that is the longstanding bifurcation between insight and relationship as curative factors. While there has not always been a contentious divide between these factors in psychoanalysis (see Friedman, 1978b), for the past 50 years or so this has been perhaps the most politicized of therapeutic issues. In this chapter I will briefly review the history of this theoretical divide, then suggest that a path towards common ground on the issue lies in the recent rapprochement between contemporary Freudian and Kleinian thought, particularly as represented in the writings of Ron Britton. Towards the end of the chapter I will present a clinical example to illustrate an application of a contemporary Freudian approach, informed by neo-Kleinian perspectives.

History of the models of therapeutic action

What follows is a brief, and necessarily selective, history of attempts to answer the question: how and why does analysis help? Of course, Freud is the place to start, and in reading through his voluminous writings it is rather striking how little this question is addressed, beyond the early years. Of course, all analysts know the familiar aphorisms: "making the unconscious conscious", "where id was, there shall ego be". There are also his statements about the importance of the positive unobjectionable transference in carrying the treatment along, which has served as a beginning point for later discussions of the importance of the relationship-factor in therapeutic action. Later Freud placed particular emphasis on the analysis of resistance and defence, and (rather vaguely) of working through. Through it all he seemed to be guided by three alternative models of what analysis aimed to achieve (Ellman, 1991): 1. we get better by dislodging pathological memories, thereby reinvigorating a previously blocked flow of associations; 2. we get better by reworking pathological defences in order to better handle life's rather than continuing to rely on solutions developed in infancy; and 3. we get better by working out alternative ways of relating to internal objects as these are encountered anew in the transference. This last view was not nearly as developed in Freud's writing during his time, but became more influential after his death when other theorists revisited this question.

When it comes to views of therapeutic action, there are three main tributaries from analysts who see themselves as more or less direct descendants from Freud. First are the classical structural Freudians (e.g., Arlow, 1963, 1975; Brenner, 1976, 1982), who attempted to construct a streamlined version of Freudian theory that would retain his fundamental vision but without the excess metapsychological baggage that they seemed to feel led so many others astray. In their view, the mind is organized in terms of compromise formations, and people who come for treatment suffer from unhealthy, overly restrictive compromise formations. Their solution is to disrupt the equilibrium of the patient's organization through interpretation, so that he/she might arrive at a healthier solution. This is one version of Freud's defence-focused theory of therapeutic action.

Second are those analysts whose work follows the clinical writings of Anna Freud, and whose primary focus is the close process monitoring of free association (e.g., Gray, 1994; Busch, 1993). These analysts steer clear of suggestive interventions, including top-heavy interpretations. They prefer to work on helping the patient learn to self-analyse, as they see the fuller understanding of how one's mind works as the key to analytic change. This is another version of the defence-analysis focus.

The third group includes those analysts whose work has been primarily inspired by the treatment of more disturbed patients, and who have drawn on the contributions of object relations theory and self psychology in order to better understand the primitive needs and experiences of these patients (e.g., Bach, 1985, 1994; Ellman, 2007; Ellman, Grand, Silvan & Ellman, 1995; Loewald, 1980; Modell, 1976, 1988). Among this "self-and-object Freudian" group, much emphasis is placed on creating a sufficient environment for patients to feel held, contained, their experiences heard and validated, and affective experiences received and articulated by their analyst.

This is the model of therapeutic action on which I will focus. One hallmark of this third contemporary Freudian group is their insistence on and articulation of the central importance of the therapeutic relationship in the analytic process, without casting aside the critical function of interpretation or insight. The other two Freudian groups largely relegate the therapeutic relationship to something incidental, not a prime ingredient of therapeutic change. In the larger psychoanalytic universe, the question of "insight" v. "relationship" has grown into a central problematic, and many of the movements that have spun-off from Freudian theory have done so along exactly this fault line. It is my view that the third contemporary Freudian position described here goes further in transcending this divide than any of the others; i.e., it aims towards a kind of parity or, at times, a convergence of interpretive and relational factors in treatment. It is in the context of furthering such a convergence that I will argue for the value offered by some contemporary Kleinian ideas.

Evolving contemporary Freudian models of therapeutic action

In retrospect, it seems prophetic that the first "modern Freudian" paper devoted to the subject of therapeutic action also legitimately belongs within the oeuvre of early modern Kleinian thought. This is the paper by James Strachey from 1934 entitled, "The nature of the therapeutic action of psychoanalysis". In that paper he draws on his experience with Melanie Klein to offer a view of pathology and therapeutic change that places considerable emphasis on the overly-cruel and primitive superego of the neurotic. This necessarily puts the primary accent on object relationships, both in the understanding of pathology and its treatment. The problem of the cruel superego is two-fold: it wreaks havoc internally, typically fuelling defences and symptomatic behaviour that are overly harsh and self-destructive. And, through the processes of introjection and projection, such an internal situation becomes self-sustaining through the mediation of contemporary external figures who become transformed through superego projection, then internalized in their now distorted, and ultimately self-hatred amplifying form. This is what Strachey referred to as the "neurotic vicious circle" (1934, p. 137).

In Strachey's description of the treatment process he offers a thoroughly relational picture, albeit one that takes place via interpretation. The key to the process is the analyst functioning as an "auxiliary superego" that becomes internalized in a transitional form, separated from other aspects of the superego. Inevitably, superego projections take place that convert the analyst functioning as a "new object", both internally and externally, into an old object (p. 143). It is at this point that transference interpretations are made (at the point of greatest affective urgency), which have the effect of differentiating the archaic from the actual, allowing the analyst to be interpreted as a more permanent superego component. One key feature of this description is the breach created in the vicious circle through the mediation of reality via interpretation that facilitates newer and more accurate internalization, along with an increase in self-understanding. Thus, both relationship and insight are fundamentally involved (neither more primary than the other).

While several articles were written in the intervening years on this subject, none addressed the subject as comprehensively as Loewald's landmark paper of 1960, titled "On the therapeutic action of psychoanalysis" (obviously reminiscent of Strachey's earlier contribution). While Strachey is nowhere directly cited in this paper, his influence is clear. Both papers offer a view of the subject that features analytic interaction as the primary vehicle for change, but without downgrading interpretation or insight. Instead, the terms are themselves reinterpreted in a way that removes the bifurcation between them. Loewald also uses Strachey's term "new object", albeit without attribution. From Strachey's perspective, the idea of the analyst as new object refers to someone outside the patient's superego projections, who is subsequently distorted via such projections, then rediscovered following effective interpretation. Loewald's usage is similar but takes us out of the range of mere superego towards the psychic apparatus as a whole. For Loewald, the psyche is always and fundamentally object-related, or (from the standpoint of the id) *environment* related. In the early parent-child relationship the environment mediates a higher level of organization to the child through what Loewald refers to as an "integrative experience", wherein the *differential* between parent and child is bridged as the mother begins to provide structure and direction to the child's uncoordinated urges through her "caring activities" (p. 24). When the maternal environment is no longer centered on the child's experience, the openness of the mother-child system closes down and this archaic situation becomes frozen and subsequently re-projected in a process that turns potential new objects into old ones. Here a vicious circle is envisaged, quite similar to the one described by Strachey, but now involving the psyche as a whole in its relation to the environment.

From Loewald's framework, the analyst offers him/herself as a new object, not only in the sense of being (potentially) free of archaic projections, but more positively, as a centering connection to a higher level of organization. This facilitates the articulation in more organized form of the more primitive experiences of the regressively organized mind of the patient. For Loewald, it is the internalization of this integrated differential that accounts for psychic growth.

It is important to note that this process is seen as taking place via progressive interpretation, timed and paced according to the patient's true level of regression. It therefore involves an indivisible mix of interpretation and internalization, insight and relationship.

From a clinical perspective, Loewald's view of therapeutic action has two central limitations. First, it does not fully address how this process takes place from the side of the analyst. What does it mean for the analyst to be at a higher level of organization? What is happening inside the mind of the analyst that allows her effectively to offer the kind of integration across a differential that Loewald describes? (He begins the paper with the caveat that he is not addressing technique, clearly side-stepping these considerations from the beginning.) Second, Loewald seems a bit sanguine about the potential for patients to respond to his integrating interventions. What he fails to address is the kind of anxiety that leads patients to continually attempt to return to a closed system, an old object (see Bass, 2002). In my view both of these limitations are answered in the work of modern (post-Bionian) Kleinians.

Modern Kleinians and therapeutic action

At the centre of the modern Kleinian perspective is the immense contribution of Wilfred Bion (1959, 1962). While his views are not accepted equally or in the same way by all modern Kleinians, I think it is no exaggeration to say that his influence within the Kleinian universe is second only to that of Freud and Klein. His influence has also been significant outside this theoretical sphere, but for many Freudians his writings have an esoteric quality that does not always easily translate into something accessible in the heat of the clinical moment.[2] While many of the British contemporary Kleinians make extensive use of Bion's ideas (Joseph, Feldman, O'Shaughnessy, Spillius, etc.), it is Ronald Britton who has perhaps been most influential recently in New York, and certainly to me personally. Not only is he a very clear and accessible writer, his ideas and way of working have a more familiar feel to the Freudian-trained. For example, Britton (1989) was perhaps the first Kleinian to assert that some patients cannot necessarily hear an interpretation right away, particularly those suffering from narcissistic pathology. This was a significant development, as the ubiquity of early and frequent interpretation has been a hallmark of Kleinian treatment from the beginning, and has long represented a clear line of demarcation separating Kleinians from modern Freudians. The latter tend to wait for patients to be able to both tolerate and utilize interpretations, whereas Kleinians have typically assumed that the inability to make use of the analyst's contributions reflects deep anxieties that need direct interpretation in order to ameliorate. Ron Britton's approach therefore feels consonant with a Freudian perspective, and his explanation offers a new conceptual framework for thinking about this aspect of clinical work.

In describing patients who are unable to hear interpretation, Britton (1989) draws on Kleinian assumptions about the early Oedipus complex to describe the development of what he called "triangular space", a description of a form of mental organization that allows meaning to be reflected upon from various perspectives. For Britton, this development grows out of the young child's acknowledgement of the parents' relationship with each other, which, when internalized, unites the child's psychic world:

> The closure of the Oedipal triangle by the recognition of the link joining the parents provides a limiting boundary for the internal world. It creates what I call a "triangular space"—i.e., a space bounded by the three persons of the Oedipal situation and all their potential relationships. It includes, therefore, the possibility of being a participant in a relationship and observed by a third person as well as being an observer of a relationship between two people (1989, p. 86).

While by no means completely unprecedented in the Kleinian literature (see Rey, 1979), this description by Britton went a considerable extent further in the direction of interests shared by contemporary Freudians in the development of self-reflection and intersubjective capacities, and in the disturbance of these as an element of narcissistic pathology (see Bach, 1985; Ellman, 2007). Further, Britton's technical recommendation that one may need to articulate to the patient his/her own point of view for a period of time before another perspective can become tolerable is certainly a new element in the

Kleinian literature, and one that fits easily with perspectives among Freudians who have benefited from Kohut's earlier contributions advocating a similar approach.

Britton's perspective is rooted in Bion's (1962) concept of the container and contained. In this conception, projective identification is conceived as primarily a means of communication between infant and mother, preceding verbal or other symbolic avenues. In early infancy the child projects into his/her mother unbearable bits of raw sensory experience, called beta elements. When the mother is functioning adequately, she receives these projections, tolerates them, and thinks about them as they relate to the child's experience. In this process she is functioning as a container of the child's experience, transforming beta elements into alpha elements through "alpha function", which is essentially, her thinking accurately and empathically about the child's experience, taking it into herself and conveying her understanding to the child through her various responses. As Bion phrased it, the mother "metabolizes" what the infant projects into her, then returns it in more tolerable form. Over time, it is the mother as container that becomes internalized, and serves as the basis for one's ability to think about one's own experience, and to tolerate distressing experience through robust alpha function.

In Bion's (1962) model, the analyst provides a function very similar to mothering, in containing the patient's unbearable (and unarticulable/non-symbolized) experience, then conveying that understanding in a form that is more bearable to the patient. It could follow from this model that the form in which this understanding is conveyed to the patient will vary depending on the particularities of the patient. For some, the most effective intervention might be an interpretation. For others, communications that stay closer to the patient's conscious experience may be needed, at least for a period of time.

You certainly hear echoes here of Strachey (1934), who based his view of therapeutic action on introjective/projective cycles, à la Klein. Perhaps more important is the parallel with Loewald (1960); I would think that alpha function is a good description of the role of the new object in functioning as a "representative of a higher stage of organization and mediating this to the patient" (p. 25). In both cases, development is facilitated through the interaction between patient and analyst, as interpretations that are felt to be accurate, more organized versions of what the patient experiences are repeatedly offered and accepted, and over time, the interpretive process itself (the analyst's alpha function, the integrated differential between higher and lower levels of organization) is internalized, so that the analytic process can continue internally and independently.

Again, Britton offers something further: a clear-eyed view of the difficulties of this process. In his classic description of Miss A, Britton (1989) describes a patient's intolerance of anything from him remotely interpretive, i.e., at all different from what she consciously thinks. He recognizes that she needs him to stay within her experiential world for a period of time, and he does this by stating back to her what he takes to be her experience. Gradually she can tolerate hearing a bit more of his understanding of her experience from a slightly different vantage point, and he can begin to explore this difficulty with her. In his framework, there was an early failure of containment by the mother that led the child to experience the link between the parents more in hate than love. In order to maintain some semblance of the mother as good, the bad/non-containing aspect is projected into father, and then their link is dreaded as it threatens the now-purified mother. As the link cannot be tolerated, triangular space cannot develop, and therefore only a dyadic connection with another, a "straight line", can be accepted. Britton's experience was that he could not "look sideways" within himself at his ideas in order to think more deeply about what was in Miss A's mind. Her thoughts could not live as thoughts within herself, and she could not tolerate them in her analyst either, the detection of which she would inevitably respond to with the command, "Stop that fucking thinking!".

Britton's intervention (or non-intervention) allowed parental intercourse to take place so long as it "did not force itself in some intrusive way into the child's mind", because to do so felt equivalent to annihilating the link with the mother, both internally and externally. Working in this way allowed the patient to find internal space for thinking, even though the thoughts were, for a long time, not elaborated upon. The analyst's ability to rediscover his own space for thinking, even when this is under attack by the patient, somehow helps the patient eventually find his/her triangular space. This is certainly a relational intervention (not primarily interpretive), although, as such space is developed, interventions that more closely resemble what are traditionally considered interpretive become more prominent in the process.

What is the goal, from this perspective? Facilitating the development of triangular space, or what I refer to as "meaning space". At some points in a treatment such facilitation cannot yet take place through interpretation, as traditionally described, but rather through interventions that stay closer to the patient's conscious experience. This form of intervention has been variously referred to as empathy (Kohut, 1977, 1984), holding (Modell, 1976; Winnicott, 1965c), affirmation (Killingmo, 1989), or similar terms.[3] Rather than view these interventions as categorically distinct from interpretive and meaning-giving communications, I am proposing an alternative perspective that unifies these therapeutic agents by viewing them in the context of the patient's ability to give meaning to experience. I would treat the interpretive relationship as primarily a meaning-giving one, and the non-interpretive phase with patients like Miss A as operating within the range of potential meaning. What are we doing with such patients? Finding space within ourselves first to think and give meaning to the patient's experience, then eventually beginning to facilitate meaning-making in our patients in a form that they can tolerate, gradually enlarging it as their tolerance expands. Over time we would hope that a patient would be able to tolerate an enlarged understanding of unconscious aspects of experience as well.

Clinical example

Mr M was a 20-year-old man who came to treatment on the advice of his academic department because he was in danger of failing out of the programme. He was having trouble writing papers, was frequently absent from class, and in his words was an "emotional wreck". At the start of treatment, Mr M decided to take a leave of absence from his studies in order to focus on addressing his emotional difficulties. We began meeting twice weekly, and after several months settled into a three times weekly psychotherapy. Mr M was eventually able to return to school, finish his degree, attain gainful employment, and begin graduate studies. While Mr M's initial treatment goals were achieved after the first several years of therapy, it became increasingly apparent that he suffered from more pervasive difficulties. He described himself as "lacking internal structure", and often found himself basing decisions, both large and small, on what he understood (or imagined) that others would want him to do. Related to this was his trouble maintaining lasting love relationships, as he so often felt both drawn to and needing to escape from the needs of women with whom he became involved. Mr M had trouble committing himself to either a relationship or a career, as he was never entirely sure who he was.

Mr M is the oldest of three children whose parents split up when he was around four, and his mother was apparently left quite depressed and overwhelmed. In a pattern characteristic of many such families, he took on the mantle of "man of the house" and set about attempting to become the kind of young man who could make his mother happy. Along the way he developed considerable skill in adapting to the needs of others (particularly women), and for some time this remained one of his most prized attributes. At the same time, he was left with a profound yearning for a father with whom to identify, as his own father remained relatively disengaged after the divorce. Mr M recalls looking to television in search of a strong, unflappable male figure with whom to identify in order to shore up feelings of insecurity and inadequacy. One way we initially came to understand Mr M's collapse while in college was his feeling overwhelmed by the familiar, internally-imposed demand that he already be the fully-formed adult, the "successful 40-year-old professional". The distance of this goal from his 20-year-old self felt unbearable, and he became increasingly anxious, depressed, and non-functional in his life.

Progress with this patient over the years has been gradual. Initially much of the work focused on simply processing and learning to think about his emotional experience, something that initially felt quite alien to Mr M. While intelligent, articulate, and highly-sensitive to the emotions of others, he had little capacity for reflecting on internal experience. When he related events that had obvious emotional importance, Mr M initially tended to convey these events in a performative mode, telling a story for maximal effect rather than attempting to give voice to an inner truth about his experience. This began to shift somewhat as Mr M's sense of having an internal "deficit" came into focus. He described lacking an enduring, consistent sense of himself, and linked this to yearning for someone like a father whom he could "push up against" and who would instil discipline and provide guidance. These wishes came explicitly into the transference, and the patient alternated between wishing and fearing both punishment and guidance. For a period of time he grew increasingly frustrated by my failure to provide the instruction and direction for which he yearned, and his new-found ability to express the extent of his rage and disappointment seemed important. However, while genetic interpretations linking these wishes to his relationship with his father made both intellectual and emotional sense, they did not in themselves alter Mr M's sense of an internal deficit, a lack of self that he had hoped to fill in through a relationship with me. This remained relatively unchanged until nearly ten years into the treatment, when we began meeting four times per week and the patient started using the couch.

The shift towards formal analysis had been my suggestion for some time, but Mr M finally took it when he returned to school and found himself incapacitated by the demands of writing papers. Whenever he began to write, he would be attacked mercilessly by what he called "the Ogre", which I took to be similar to what Britton (2003) has referred to as a "chaos monster", the basis of an ego-destructive superego. This refers to an internal figure that attacks the patient's internally-generated meaning. It is particularly at moments of creativity that these attacks occur, and, as we have moved into a more analytic mode, it has grown increasingly clear how often I become, in Mr M's mind, the voice of this attacking, envious internal presence. As he has found the words to express this experience of me, it has become apparent how pervasive this experience is. I become an internal presence who serves the function of preventing meaning by attacking his mind during moments of genuine self-expression. He experiences me as allied with an internal object hostile to and envious of the creation of meaning or expression of personal initiative. He experiences me as issuing hidden directives through my interventions, and of secretly manipulating him to maintain a position of control. Alternating with this experience is a conscious wish to comply with me, to be told what to think and feel. I would now speculate that this has probably been a hidden dynamic in our work throughout the treatment, only now available to conscious reflection.

As we have begun to address the pathological way in which Mr M internalizes my interventions, he has become increasingly spontaneous and genuinely self-reflective in sessions, and simultaneously, has described a new-found sense of initiative and assertiveness in both professional and personal settings. He feels a greater sense of structure within himself, and links this to the way our relationship has evolved; he more often experiences me as someone with whom he discovers the workings of his mind rather than someone from whom he seeks gratification or reassurance. With respect to the process of therapeutic action, it seems to me that what has helped this patient is not, in fact, merely (or mainly) the content of interpretations, but rather, his sustained exposure to the *interpretive attitude* itself (Poland, 2002), which I would define as a consistent attempt at understanding and giving meaning to his experience, despite his nearly continuous unconscious effort to prevent this from occurring. This effort was the primary source of resistance; rather than warding off any particular insight, he fought to prevent the experience of me as a separate other engaged with his mind, and did so mainly through processes of projective and introjective identification. This dimension of his experience had not been clear prior to the beginning of formal analysis. While much of our early work focused on analysing the transference, this was typically done with an interpersonal focus, i.e., with primary attention on the role relationships enacted or wished-for. For example, Mr M spoke frequently of his conflicting wishes and fears of finding a man to provide guidance and structure, in order to compensate for what was missing with his father and within himself, and we took this up in the transference. Sometimes I found myself wishing to be such a father to him, and, at other times, I found myself caught in enactments that symbolized to the patient the opposite, that I felt no genuine concern for him at all. In retrospect, this aspect of our work was both important and slightly off the mark. It reflected some of the very real calamities of his childhood, and his various wishes and fears around this were significant. But, at the same time, much of this work felt strangely non-spontaneous and performed. Not completely pantomimed, but neither fully authentic either. This was something I found difficult to articulate with the patient for some time, as there seemed to be no other way of being for him, no real experiential counterpoint. In retrospect, it was only the intensification of treatment and shift to formal analysis that made available the more subtle processes that prevented this patient from finding greater authenticity and spontaneity, and from developing a more structured sense of self and capacity for intimacy with others. What became visible was the way he systematically denuded his own ability to make use of my help and to genuinely reflect upon his own experience. In Bionian terms, we might say he fragmented and expelled his own mental capacities. As we came to discover, this active resistance served the function of warding off the threat of catastrophic anxiety that he believed would ensue if he left himself open to the full registration of his own experience. He neither felt equipped for thinking, nor felt any possibility (or hope) of help from me. Rather than merely feeling hopeless about my help, he seemed to have no available prototype for the possibility of someone actually bearing with him the full force of his anxiety and distress. It was simply unimaginable, and therefore unthinkable to allow room for greater openness to his own experience, which in his mind would be tantamount to a kind of psychical suicide. While Mr M ostensibly used treatment to facilitate a greater range of experience, he was all the while recruiting me internally to do the opposite, to attack the possibility of affectively enriched experience and the generation of personal initiative. He actively attacked the possibility of "meaning space", an internal clearing where his own spontaneously generated meaning might emerge.

Discussion

So, how did this rather profound change in Mr M take place? This is perhaps the most vexing of questions in psychoanalysis, as we are so often left with theories inadequate to the phenomenon, and no other way of knowing or explaining. How did it happen? I am here tempted to paraphrase Loewald's (1960) disclaimer, that I am not actually advocating a change in psychoanalytic technique as much as offering a way of thinking about some of the processes involved in standard psychoanalytic treatment (albeit with more disturbed patients). With this particular patient, there were no major modifications of what would be considered standard practice in psychoanalytic psychotherapy, followed by psychoanalysis. Having said this, there are of course the many subtle "deviations" that we all engage in when treating patients—I doubt anybody would now dispute the notion that there is no single technique, as in every case much of what goes on is shaped, in the broadest (and largely unconscious) sense, by transference and countertransference. Even so, I do think there were several things that I learned from my own conduct of this treatment. First (as relates to the central thesis of this paper), I conducted a thoroughly interpretive treatment in this case, although I grew sparing with my interventions as I became aware of the "put on" quality that would sometimes pervade the treatment room when I had made an interpretation that I found particularly noteworthy. What felt more useful and real was staying closer to this patient's experience, not to offer extensive interpretations unless they were directly inspired by the immediacy of the clinical moment, usually in the transference, and typically without making extensive genetic links. The focus would be on what was happening between us, the language more often descriptive than explanatory. At the same time, I laboured to maintain an interpretive mindset about the content of the patient's mind, despite sometimes great difficulty thinking about him in much depth. Eventually I did find the words (and space) to articulate the qualities of falseness and two-dimensionality, but saying the words did not immediately lead to change. Second, there was no single interpretation or topic of interpretation that made the difference with this patient. Rather, the important variable seemed to be the cumulative effect of being in a particular kind of relationship over a long period of time, i.e., with someone steadfastly devoted to thinking about his mind, and with helping him eventually face the tremendous sense of risk he associated with such a relationship.

Over a long period of time he grew to trust our relationship enough to face the danger of shifting to a modality that would increase his exposure to his own experience (and my separate but connected presence), through use of the couch and more frequent sessions. In this situation the defences intensified, but also more clearly announced themselves, and by finding voice were also eventually interpretable within the transference. In essence, this patient got better because he could trust a relationship that was based on an attempt to know his mind at a fundamental level.

While some might identify the earlier phase of treatment with Mr M as one in which I was primarily engaged in empathy, or functioning as a "self object", I think these descriptions, while accurate at some level, critically obscure the extent to which maintaining an interpretive frame of mind remained essential for the treatment to progress. For a patient who needs to defensively collapse the possibility of meaning, experiencing the analyst as merely serving a function (e.g., providing empathy) is greatly reassuring, and the analyst may need to limit his/her range of interventions so as not to disrupt this needed experience. At the same time, as Britton (1989) showed in the analysis of Ms B, the analyst needs to continue the very difficult work of privately locating the interiority of the patient's mind amidst defensive attacks on exactly this possibility in order to safeguard the potential of a space for meaning within the patient.

What the modern Kleinian concept of containment offers to Freudians is an elaboration of Loewald's (1960) conception of the "new object" that adds the connotation of the analyst actively holding and processing the patient's experience while simultaneously protecting the patient from more of it than she can tolerate. While some of the most important Freudian writings on the treatment of more disturbed patient have emphasized the importance of abstaining from interpretation for a period of time and remaining emotionally resonant with the patient's experience (e.g., Grunes, 1984; Bach, 1985), it is my view that the contemporary Kleinian insistence on the "mentalness of mind" (Alvarez, 1992) offers a needed conceptual bulwark against the regressive pull towards collusive non-thinking with patients who are currently too disturbed to tolerate space for meaning, both internally and within the analytic relationship.

Summary

The focus of this chapter has been on an approach to thinking about therapeutic action that integrates aspects of contemporary Kleinian theory as a way of transcending the time-worn distinction between interpretation and relationship in psychoanalysis. I began with a review of important Freudian contributions to the theory of therapeutic action, then discussed Bion and Britton as their ideas relate to those of Strachey and Loewald. The main point I hoped to distill and perhaps refine through this theoretical comparison was the role and function of the "new object" in an interpretive treatment. I also hoped to prepare the way for thinking about interpretation that is not reducible to the transmittal of information, but instead refers to a particular mode of relating that facilitates what I refer to as "meaning space". In my clinical presentation I offered the example of a man who was treated extensively in psychotherapy before transitioning to psychoanalysis, and whose treatment illustrates the view that, at least for some patients, relational and interpretive dimensions are inseparable. For Mr M, it was his mind's emerging openness to the knowing of another mind that was essential to the development of internal reflection, and the absence or distortion of this that proved most crippling. If nothing else, keeping this in mind can hopefully provide a framework for maintaining this essential interpretive stance with patients who cannot tolerate or make use of formal interpretation, sometimes for a very long period of time. Rather than thinking of these treatments as *only* involving relational factors, i.e., as supportive, holding, self-object, etc. I believe we (and the patient) are best served in thinking of them as, at least potentially, somewhere on the continuum of an interpretive treatment, cultivating the gradual development of meaning space.

CHAPTER TEN

"Secretly attached, secretly separate" Art, dreams, and transference-countertransference in the analysis of a third generation Holocaust survivor

Michal Talby-Abarbanel

Ann is a 32-year-old Jewish woman, a painter. She was raised in France and immigrated to the States several years ago. In our first consultation session she told me that she had considered entering treatment for several years, as she was aware that since she left home, ten years ago, she has been experiencing complicated emotional processes she needed to work through. She felt she needed someone to help her to reach better integration. She told me in the first session: "My experience is sometimes like I have many parts to myself that I need to put together."

I could feel Ann's un-integrated parts through her appearance and the way she dressed. Her somewhat sweet and childish voice did not fit her mature and strong presence. She dressed in a Bohemian style, an amalgam of contemporary fashion with old-fashioned items that looked as if they belonged to a different period. I learned later that these antique dresses belonged to her grandmother, who wore them when she was Ann's age.

Ann is an intelligent, verbally rich woman, who quickly formed a very good rapport. She is articulate and insightful. At the end of the consultation process I offered her analysis and she agreed enthusiastically to my offer, demonstrating a somewhat innocent, immediate trust.

Ann explained to me that her main concern was in the realm of forming close relationships, especially a romantic relationship with a man. She had had several intimate relationships, which she perceived as "frustrating, limited, and crippled". She was aware of the fact that she tended to choose men who were not available or not suitable for her and that she was not able to be authentic and spontaneous in these and other close relationships.

Ann described another pathological pattern in her life which she only vaguely understood. In the past few years, she continually created separations by moving on every two to three years. She usually enjoyed the first year in the new place and then her enthusiasm gradually diminished, and she started to feel a kind of deadness and developed an urge to pack her belongings and move on again. In one of the first sessions she told me: "I am like a street cat that has no home and gets along everywhere … or maybe I am more like a turtle whose home is always with him." I need only a small suitcase in which I can easily pack myself; several clothes, some books, my art creations and here I am on my way again."

Ann was aware of her ambivalent attitude towards separations. Although she created them all the time, they were actually very difficult for her. In the first few sessions she remembered that when she first left her home to live by herself, she suffered from psychosomatic symptoms, especially stomach aches. These symptoms recur every time she is about to leave. Ann wondered why she could not put down roots anywhere and create her own home. She felt that for her the only home was still her childhood home.

* * *

Ann described her mother as devoted and caring but felt the relationship was too close and "dangerously emotional". She felt that her mother had difficulty letting her go. Ann felt it was impossible to share emotional things with her mother. Whenever Ann was sad her mother became depressed, and whenever Ann was anxious her mother became panicky. Ann felt that there was no space between them and later in the treatment she named this situation "no membrane". Ann said that her mother has always suffered from existential anxiety and has had apocalyptic fantasies about death and loss. At the same time, Ann complained that there was no real closeness between them. Her mother was very passive, refrained from expressing her own ideas and feelings and was not really present in an authentic and lively way. Ann was always very sensitive to her mother's emotional responses and feelings, especially to her indirect, non-verbal messages—which were actually the main communicative channel between them.

Ann's father is a lawyer. He is a well-read person from whom Ann learned a lot. He was always willing to help her with any practical problem but was emotionally detached. He has had difficulty dealing with negative feelings and is easily hurt when criticized. When he feels offended, he tends to express a kind of restrained rage, which was always very frightening for Ann. She felt her relationship with him contributed to her own difficulty dealing with her anger and she has always tried to avoid conflicts in her relationships.

Ann has a sister, four years her junior. She describes her sister as very demanding and angry and I have sensed that Ann often projects onto the image of her sister split-off parts of herself, which she cannot accept or contain.

* * *

With this initial information Ann and I embarked on the treatment. We started a once a week therapy and planned to move to a four times a week analysis on the couch, three months from then, when our schedules were going to allow it.

Ann's concerns over close relationships were expressed with me from the start, in the form of a wish-fear dilemma regarding starting an intensive therapy. On the one hand, she had many indirect associations about things that were not frequent enough and talked about her need to have a firm structure and constant feedback in order to feel involved. On the other hand, when I suggested that she come twice a week, she refused and said she preferred to wait for the analysis. Her fantasies about the analysis seemed to be a compromise solution to her intimacy dilemma. She imagined that when she began using the couch she would not have to look at me and would be able to immerse herself in her internal world without having to relate or be influenced by me. The analysis symbolized clear and safe boundaries that could protect her from her fear of engulfment.

Around two months into the treatment Ann met her current boyfriend. It was the first time that Ann had a real, stable relationship with a man. I wondered about the timing: was this a need to form a kind of triangle to defend against the dyadic relationship with me? Or was the relationship with me protecting her from engulfment with him? It seemed that in order to avoid being engulfed she had to form two close relationships at the same time.

In this way Ann tried to create the conditions she needed to immerse herself in the treatment. Yet, when we started the four times a week analysis the conflict intensified. Ann had difficulty modulating the level of closeness and reported that she felt as if she had no skin and everything was experienced as too intense. On her way to one of the first sessions she had an anxiety attack in the subway when the train was stuck in a tunnel. In the small closed cabin in the subway carriage that had no open windows, she had a frightening thought about the sour air that everyone there was breathing. While listening to her, I became aware of the smallness of my office that had no windows and could feel for a moment a concordant claustrophobia: both of us trapped together in a too close, "emotionally dangerous" relationship, each of us inhaling the carbon dioxide that the other was exhaling. When I tried to make a comment about her fears, she experienced my interpretation as an unwelcomed intrusion and had a moment of anxiety again in the session. We were then able to talk about her fear that the relationship with me would be too close and intrusive and that she would not be able to find her space and freedom in it.

* * *

Gradually, Ann began to talk more about her difficulty expressing herself as a separate individual in my presence. She told me that she felt inhibited. It was difficult for her to initiate the sessions, to shift to another topic, and to be spontaneous. She remembered that it was always especially hard for her to express her feelings and needs with her mother. She began to talk about a discrepancy between what her mother said and her non-verbal communication and messages. Beneath her mother's tense silences Ann discerned unpleasant feelings and distress. She had to guess what her mother meant to say and tended to interpret everything the mother expressed as a sign of her disappointment. It was very difficult for Ann to have direct communication with her mother.

In our own moments of silence Ann felt a similar discomfort and told me that this had been present from the very first moment of the treatment. When I wondered out loud why Ann did not share with me this experience until now, Ann said: "I cannot even imagine myself telling you such a thing. It is so automatic for me to avoid talking directly about unpleasant experiences." She explained to me that as with her mother she feared I could get hurt by her or be disappointed with her.

During subsequent sessions we gradually explored this maternal transference and Ann realized that she was always worried that something bad would happen in our relationship if she expressed herself in my presence. Every moment of silence was an indication that there was something wrong and the relationship had been damaged. She was always very careful, as if she was walking on egg shells. When she initiated more active interactions, she felt as if she "intruded into my privacy" or "ate away" my existence. She told me that that is why she cancelled her own wants and needs in close relationships. "I totally lose myself in the relationship. Maybe that's why I am kind of autistic, I always escape to my aloneness," she added. I said to her: "It is as if you have only two available options: to be in a relationship where you renounce your needs, or to be alone. Maybe your wish in the treatment is to find a way to be together without losing yourself, to find your autonomy and freedom in the relationship." She later told me that this interpretation was very meaningful to her.

*　*　*

As a result of our initial work, Ann dared to express her wish to bring in some of her art creations, since "until now I kept my art outside of the treatment". She brought in one of her drawings that shed additional light on her core conflicts and defences. In this drawing Ann is depicted as a piece of paper, which is being folded in the middle, divided into two symmetrical parts. Each part still has a leg and a hand but her heart is being squashed. "I have only one heart," she said, "and it is painful." Her associations led to her experience of being torn between her two worlds. France, where her family lived, represented closeness, care, and warmth. She feels the need to go there every few months to "charge her batteries". In London, where she lived and studied when she drew this picture, "which was so cold", she felt very lonely and deprived of connectedness, but there she had her other world: her studies, her art, her true self. She felt that the two worlds could not be combined. While telling me this, she suddenly had an insight. She realized that it was impossible for her to develop herself near her mother and that she had to distance herself and go abroad in order to start exploring her internal world and to begin a meaningful process of personal development.

During that period, I tried to understand the nature of Ann's conflicts and defences better, and assess the level of her psychic structure. Ann's fears of engulfment, her difficulty modulating affect, and the sense of blurred boundaries between her and her mother suggested an intense and almost symbiotic relationship with the early mother. At the same time, her ability to talk about these subtle and complex internal processes in a very articulate and self-reflective way suggested a more developed and differentiated level of development. It seemed that, for some reason, she could not express her rich and creative self with her mother, as if expressing her individuated self might in some way destroy her mother. I wondered about the nature of this life-long bond with her mother that now kept her from self-realization and intimate relations with others.

* * *

We began to understand more about the bond with her mother and her need to protect her, through dreams she reported before one of her trips to France, five months into the analysis. Throughout the first year of the treatment, Ann had a characteristic way of responding to our separations. Her reaction usually began with detachment and withdrawal and a kind of emotional numbness. There was a sense of deadness in the sessions. She usually felt a vague feeling of distress, which she could not verbalize or connect in any way to the fact of the separation. She severed the links between affect and thought, her characteristic defence whenever she was overwhelmed.

Before that specific break, her dreams reflected extreme distress and anxiety. They were a series of nightmares about huge tidal waves that were threatening to drown her. In the dreams, there was always another person for whom she felt responsible and whom she tried to instruct how to dive beneath the waves. There was a sense of helplessness, despair, and frustration since the other person was very passive and did not manage to do it and they were both in great danger. We explored the associations to the dreams and Ann started to talk about her fear of visiting her parents, whom she always felt she had to take care of. Her mother has been depressed. She flooded Ann with detailed descriptions about her bad mood, her bodily pains, and her pessimistic stories and apocalyptic fantasies about the future. Ann felt as if her mother got under her skin. She also got depressed whenever she listened to her mother, as if there were no boundaries between them, no membrane.

This experience of lack of emotional boundaries, where the other's pain becomes hers, made her reflect on this tangled bond she had with her mother. She realized that she had distanced herself from her mother in a physical sense but had not managed to separate from her emotionally. She came to the following session very excited and told me about a dream she had had the previous night. In her dream she saw a young bird in a nest. The bird starts to fly high in the air but then realizes that she cannot go too far because there is a string connecting her to the nest. Ann's associations led to her intense and limiting relationship with her mother. She used a metaphor of an umbilical cord (the string), to explain how she and her mother were connected in a mysterious way and how things have been transmitted between them non-verbally and through this imaginary umbilical cord, creating a private language that only they understood. I said to her: "You wish to free yourself" and she responded: "Yes, but if I do so, will I survive?" We talked about this dual experience of the bond with her mother that limited her freedom but was also life sustaining.

Ann's growing ability to symbolize her relationship with her mother led to further insights into the nature of their bond, captured in another dream the following week. She dreamt about a young woman who needed psychological treatment. Ann gave the woman a chocolate bar and told her to break it into two parts. The woman, who was very attached to that chocolate bar, was reluctant to do it and Ann forced her since it was the only way to help her. The woman cried and said that her mother did not allow her to do so. Ann added that actually in the dream the bar was already broken. She could feel the two separate parts through the wrapper that was still holding the two parts together.

The main theme in her associations was the difficulty she was experiencing in treatment. She felt that her attitudes were changing.

She talked mainly about the change in the way she saw her mother. She started seeing negative aspects in their relationship. "It is difficult to criticize something that is part of you, values and attitudes on which you were raised," she said to me guiltily. I related this to the sense of loss in the dream, the fear that her negative feelings would destroy something precious. Ann agreed and added: "But actually the chocolate bar is already broken. Maybe I just have to acknowledge and accept something that already happened."

I was taken with the rich image of the chocolate bar. It confirmed my sense that Ann felt secretly separate from her mother but, still wrapped together; she was not allowed to admit or announce their separateness. As she was progressing in the treatment towards accepting her separateness, she felt guilty about this "betrayal".

The chocolate bar metaphor seemed to convey the essence of Ann's core object relationship in a condensed and rich way. As the treatment progressed, this metaphor grew richer, revealing more meanings that were gradually unfolding in the treatment. It also became a kind of touch-stone: every time I understood something new about Ann, I could see how it was represented in this condensed and creative image of the chocolate bar.

* * *

Over time, as Ann continued to talk about this complicated maternal bond, one that she tended to re-create in all her close relationships, I became aware of its actualization in our relationship as well, a non-verbal facet of the transference-countertransference that usually preceded understanding and symbolizing. During this period, which lasted a few months, I realized that I was constantly feeling uncomfortable about my interventions. On one hand, I felt that I was pushed to be active and say a lot because Ann was passive and laconic, but, at the same time, I felt I was too active and sensed that my interventions were too intense or too intrusive. I found myself trying to tone down my voice or to slow it down in order not to overwhelm her. Ann usually agreed with my interpretations and even added associations, but I was not sure whether it was an authentic participation, or her way of adjusting herself to me. She is extremely sensitive and usually a single word of mine was enough for her to understand my whole perspective, which she too easily adopted. On several occasions, after I said something, she stayed silent for a long time and then explained that my interpretation was too accurate and left her speechless. In such moments I felt as if I robbed her of her own ideas or feelings. It felt impossible to find a good place to be. It seemed that Ann had managed to draw me into that chocolate bar wrapper with her and through this projective identification I could feel her fear of expressing her separateness and being herself. Like her, I felt that expressing myself freely could hurt the other's feelings or damage the relationship. Through this identification with her experience I began to be able to understand it more deeply and put it into words for her.

As I did so, Ann began to verbalize similar themes in all her close relationships, especially with her boyfriend. She talked about this entangled dyad of two people who are afraid to act as individuated individuals, because any one's act affected the other too intensely. The process of making any decision together became exhausting, because each person tried to guess what the other person liked to do and then comply. The result was a total paralysis in the relationship exactly as it was in her relationship with her mother. She brought up another image to explain her experience in close relationships. She felt as if the other person was the container and she was a kind of fluid that always took the shape of the container. She was afraid to be the solid container since then she would force the other person to take her shape. She started to realize that something here in the treatment reminded her of this frustrating and impossible atmosphere she had with her mother.

*   *   *

As she reflected on this kind of entangled relationship, she gradually began to react to my existence as a separate being. These moments occurred especially when I made a change in the setting; for example, I once had to cancel a session at short notice because of a snow storm, revealing that I live out of town. Ann's reactions to these events were very charged and complex. On the more superficial level, she felt relief and even joy. She told me that the fact that I could express my own needs and assert myself enabled her to express hers and be more comfortable with herself. At the same time, on a deeper level, these occasions stirred up a lot of anxiety that was reflected in a series of anxiety dreams about the treatment. In these dreams there was a disruption of the treatment and everything went wrong. In one dream, we were sitting in a corridor with no privacy. I almost fell asleep in the middle of our session and was not available. In another, she dreamt that I had a baby who was screaming and Ann had to soothe her but did not manage to do so. When I directed Ann's attention to the anxiety, Ann said: "I have this feeling that when I think of you outside this room, our togetherness becomes impossible. Knowing something about you undermines my attempts to ignore that you have a life of your own." She added that whenever she saw my needs, she felt an immediate need to protect me and our relationship.

In the following sessions, Ann became more aware of this need to protect the other. She reflected again on the relationship with her mother and asked herself and me: "What is it that I have to protect her from?"

In the following week she tried to get an answer to that troubling question, by initiating a series of conversations with her mother. For the first time she dared to share with her mother her frustration in their relationship. She talked with her about their shared passivity, both of them walking on egg shells, trying to protect the other all the time. Her mother's response was surprising for both of us. The mother began to talk about her history as a daughter of Holocaust survivors. It was the first time in the nine months of treatment that Ann talked about her family's Holocaust history. She told me that her mother's parents escaped to France before the Second World War. They both lost both parents, who were probably killed by the Nazis. Ann's mother explained to her that maybe that is why she was always fearful that the family will fall apart and felt a constant need to protect everyone from bad things. I suggested to Ann that maybe she absorbed the unspoken message that negative feelings could destroy and endanger relationships. In that session, Ann dared for the first time to express anger towards her mother about burdening her with her own traumas. Her mother's parents never spoke about the Holocaust and her mother brought this unspoken and unspeakable loss and terror to her own family. Ann told me that as a child she had been obsessed with reading books and watching films about the Holocaust. She never knew why she was so attracted to this subject and never connected it to her own life. Now she understood that through the books she was trying to give words to her own personal holocaust. Her holocaust involved a lack of meaning, lack of words, feelings without content, horror without a story.

The discovery of her traumatic history shed light on many of Ann's issues: her intense sensitivity to her mother's distresses and her need to protect her; her sense of so many unspoken issues that she could not understand; her sensitivity to issues of separation and loss; her developmental guilt about having her own life; and her anxiety about expressing negative feelings, which she perceived as dangerous and destructive.

The story of the Holocaust added a new dimension to the chocolate bar image. Suddenly I had a picture of two people hiding together in the war, keeping their independence underground, hidden from the enemy. I thought again about Ann's relationship with her mother. Most probably every expression of Ann's separateness and the mundane small losses of a normal separation process between a mother and child were unbearable for Ann's mother as they stirred up the terrible separations, loss, and unresolved mourning of her own parents. I shared these insights with Ann.

* * *

During this period, around a year into the treatment, the issues of separation and separateness took centre stage in the treatment. Whereas in previous breaks from the treatment Ann expressed overwhelming, diffuse distress that she could not verbalize or connect in any way to our separation, during this period, this wordless experience was gradually filled in with content: memories, fantasies, and more differentiated feelings.

She remembered that during her childhood, separations always stirred up fantasies about death and loss or feelings of abandonment and guilt. She realized that she typically "emptied" her relationships a long time before she was going to leave. Now she became aware that she was doing the same with me before our breaks, trying to turn our relationship into an unimportant one to make it easier to leave. "It is unbearable to miss something that you cannot have," she told me, when she realized with some pain that our relationship has really become important to her. "It is the first time I am forming really meaningful relationships, with my boyfriend and here in the analysis." She could not as yet say "with you".

Ann now began to explore her need to create separations all the time and to live far away from her family and friends. She remembered that her parents had the same need to distance themselves from their own parents, both physically and emotionally. She speculated that they needed to escape from the unbearable atmosphere they absorbed in their post-traumatic environment. Ann added that by avoiding the trauma and by refraining from working it through, they paradoxically re-created the same atmosphere in their own family, from which she now needed to distance herself. Indigestible non-verbal terror, unbearable pain, and apocalyptic fantasies were always in the air.

Ann felt she has been "re-creating" her family history all her life, and began to explore the original trauma of her grandparents that had been unconsciously transmitted through the generations. Each of her maternal grandparents lost both their parents in the Holocaust. Her paternal grandparents did not lose their loved ones but they suffered other kinds of losses when they escaped to France. They lost property, status, and a sense of belonging, and experienced uncertainty, estrangement, and identity confusion. Her paternal grandfather had artistic talents which he gave up. He never adjusted to living in France and suffered a deep narcissistic injury from being expelled from his home land.

* * *

Ann's associations led us to her art and she asked me to look at some paintings she brought in. I was astonished to see the enormous impact this central conflict had on her art. The main theme in all the paintings was leaving, moving, and searching for a home that could never be reached. In several of them, you could see an old, funny-looking man, wearing old fashioned clothes and holding an old worn-out suitcase. The man looks as if he is walking on a seemingly endless journey. Another group of paintings centered around a lone figure lying on a raft, floating in the middle of the ocean, looking frightened and confused. The atmosphere in all these paintings is one of total loneliness and estrangement. Ann told me that while working on these creations in London, she did not have the slightest idea that it was connected to her own history, but she now realized that maybe it was her own identification with the story of her paternal grandfather. As a child, everyone in the family told Ann how much she resembled this grandfather and she was seen as his successor.

I said to her: "You carry within yourself the history of the family, the unbearable unspoken experiences that you absorbed, and you unconsciously tell these stories over and over again". I reflected on her need to be the "wandering Jew". Her solution to her personal holocaust was a compromise formation between her need to save her family on the one hand, and her need to renounce that role on the other, between her need to escape the transmitted trauma as well as the need to relive it again and again.

* * *

Gradually, as we moved into the second year of the analysis, the fruits of our work were reflected in Ann's becoming more separate and more expressive while her clothing and appearance became less eccentric. I thought to myself that maybe she was able to give up the external proofs of her uniqueness, now that she was developing a clearer sense of autonomy. I noticed a new autonomy in her relationship with her mother, with her boyfriend, and with me. During that period Ann's mother was again depressed and panicky after Ann's sister got married and moved to another town. The mother was overwhelmed and reacted in her "Holocaustic" way (Ann's expression) as if it were a disaster, and had no "membrane" when she shared with Ann her unbearable distress. But this time, Ann was able to set emotional boundaries and was not consumed by the mother's distress. She confronted her mother and explained to her that she needed to distance herself in order not to get depressed too. She said to her mother: "I am not willing to sacrifice myself. I need to protect myself". She also told the mother that "getting married is not a disaster. It is actually a happy thing". In sessions she expressed a wish to renounce her special role with her mother and said humorously that she wanted to "divorce her mother" but was afraid to do so until she could find a substitute, who would be willing to listen to the mother's distresses.

Ann also started to express her need for boundaries and space within the treatment. In one session, after I commented about her need for boundaries and her fear of setting boundaries in a more direct way, she stayed silent for the last ten minutes of the session. I felt it was important not to interrupt the silence. I felt she was starting to signal her boundaries with me, showing the first signs of being able to be alone in my presence.

In subsequent sessions, there were many moments of silence when Ann chose to be alone. She also set boundaries by telling me when she wanted to change the subject or wanted to stop talking about something that was too distressing for her. There were several instances in which she expressed anger with me when she felt that my interventions forced her to deal with the emotional meaning of something when she still needed to deny or ignore it. I felt it was important not to interpret these reactions as resistance since I saw them as precious buds of autonomy.

* * *

During the second year of the analysis, our focus moved to Ann's wishes and fears regarding closeness and togetherness. She told me that in her family there was no real intimacy and the relationships were kind of shallow. From very early on, she got used to automatically warding off intense feelings and wishes. She realized that her current relationships were also shallow and unsatisfactory. She became aware of a wish to really give herself in the analysis and expressed pain and frustration about not being able to do it.

I became aware of sharp fluctuations from session to session. On occasion, she would suddenly begin to talk in a more direct way about her feelings and about the transference and then, after these more intimate sessions, she became detached and withdrawn again, severing the links between affect and thought. These estranged sessions threw some light on Ann's fears of intimacy which had to do with primitive oral fantasies about intrusion, engulfment, and fusion. She talked about these fears in a concrete way. She told me about her various somatic symptoms like stomach aches and mysterious viruses that infiltrated her body and disrupted her ability to function. She gradually realized that these fantasies came to her mind after intense interactions with people with whom she was close. In her fantasy, close interactions with her intrusive and demanding objects were experienced as if a foreign body intruded into her and disrupted everything from within. We could then better understand an eating ritual that we had discussed many times before. Every couple of months she goes on a severe diet for several weeks. Now, we connected it to her experience of being engaged in too close and overwhelming relationships with her mother, her boyfriend, and with me—the toxic effects of which she needed to empty herself of, in order to regain a clearer sense of self.

During this period, especially in these estranged sessions, I also found it difficult to talk to Ann in a direct way, especially about our relationship. For example, in one of the sessions she mentioned a wish to move back to Europe and shared with me some of her tentative plans. She did not mention her plans for the future (and the future of the treatment) again for a long time, and I did not raise the issue with her. I realized that I was colluding with her defences and participating in a kind of an unspoken agreement not to talk directly about it. Sometimes I felt that when she talked about other relationships, we both knew that we were actually talking about our relationship, in a displaced way.

When I tried to direct Ann's attention to these issues, she tried to explain to me how she experienced our relationship. She said she did not experience me as a real object that existed outside her. She felt as if I was just reflecting back her own thoughts and feelings and the interactions between us were experienced as a kind of virtual dialogue within herself. "Maybe", she said, "I am afraid to see you as a real person and to see our relationship as a real, vivid, and significant one." She added that that is how she felt with her mother and commented that she felt as if her mother was always with us in the room. She had a dream that her boyfriend proposed to her and showed her a plastic dog that he was carrying around. She commented that dogs for her were symbols of attachment but in their relationship the attachment did not always feel real. She expressed frustration and despair about being stuck in this plastic and unreal kind of experience.

* * *

I began to look at the chocolate bar image from another angle. It was not just that Ann's *separateness*—symbolized by the two separate pieces of chocolate—was hidden and unacknowledged. She also hid her secret *attachment* to her mother—the fact that the two of them were inextricably and suffocatingly wrapped together, bound in a secret agreement not to speak, and even not to know, about the Holocaust trauma they were living out with each other. Now as this was actualized in the transference-countertransference relationship, we both felt the entangled bond and the intensity of the dilemma— the wish to break out of the wrapper and feel our connectedness as real and significant, as well as the resistance and fear to do so. I reflected on this style of attachment that was probably transmitted through the three generations. I could imagine how, after the unbearable loss that her grandmother had suffered, it was so frightening to get attached again, to take the risk to feel one's own neediness, and to love again. Maybe that was why Ann and her mother formed this compromise formation—to be secretly attached but not really attached, and at the same time to be secretly separate but not fully separate.

Ann's frustration about being imprisoned in the analysis and within herself grew from session to session and I began to feel a little frustrated and impatient too. In one of these sessions, I found myself making a very long interpretation, telling Ann about my new insight and reminding her of the chocolate bar dream, which she had already forgotten. I suggested to her that the avoidance of talking about the relationship has been re-created between us. I felt that I was less cautious than usual at that moment and that my tone of voice was much more passionate and emotional. Ann stayed silent and I became a little worried that I was overwhelming her, but, when the session ended, at the door, Ann looked directly into my eyes and said in an excited voice: "Thank you". It was a unique moment of a more direct interaction between us.

In the following session, Ann expressed feelings of joy and hope. She told me that when I talked in such an emotional way, she felt that I liberated her for a moment from this frustrating feeling of imprisonment. She said that she suddenly could feel me as a separate person who was very different from her mother. She could sense my personality and experienced our relationship at that moment as alive and real, one in which I really dared to express myself.

In the following week Ann was excited and felt a little "hypo manic". She had detailed and excited dreams. In one of them she gave birth to a baby daughter and in another she dreamt about both of us practising gymnastics together and felt that we had a much more intimate kind of physical contact in the dream.

She also had many important insights about her relationship with her mother and about the prohibition against verbalizing conflicts and talking directly about their relationship. She realized that they had a kind of a secret language—a code—through which they communicated what was going on between them. She gave me an example of such a dialogue. She recently wondered why her mother had not answered her letters in a while and was worried that her mother was angry with her about her decision not to go back to France yet. She called her mother and asked her how the weather in France was. Her mother responded in a cold voice that the weather was bad and complained about a terrible headache. Ann felt that they were actually talking about the atmosphere between them. The real conversation went something like: Ann: "I feel guilty about wanting to stay in the States. How do you feel about it? Are you OK?" Her mother answers: "I am sad. It is painful ... ." Her description also accurately reflected our mode of communication over the prior few months. I felt that we had also been talking in code.

It seemed that this kind of relationship protected Ann and her mother from the "dangerously emotional relationship" they both feared. We gained a better understanding about these primitive fears of closeness through a 19th century story that Ann had read. She brought this story to a session without really knowing what she was trying to communicate. The story was about women vampires who formed intimate, erotic kinds of bonds. The narrator is a young woman who was a victim of the beautiful woman vampire. Gradually and patiently, the vampire tempted her into a love relationship and would secretly bite her on her breast while she was asleep. Every bite made the victim more ill, since in this process the illness of the vampire was transmitted to her. The illness was a kind of depression since the woman's vitality was sucked out by the woman vampire. The victim was about to die and to turn into a vampire herself, as it had always happened in the previous generations of the vampires, but this time the woman was saved, at the last moment, by her father.

I thought it was a beautiful metaphor for the way the Holocaust trauma was transmitted through the generations of Ann's family. Through merger and love and in Ann's fantasy maybe through the incorporation of mother's milk—(the bites were on the breast)—the trauma was transmitted to the next generation, creating a new agent to carry the trauma forward. In Ann's unconscious, it was dangerous to love because love was poisonous and deadly.

We talked about Ann's fears of closeness that were reflected in this story. Ann told me that when she gets close to another person, an open channel is formed between the two people and things are transmitted between them without her being able to choose what to take in and what to leave out. She was afraid that she would absorb bad things that belonged to the other person or that good things would be drained out of her. That was how it was with her mother, who projected into her the unbearable trauma and also robbed her of her vitality when she (the mother) was depressed. She used a metaphor about breathing saying: "You cannot choose to take in just the oxygen and leave out the carbon dioxide." She smiled when she commented that we were also sitting together in a closed room with no windows, breathing the same air. I felt that this time the anxiety about our relationship was less overwhelming and Ann could relate to it with a sense of humour.

* * *

More recently, Ann began talking in a more direct way about our relationship. She had a fantasy of coming to a session and saying to me in a direct way: "Michal, let's talk about us." She started very hesitantly to express her own wishes as well as the variety of emotions that the relationship with me stirs up in her: dependency needs and longings, wishes for autonomy and for closeness, sadness, anxiety, and anger. She has become more present and lively and the dissociative states and moments of traumatic affect have become less frequent and less intense.

In one session she compared herself to a snail who dared to take his head out and see the world. She felt she was coming out of the "prison" and said she could not understand how she avoided relating to me in a more direct way for such a long time and how she refused to perceive our relationship as a personal one.

We are now in a really exciting period. She seems to be emerging from the confines of the wrapper and discovering me, a real object outside her, who she can desire. Or maybe it is more accurate to say that we have both emerged from our transference-countertransference wrapper, and have begun to be able to talk more directly about our relationship.

* * *

I would like to share with you one last aspect of the work with Ann. Throughout the process of writing this case, I found it hard to share the experience with my imaginary readers. I struggled with many dilemmas: how would I be able to describe this complex and intuitive process and put into words this unique experience that has to such a large degree been non-verbal? I reflected on my resistance to sharing my story with a third party and realized how it reflected once more the chocolate bar image. I felt that Ann and I were wrapped together in our intense transference-countertransference relationship, feeling a need to hide our togetherness from the world—at times perceiving any third party as the enemy. But at the same time, in Ann's story about the vampires, the third person is the saviour. In her fantasy the father takes her out of the dangerous fusion with the mother. Maybe the analysis itself is a kind of a third, and the process of analysing and verbalizing the "un-thought known" was what helped her to hatch from this disabling symbiosis and to consolidate her own autonomy and develop more capacity for intimacy.

DISCUSSION OF "SECRETLY ATTACHED, SECRETLY SEPARATE"

Trauma in action: the enacted dimension of analytic process in a third generation Holocaust survivor

Gil A. Katz

As background to my discussion of Michal Talby-Abarbanel's rich and evocative case presentation, I will present and expand on the contemporary Freudian concept of enactment. The term was introduced into the psychoanalytic lexicon by Ted Jacobs (1986) over two decades ago and continues to generate a large, productive literature on the subject (e.g., Chused, 1991; Jacobs, 1991b, 1993a, 1994, 1997, 2001b; Johan, 1992; McLaughlin, 1987, 1991, 1993; Renik, 1993; Roughton, 1993; Smith, 1993a, 1993b, 1997). More recently, I introduced the concept of the "enacted dimension of analytic process" (Katz, 1998, 2002). As I will now further explicate, I prefer thinking in terms of a dimension of experience, because the word "enactment" has the connotation of a discrete, behavioural event, whereas the essence of what needs to be conceptualized is a dynamically evolving, unconscious process.

In all treatments, a new version—what Freud (1905) called "a new edition" and what Poland (1992) has termed "an original creation"—of the patient's early traumas, conflicts, and formative object relationships is inevitably created, without awareness or intent, in the here-and-now of the analytic dyad. This new treatment version may evolve over long stretches of time, sometimes years, only becoming available for verbal symbolization and analytic use at unconsciously determined meaningful junctures in the treatment process. As noted above, I previously described this process as taking place in the treatment's enacted dimension. Analytic process, I conceptualized, comprises two interwoven dimensions: the familiar verbally symbolized dimension (free-association, interpretation, etc.), and the enactively symbolized dimension in which unconscious, non-verbal communications are continuously taking place. These are not dichotomous dimensions or processes, but are inextricably interwoven at all times: patient and analyst are continuously expressing transference and countertransference on both the enacted and the verbal levels simultaneously. What we have come to refer to as interactive enactments are often the inevitable result of the patient's unconscious efforts, in the enacted dimension of the treatment, to induce the analyst into playing a part in, and thereby actualizing, an unconscious object relationship (Sandler, 1976). This process thus constitutes more than projection or projective-identification alone, because it specifically includes the involvement of the *analyst's* unconscious in its creation. These spontaneous creations in analytic space are crucial ingredients of the therapeutic action of psychoanalysis, because, as Freud (1914) said long ago, "One cannot overcome an enemy who is absent or not within range ..." (p. 152). "We must treat the patient's illness," he said, "not as an event of the past, but as a present day force" (p. 150). In an enacted process, the past is not just remembered, it is re-lived—past experience and current experience become linked with an immediacy and affective vitality that inspires enormous conviction. When these actualization processes become conscious, they form the basis for experientially-based interpretive work in the verbal dimension of the treatment, creating the kind of *experiential insight* that produces meaningful psychoanalytic change.

For many contemporary Freudian analysts, the concept of enactment has gradually supplemented the traditional understanding of transference and countertransference. For these analysts, the traditional conceptions of transference and countertransference denote too much of an artificial separation from the process by which the patient's unconscious fantasy is brought to life in the unconsciously lived-out drama of the analytic pair. The Freudian idea of an interpenetration of transference and countertransference does not, however, embrace a social-constructivist epistemology or an intersubjective psychoanalytic theory, which view the analyst's subjectivity as "co-constructing" or "co-creating" the patient's transference. In the Freudian perspective, it is only one part of an enactment—the overt manifestation of the transference-countertransference intertwining—that can be said to be unconsciously co-constructed or co-created. The patient's transference and the analyst's countertransference themselves, however, are not co-created. Each is a unique, separate entity, each the product of a unique psychic organization. The genetic origins of the patient's transference are not the same as those of the analyst, each party has a different unconscious need to create the enactment, and each has his or her own separate experience of the enactment they created together. The transference and countertransference are similar enough, however, that when each is unconsciously actualized by the other, two intrapsychic dramas blend to look like one interpersonal play.

Also central to the Freudian perspective is the understanding that enactments are not a part of technique. Technique is what we consciously, intentionally strive to do; enactments are the observable aspect of a continuously evolving *unconscious* transference-countertransference *process*. To put it another way: enactments are a descriptive part of analytic process, not a prescriptive component of technique. There is a line in a John Lennon song (1980) that goes: "Life is what happens to you while you are making other plans." To paraphrase: enactments are what happen to you while you are doing psychoanalysis. They are an inevitable part of analytic process and, after they become conscious, they are analysed as are any other psychic phenomenon, such as a dream or a fantasy. In fact, an enactment, as a product of the mind (in this case, two minds), can be usefully likened to a dream (in this case, a two-party, waking dream (see Kern, 1987)). The overt, visible, manifest component of an enactment bears the same relationship to its dynamically unconscious transference-countertransference component that the manifest content of a dream bears to the latent content of a dream. Dreams use sensory images as the vehicle to provide unconscious wishes with disguised, but experientially "real", expression; enactments use action (both motor action and verbal action) to provide unconscious transference and countertransference wishes with disguised, but experientially "real", expression.

There is one sense, however, in which enactments can be said to be a part of technique. A central component of analytic technique is the frame. Setting up and maintaining an analytic frame (as opposed to, for instance, a behaviour therapy frame) is what creates the space for these unplanned enacted processes to occur and be explored. And it is in reference to the frame that enactments attain their analytic meaning: enactments are *unintended but meaningful departures* from the optimal analytic attitude that the frame is designed to promote. Additionally, while not a *formal* component of technique, an increased sensitivity to enacted processes expands the array of data available for analytic investigation to include the world of transference actualizations that are unconsciously created and communicated through action, both verbal and non-verbal, by both patient and analyst.

Psychoanalysts have long debated the question of what is mutative about the process, and contemporary discussions continue, unfortunately, to be dichotomized along theoretical/political lines. There is the belief, generally associated with Freudian analysis, that psychic change occurs through insight gained via transference interpretation; there is also the belief, generally associated with relational-interpersonal analysis, that change occurs through new experience within the analytic relationship. This dichotomy is related to another, the one between one-person and two-person models of mind. Both of these polarizations are unfortunate. Regarding insight versus experience, in actuality both operate together and potentiate each other (see Jacobs, 1993a). Insights are often needed in order for new experiences to register as truly new and break free of the sway of transference. New experiences, both inside and outside the treatment, often promote insight. And, in my opinion, one-person *and* two-person models are *both* valuable and informative perspectives on the treatment process. Enactments are noteworthy phenomena because they illustrate the therapeutic interweaving of insight and experience as well as the need for both one-person and two-person perspectives.

In an enacted process, the patient's unconscious world of self and object representations (a one-person perspective) comes to life in the unconsciously experienced enacted dimension of the treatment relationship (a two-person perspective). (Again, by "two-*person*" I refer not to two *people* and their overt interactions; I am referring to the *inter-psychic* (see Loewald, 1960) component of that interaction—the unconscious effect each psyche has on the other.) In a Freudian analysis, when this unconscious interactive process finally becomes available for conscious reflection, the primary focus is the one-person perspective, that of the *patient's* experience. Through verbal symbolization and interpretive work, the patient's experience is given new meaning. The therapeutic process here is as follows: the patient first has the experience of the analyst's becoming, inadvertently, his or her old object (which the analyst inadvertently does to an extent) and then, via the interpretive function of the analyst, the patient has the experience of the analyst's becoming a new therapeutic object (at first a partly-old and partly-new object, gradually becoming ever more new and ever less coloured by transference). Interpretations not only convey content (insight), they are also themselves new object-relational experiences. At one and the same time, the analyst's timely interpretations also provide the patient with greater understanding and mastery over his or her relationship with his or her internal objects, which can eventuate in new ways of understanding and experiencing him- or herself and more adaptive and more satisfying relationships with other people. Experience *and* insight operate *together* to promote therapeutic change.

Analytic treatment of patients with significant early trauma or object loss illustrate the enacted dimension of analytic process with particular clarity, as they often centre around dramatic treatment experiences that are the manifestations of an elaborately developed, enacted transference (and countertransference) process that tends to remain, sometimes for long periods, inaccessible to verbal symbolization and unresponsive to interpretive work. The treatment of such patients typically requires an extensive period for the trauma to achieve symbolic actualization within the transference-countertransference matrix, during which time patient and analyst may remain unaware of crucial aspects of the re-creative meaning and analytic significance of the patient's (and the analyst's) behaviour.

The treatment of Ann, so beautifully described by Michal Talby-Abarbanel, illustrates how aspects of unspeakable trauma—trauma that must be dissociated because it cannot be symbolized in words—can be passed on, unconsciously, from generation to generation. In this discussion, I will try to illustrate the particular nature of Ann's trauma, the dissociation evident in her psychic make-up, and the ways in which her unmetabolized, unverbalizable Holocaust trauma gained representation and expression through alternate channels—her life-long somatic symptoms and behavioural patterns, her many artistic creations and, within her analysis, in the enacted dimension of the transference-countertransference matrix.

The treatment of Ann

As Talby-Abarbanel described, a striking feature of the early work with Ann was her frequent states of traumatic affect that she could not process or digest. Ann would feel flooded and overwhelmed by unnamed and unnameable affects in one session, followed in the very next session by pervasive emotional numbness and detached ideation. To Talby-Abarbanel, these detached thoughts, by virtue of their content, were clearly related to the intense affect of the previous session. Ann, however, experienced no connection. The nature of this splitting and dissociation became understandable only much later, nearly nine months into the treatment, when the material emerged about the annihilation of much of her mother's extended family, and the dislocation of much of her father's extended family, in the Holocaust. Because the emotional sequelae of these devastating traumas were transmitted from generation to generation—from her grandparents, to her parents, to Ann—without ever being put into words, the unmetabolized emotional experiences became sequestered in an ego state that was completely dissociated from Ann's otherwise intact symbolizing capacities. Unable to be accessed on the verbally symbolic level, the family Holocaust trauma was, instead, encoded and expressed on the sensorimotor level—in Ann's unmetabolized affect states, her somatic symptoms, and her eating rituals—and, more globally, in her propensity to live her life as a "wandering Jew", her near-compulsive need to move to a different country every couple of years. These modes of experiencing and regulating the trauma organized virtually every aspect of her functioning, influencing relationships and decisions, large and small, in her daily life.

The split-off experience of her family's Holocaust trauma was also represented and expressed, throughout Ann's life, and without any conscious awareness, in her paintings and her many artistic creations. These became a key feature of her analysis as well: drawings, paintings, and stories all supplemented Ann's equally rich dreams and associative images and metaphors. The treatment was a veritable multimedia presentation. Being blessed with artistic talent from birth provided Ann with a channel for the expression of the unsymbolizable experiences she was forced to carry, and they no doubt saved her from more severe psychological disruption in her development. And, equally fortunate for Ann, was finding Talby-Abarbanel, an analyst who could understand these dissociated symbols, tolerate her psychic split and emotional dilemma, and then, with enormous empathy and sensitivity, enable her gradually to come to terms with her world and begin a process of integration and repair.

A third, powerful, way the dissociated aspects of the trauma found symbolic representation in the treatment was in the non-verbal, enacted dimension of the transference-countertransference matrix. What found symbolic actualization was both the dissociated and un-symbolized existential anxieties of the Holocaust, as well as the non-verbal and unacknowledged arrangement with her mother that maintained the dissociation. From the treatment's inception, and for the better part of the treatment to the date reported, this powerful, non-verbal aspect of the analytic relationship formed its continuous backdrop—but again, it was only understandable much later, in retrospect. As described by Talby-Abarbanel, it constituted the essence of those long and intense periods in the treatment in which patient and analyst literally felt enveloped in that chocolate bar wrapper—secretly attached and secretly separate—a tortured relationship, or to use Ann's phrase an "emotionally dangerous" relationship, that neither wanted to be in, but from which neither could leave. Before the material about the Holocaust emerged—that is, before Talby-Abarbanel could have any clear idea what this transference-countertransference configuration was about—there were those long periods, as Talby-Abarbanel reported, in which both felt like they were walking on eggshells with each other—Ann fearful that any expression of her autonomous self would destroy her analyst, and her analyst fearful that any intervention, or any non-intervention, would destroy the treatment. So sealed in their wrapper were they that, at moments, Talby-Abarbanel actually felt Ann's unformulated, inchoate terror and could not be sure from who, or from where, this experience originated—there was "no membrane", to again use Ann's phrase. As Ann and her mother had long done, Talby-Abarbanel also found herself speaking with Ann in code, not talking about the real thing or else talking in displaced arenas, both of them fully knowing, but never acknowledging, what they were really talking about. And even after the material about the Holocaust finally began to emerge, Talby-Abarbanel found herself feeling that discussion of any experience of attachment and loss—particularly as experienced in the analytic relationship—was inadmissible, a dangerous and forbidden subject in the analysis, the same taboo under which three generations of holocaust survivors had suffered.

This re-creation in the transference-countertransference was abruptly shattered when Talby-Abarbanel, without conscious planning, suddenly found herself putting into words for Ann—in one lengthy, powerful intervention and with, what was for her she tells us, an atypical degree of intensity and comprehensiveness—everything she had actually come to understand for a while, but from her position within the transference-countertransference wrapper could not previously utter. Talby-Abarbanel states that she worried about her unusual intervention, but she could also see that she felt freed and more alive—it was as if the allied forces had suddenly liberated the camps and a new world became visible and possible. I see Talby-Abarbanel's intervention as *an inseparable* part of the enacted process, a response to what was likely Ann's communication, both conscious and unconscious, that she was ready to emerge from the maternal transference-countertransference wrapper both had been in for nearly a year and a half, and to begin the process of bearing witness to and integrating—integrating, rather than dissociating—this aspect of her psychic heritage and coming to terms with it as best she might. Through this enacted process, Ann was afforded the opportunity to convert what had been passively endured in childhood into something that was actively (even if unconsciously) intended and which, through this "new edition", could now be actively mastered. To return to the theoretical point I made earlier about co-creation: while the particular shape of this new analyst-patient interaction was co-created by the analytic pair, Ann's transference issues and Talby-Abarbanel's countertransference issues were unique to their individual history and internal dynamics.

This entire process—the creation, and the analysis, of the new edition of the trauma in the enacted dimension of the transference-countertransference matrix—was thus a necessary transitional state that allowed the dissociated trauma to achieve a higher level of symbolic representation, and thereby become available for analytic consideration and working through. It was also a *formative* psychic activity. It was an analytic process in which new psychic representations were constructed as Ann's dissociated ego states were gradually integrated, rather than an analytic process characterized by a lifting of repression and the recall of a once conscious representational memory. That aspect of analytic treatment of patients with such severe, dissociated trauma only begins to be possible at this point.

A final word about Ann's analyst. In addition to her analytic fortitude and commitment to her patient, Talby-Abarbanel brought to this analysis a well-developed capacity and talent for using her *self*—her own fantasies, reveries, and emotional states—in the service of understanding her patient. Her capacity to oscillate between, on the one hand, an immediate, intense, and direct identification with her patient and, on the other hand, a differentiated state of observation and analytic assessment—evident in her presentation—was a key ingredient in the creation, sustaining, and ultimate emergence from the enacted maternal transference. These qualities enabled Talby-Abarbanel simultaneously to be a participant in the undifferentiated wrapper experience—going to the edge, even, at moments, a bit over the edge—and also to be a separate, differentiated self, one with which Ann could ultimately identify. I have been privileged to discuss her work.

CHAPTER ELEVEN

A new Freudian synthesis: reflections and a perspective

Norbert Freedman

With the publication of this volume we are celebrating 100 years of Freud's manifest presence in America. It was in 1909 that Freud delivered his Clark lectures on "The Origin and Development of Psychoanalysis". While Freud's teachings had been well-known, and indeed they had led to the invitation by G. Stanley Hall, president of Clark University, these papers have marked the constant presence of his work in the United States. This past century has brought with it a marvellous history of reworking and reformulation. These modifications have reached their culmination during the second half of the 20th century, particularly in the work of those second generation analysts who embraced an object relations perspective, namely, Kohut, Balint, Winnicott, and Loewald. It is on the shoulders of these contributions that this current new 21st century contribution has been built.

The title "*A New Freudian Synthesis*" is evocative and provocative as well. It is evocative because it immediately conjures up the question: "What is Freudian about these papers?" It is provocative because it also elicits the question: "In what ways are they no longer Freudian in the original sense?" And the title of this book challenges us to arrive at a synthesis that might tell us how divergent views can be brought under one umbrella.

What is Freudian about these contributions?

Every paper in this book deals with the recognition of the importance of unconscious fantasies or minimally of unconscious processes that need to surface in the course of psychoanalytic work. To be sure, these papers are not concerned with the topographical unconscious but with a state of consciousness within a structural perspective. All papers find the transference concept indispensable, as an intrinsic agent of working through. Transference is viewed as the transposition and replay of derivatives of infantile fantasies in the here and now. In psychoanalytic technique, they all include a reliance on free association as facilitating and eliciting unformulated fantasies. Anticipating recent developments, free association facilitates, as Bach notes, a bringing together of alternate states of consciousness, objective and subjective self-awareness, and is intrinsic to meaning making (Vorus, chapter 9). Most important, every clinical contribution makes explicit a reliance upon the analytic frame, which emphasizes constancy, the value of abstinence, and the general judicious preservation of anonymity (Ellman, chapter 7). They all recognize that sooner or later interpretation marks a defining moment in mental transformation but the when and how of interpretation is a continuing source of dialogue and leads to a consideration of recent revisions. Finally, from the point of view of pathogenesis, they all recognize the importance of Freud's early notion of the traumatic moment (notably Hurvich, chapter 4) and these traumatic moments are situated in the earliest phases of object relatedness recapitulated in the transference.

What Freudian concepts have been excluded or revised?

This question is best answered by Druck's chapter 1 on "Modern Conflict Theory" and with it he sets the frame for the entire book. The phenomenon of conflict and compromise formation is not denied but a reliance in analytic technique on analysing pathological compromise formations through interpretation and confrontation is avoided. While in the current intellectual climate there indeed is an appreciation of developmental phenomena, a reliance on fixation points (oral, anal, genital) is eschewed for such a focus tends to fragment psychoanalytic listening. In its earliest days psychoanalysis was deeply rooted in Bleulerian diagnostic thinking, notably Freud's (1894) paper "The Neuro-Psychoses of Defense". Today pathology is defined as varieties of narcissistic states of consciousness. Hence, emphasis on diagnostic classifications is minimal. The focus on the resolution of the Oedipus complex as an ideal for analytic working through is replaced by an aim of resolving the earliest aspects of object relatedness. Disruption in the early mother-infant interactions is a theme throughout. The classical analytic patient with a fixation point on Oedipal triangulation has disappeared. In Druck's language, there is not a single paper in this volume that embraces the "Modern Conflict Model" and all that is to follow are variations and particularization of what Druck calls the "Modern Structural Theory".

With the internalization of a structural perspective, new visions of clinical change have been introduced. Throughout this volume, explicitly or implicitly, clinical change is described as a shift in mental states from experiences that are at first implicit and unformulated and which then become formulated in spoken language. In my vocabulary, they have been symbolized. I will end this discussion with a proposition: "Working through is repetition transformed".

In what way is this an innovative Freudian synthesis?

The term particularization of the structural model, with a focus on developmental deficit, is crucial. All but one of the papers rely on the second generation of analysts whose work emerged during the second half of the 20th century, as stated previously: Winnicott, Balint, Kohut, and Loewald with the exception being Ferenczi, who belongs to the first generation but whose work, in spirit, anticipated current trends. Each contributor offers his or her own particular readings of these authors. In what follows I will develop the main thesis that, whereas each of our authors closely internalizes their own rootedness in the respective second generation analysts, they do so by suggesting specific innovative "vehicles of transformation", which I see to be specific to each of the contributions. As I read them, I perceived in their particularity a quality which allows us to recognize a third generation of analysts built upon the shoulders of the preceding ones. Inherent in this new version of a "Modern Freudians" vision is also both an appreciation of and differentiation from the contribution from recent relational analysts (cf. Aaron, Benjamin). The role of intersubjectivity as a defining baseline for all analytic work, so much emphasized by these authors cannot be gainsaid. However, each of the authors in the present volume also advanced a distinct line of differentiation that eschews the intrinsic narrowness inherent in the exclusive reliance on action and interaction.

A gradient in the vehicles of transformation

In these essays, in spite of consensus, I perceive a gradient in which the authors chart the pathway of overcoming the agony of primitive mental states. These I shall term "vehicles of transformation". I shall single out three of these vehicles, as they are shared by all authors but singled out by some and not by others. The goal of all analytic work is one that aims towards re-integration (not conflict resolution per se), and relatively distinct pathways towards this attainment can be distinguished. One strand derived from a reading of these papers stresses the inevitable confrontation with the abyss of object loss through the experience of a state of absolute dependency as the starting point towards working through (as it is explicit in chapter 5 by Thaler but is also suggested in chapter 6 by Libbey). A second strand inheres in the focus on the selected active and judicious analytic engagement as articulated by Ellman in chapter 7 on what I shall call the selected unexpected fact leading to selected self-disclosure. In chapter 8 Frankel similarly relies on the phenomenon of selected engagement at those moments in which the analyst realizes that countertransference might be a repetition of compliance generated by the patient's "identification with the aggressor". Thirdly, there is an implicit interpretive mode of listening most clearly illustrated in Vorus's reconciliation (chapter 9) between modern Kleinian and Contemporary Ego Psychology. This implicit interpretive mode of listening is also present in the work by Katz and Talby-Abarbanel (chapter 10), and reached an innovative peak in Hurvich's introduction of the concept of "Annihilation Anxiety".

The discovery and specification of those pathways that lead to transformation of "primitive mental states" addresses crucial issues in contemporary psychoanalytic thought. The vehicles of transformation spell out modes of overcoming the roots of early pathogenic trauma. In the current psychoanalytic literature, there is precisely this focus on primitive mental states (Mitrani, 2001), but the pathways towards re-integration have not as yet been sufficiently charted out. In this book, the vehicles of transformation are 1. the task of metabolizing the agony of the abyss of object loss; 2. the use of a mode of selected self-disclosure leading to the re-finding of a new inner object; and 3. the maintenance of a continuous mode of interpretive analytic listening. These steps, cumulatively, give new shape to the direction of analytic work. It is in this sense that this is a third generation Freudian synthesis. And now to the details.

The inevitable agony of the abyss of un-integration and disintegration

This crucial component of transformation is of course rooted in the work of Winnicott but here it is spelled out in vivid particularity in Thaler's essay. He traces a sequence of recovery: it begins with the phase of un-integration—severe disturbances of continuity and ego integration; followed by explicit transference regression, projection, and dissociation; a phase of reversal—of apparent re-integration; then bursting forth in "the breakdown phase proper", the pure culture of disintegration; culminating in a series of eight powerful dreams, which offered a symbolic reconstruction of earliest developmental trauma. The theoretical foundations of this work can also be understood through the broad theoretical perspective offered by Bach (chapter 3) but in its particularity and its innovative depiction it is a unique synthetic achievement by Thaler.

The phenomenon of breakdown at its peak is marked by a process of disintegration, which to my mind is also a manifestation of de-symbolization, that is, it marks not only the absence of the symbolic but the active destruction of meaning, of significance, and of cohesion (to my mind the distinction between the de-symbolized and the un-symbolized sub-symbolic experience is an important one). Prior to breakdown we observed several oscillations, namely, transference regression followed by momentary reconsolidation. It is of interest to me that the oscillation between projective—introjective states so crucial in the Kleinian view of the "paranoid schizoid position" as viewed by Thaler's presentation can be distinguished from the breakdown phenomenon, which to my mind is a state of disintegration. Here two primitive mental states need to be distinguished. Only after confrontation with active transference regression do we observe the emergence of communicated symbolic forms. This is thematically illustrated in eight successive dreams reported by Thaler. These give flesh to the recovery process.

This entire evolution is governed by several assumptions, namely that first even in the face of disintegration phenomena there must be present in the patient some healthy component towards object seeking. There is an implicit wish towards re-finding the object; that secondly the very presence of mobilization of a shared state of consciousness facilitates the transformation from an object of absence to an object of presence; and that it is this reactivation now only through active engagement with the analyst that allows for the symbolization to arise: "Darkness precedes dawn."

The progression just outlined is rendered persuasive through Bach's notion of unification of fragmentation through the establishment of a mutual state of consciousness, and the ability to enter into another person's life. Bach in this line of thought provides a generic principal for all analytic encounters and is shared by all authors. Most recently the same theme has been enunciated by Steingart's (1995) emphasis on *analytic love*, Ellman's (2007) emphasis on *analytic trust*, and Grunes' (1984) emphasis on the *therapeutic object relationship*.

* * *

This pivotal proposition advanced by Bach has been documented and confirmed in numerous quarters over the decades. This proposition has been given an innovative form by Libbey in her "Narcissistic States, Shame, and the Treatment Process: a Case Illustration".

Libbey organizes her presentation around the idea that change arises in a particular state of transition; not a state of absolute dependency, as in Winnicott, but in the confrontation with mortifying and paralyzing bursts of shame—an overwhelming experience of object loss. Further, the process of recovery had as its starting point not that of "breakdown" or un-integration, but in Libbey's case it was observed in a patient with relatively intact ego functioning. Such a finding suggests that the processes of transformation described in this volume have generality and hence can be applied to a range of psychopathological syndromes.

Most important, Libbey's chapter offers a unique variant of analytic technique, namely, a distinctive version of the intra-and inter-subjective engagement by both participants. Thus, in reading the material we are treated to a micro-analysis of the patient's implicit subjectivity, the analyst's subjectivity, the analyst's reflections about her inter-subjective experiences and the patient's reception of that dialogue—and further as these are evoked in the four distinct phases of analytic discourse. In this account she makes vivid use of a line of psychoanalytic thought articulated by Smith (1993b) in a defining paper on *conflictual listening*, and especially through her account of the analyst's subjectivity she describes a method that was first formulated by Jacobs's (1993b) contribution and which has influenced our field over the last two decades. I shall centre the remainder of my comments on this aspect of her work.

This is a story of an English professor suffering from writer's block. He experienced himself caught in complete paralysis of objectification. He felt himself to be trapped in a plaster cast so that his subjectivity did not exist. Yet, these irreconcilable self states were resolved through an agonizing experience of shame, which the patient called a "blast furnace". Indeed, such powerful affects have their paralyzing impact on resistance, especially in narcissistic patients, and this potential impasse was challenged through Libbey's use of her own subjectivity.

In four successive phases, she first sensed the patient's thrust towards aliveness within herself, which he himself could not lay claim to; she next describes excitement within herself and then notes that the patient felt unconsciously pleased to be able to excite the analyst; a new "we" feeling arose in the transference and with it the analyst initiated a new interpretive stance; in the fourth phase close to termination, this patient, who had sought analysis to conquer his writing block, was now able to claim for himself to speak with "an authentic voice". Now the analyst interpreted directly which led to a re-interpretation of shame, which had been transformed. Through language we can have a voice that is interchangeable.

In this essay we observed the re-symbolization of the experience of shame through a process of reciprocal reflective dialogue. It was achieved as the patient discovered a mind of his own but he did so through a unique process of analytic engagement. As the patient passed through the various phases of analytic work, he was joined by an analyst who allowed us to share her alternating states of consciousness: the inappropriately distant, absorbed, fascinated, marvelling, excited analyst, capturing implicit meanings through the gaps with words and rejoicing in mutual identification.

A final comment on the concept of shame. Libbey's account of the patient's experience of shame underscores an important recent shift in psychoanalytic thought. The affect of shame has been a favourite signifier of a libidinal fixation point, namely, the anal phase. Diagnostically, it is a signpost of obsessive-compulsive neurosis, a manifestation of a cognitive style of field dependency (Lewis, 1971), and developmentally a key component of the separation-individuation process (Mahler, Pine & Bergman, 1975). But in this paper shame has been deconstructed from self-consciousness to embarrassment to humiliation to mortification. However, at the end point, mortification was not linked to an anal crisis but to a powerful traumatic moment at birth: the absence of the breast. Here, once more, we witnessed a transformation of primitive mental states of consciousness.

The re-finding of the new object through selected unexpected self-disclosure

This notion of a selected form of self-disclosure is guided by Bion's concept of the *selected fact*, which is the "creative integration of disparate facts into a meaningful pattern" (Britton & Steiner, 1994) preparing for an interpretation. I do consider Ellman's use of the analyst's selected self-disclosure as an instance of a selected fact. This instance of the seizure of a critical moment must be understood as a step in the development of analytic trust. The goal of analytic work is the ever deepening of the transference.

Ellman entitles her paper "Anonymity: Blank Screen or Black Hole". It stresses her commitment to the analytic frame, to regularity of sessions, payment of fees, and with it also the preservation of anonymity. Self-disclosure is not a cure-all; it is only justifiable if it opens new aspects of an unconscious fantasy. It is important to distinguish the use of self-disclosure from the way this term is used by relational analysts. The recurrent use of action and counteraction prevalent in the relational frame, while it intensifies the vitality of the immediate analytic interchange, it might do so at the expense of throttling fantasies of endogenous origins leading to the re-finding of the lost inner object. The selected use of self-disclosure is a vehicle for opening analytic space, especially when it is designed to overcome the impasse of early developmental trauma.

Ellman in her essay illustrates her commitment to anonymity as she cites a treatment experience of a lesbian patient treated by a lesbian analyst (a supervisee of Ellman's). Although the patient repeatedly requested to learn about her analyst's sexual orientation, even when they both met at a Gay Pride Parade, the analyst withheld the information for the sake of anonymity. The blank screen might have become a black hole. What mattered was not the self-disclosure but its sequelae. It opened up a veritable avalanche of sadistic feelings, shame and then a realization that these were defences against loving herself, her analyst, and her partner. These discoveries had profound implications for the integration of dissociative experiences rooted in early object relations. It signified the deepening of the transference. The black hole was avoided.

Ellman cites Stone (1961) that it is crucial not only to affirm the transference but also to avoid the non-presence of the other. While many of her other examples involve patients engaged in a triangular conflict, the dynamic conflict is rooted in earliest object relationships. In other instances, patients are able to share their grief and pain over the loss of love and not only the terror of the abyss but the re-finding of a new inner object. Here the selected self-disclosure to preserve analytic trust is rooted in a deeply Freudian position.

* * *

An analogous use of selected self-disclosure can be found in the work of Frankel, although his thinking is rooted in a very different line of psychoanalytic history. His formulations are based on a profound understanding of Ferenczi's work. He traces the evolution of Ferenczi's rejection of active technique, and the embracing of indulgence technique, to Winnicott's notion of transitionality. A guiding principle that permeates all Frankel's work is the preservation of a sense of psychic safety for the patient. Active interpretation can be an unwanted way of inducing trauma. In this respect, Frankel's analytic stance matches that of Thaler, who traces the progression from breakdown to recovery viewed from a Winnicottian perspective.

Rather interestingly, he designates this progression of analytic work as one of symbolization of excluded experiences.

However, I believe that he also introduces the conditions of selected self-disclosure as a vehicle of transformation. This is contained in Frankel's unique understanding of Ferenczi's notion of identification with the aggressor. Identification with the aggressor is created by a deceptive object relationship emanating from the emotionally unavailable other, which reappears in transference. Identification with the aggressor is a form of complementary identification with the analyst in Racker's sense. In identification with the aggressor, the patient has been guided by excessive compliance and has been robbed of his/her own autonomy; when it occurs in transference and arises in countertransference it must be challenged. It is a fundamental condition for non-trust. In this conception of identification with the aggressor, Frankel introduces a highly contemporary theme of pathological compliance, which we encounter in the social phenomenon of "obedience to authority" (Milgram, 1974).

Historically, Ferenczi countered the dangers inherent in identification with the aggressor through mutual analysis. While mutual analysis is a historical icon, the very idea makes the case that at crucial points the analyst must make his presence felt. This is especially signalled by the analyst's awareness of his/her own countertransference. In that interaction, the analyst's actuality can be differentiated from the representation of the inner object.

Like both Thaler and Ellman, Frankel is committed to the preservation of receptive non-intrusive listening, which guarantees maximum patient safety. He introduces the notion of a "relational dialectic" in which he stresses the narrowing impact of excessive interplay and yet the defining in crucial moments of the analyst's presence: "At these times, the patient needs something else—some more active manifestation of my presence in a personal way—a simple personal statement about myself, for instance, or an acknowledgement about a fault or error I have made that will re-establish me as a safe and protective object". While Ellman's selected use of self-disclosure is a means of deepening the transference, Frankel uses it to challenge the pathogenic sources of identification with the aggressor and in this fashion to achieve a more differentiated psychic space.

The use of a differentiated gradient of intervention is implemented by Frankel's notion of play, which is his conception of the analytic frame. His is a metaphoric use of play. The analyst is able to speak to the patient openly in the spirit of genuine self-examination. Play exists in a separate reality and it can exist in the analytic frame as "A Thing Apart" to use Steingart's phrase (1995). It thus enables the patient to explore and absorb alternative realities. The analyst is invited to play together, connected, yet each experience is a mutual experience of disbelief. Steingart uses the notion of a thing apart as a metaphor for psychoanalytic love; two forms of psychic reality that are present in the psychoanalytic dialogue.

The implicit interpretive engagement

In addition to metabolizing a state of helplessness, or of affirming the analyst's presence through selected self-disclosure, a continuing mode of interpretive analytic listening as a form of engagement becomes another vehicle for transformation. Implicit interpretive listening (apart from explicit interpretation) has a long history in psychoanalytic thought. It has recently been articulated in Lasky's (2002) concept of the *analyzing instrument*, in Poland's (2002) *interpretive attitude* as well as in Smith's (1993) emphasis on *conflictual listening*. We may not interpret the conflict but we need to be attuned to incompatible irreconcilable promptings. This attitude is well exemplified by Vorus's essay in which he describes the task of analytic work as one of "meaning making".

The issue of interpretive listening is exemplified in Britton's citation that in order to appreciate triangular space we must distinguish between a straight line of listening in contrast to looking sideways. By that Britton introduces a distinction between two states of consciousness, one that involves total absorption in the patient's subjectivity, and the other absorbed in the meaning structure. As we hear the patient's oscillation between projective and introjective states of consciousness, between alpha elements and beta elements, the analyst cannot help but contextualize what is proffered. This appears to be especially true in Vorus's attempt to reconcile the inevitable conflicts suggested by Kleinian theory and the goal of unification.

At a crucial phase during a long psychoanalytic treatment, Vorus cites a patient suffering from a writing block who felt himself attacked by "the Ogre", Britton's "Chaos Monster". Increasingly, it became evident that the analyst assumed the voice of this internal attacking presence. As the patient became aware of the force of the destructive superego, Vorus notes: "I become an internal presence who serves the function of preventing meaning, by attacking his mind during moments of genuine self-expression".

This path towards "meaning making" is unthinkable without Vorus's implicit awareness of the sadistic force of the destructive superego, its projection, and introjection, in the path towards working through. It was discovered by the patient but it was also co-constructed through the analyst's implicit psychoanalytic theory. The distinction between implicit theory and explicit theory stressed by Canestri (2003) needs to be emphasized.

* * *

This implicit mode of interpretive listening is also present in the very evocative material presented by Talby-Abarbanel and further discussed by Katz. In "Secretly Attached, Secretly Separate", the analyst tells a remarkable story of the intergenerational transmission of trauma, unconsciously registered in three generations of Holocaust survivors.

Talby-Abarbanel cites a remarkable progression of psychic events: starting with the symptom of restlessness, moving from place to place, "a street cat that has no home and gets along everywhere", and yet being unable to tolerate separations. This phase marked an initial transference regression with the presence of somatic symptoms. She revealed a tangled relationship to her mother emanating from a dream containing a powerful metaphor of a chocolate bar broken into two parts contained by the wrapper. The patient became aware of her yearning to both protect and separate from her mother, which forced her to confront her mother and reveal her biography. She discovered that the mother herself was a daughter of Holocaust survivors, whose parents in turn were probably killed by the Nazis. Subsequently, she realized that even in her childhood she had recurrent fantasies of death. After an expression of indigestible non-verbal terror ... there was an evocative emotionally charged interpretation linking her biography to the chocolate bar dream ... the analyst and patient for the first time established a connection, to be followed by interpretive dreams where both analyst and patient were practising gymnastics together.

In its barest outline this progression revealed a shift from somatic experiences unformulated to the evocation of metaphorical thought.

This process of organization and re-organization, memories recovered, resulted in the consolidation of an integrated relationship and integrative dreams. It all occurred in less than two years of analysis and in an articulate, artistic, talented woman. It is of interest to me that in this progression, it bears a similarity to Thaler's account of structural change. There is a parallelism that suggests that in spite of such wide variations in cognitive style, in biography, and in the unique quality of the analytic dyad, they may well be a common strand, which we call structural change.

Returning to the theme of interpretive listening, it may well be that this demonstration of this intergenerational transmission of trauma may also have been created by both participants in the analytic couple. The historical origins, the recourse to metaphor, the facts of the past were indeed discovered by the patient and yet it may have been co-constructed. At a crucial moment of countertransference enactment, the analyst countered the patient's transference and made her crucial intervention. Indeed, it was a form of selected self-disclosure although, unlike Ellman's example of the same species, it was guided by an intense affective burst. It is this forceful intervention that seems to unravel the patient's integrative associations. There is a substantial literature that has affirmed the phenomenon of intergenerational recollection in the transmission of trauma (e.g. Fonagy, 1993). It is of interest to note that such an experience can be both re-created and co-created in the analytic dyad.

Katz's view of this progression is enhanced by his frame of the enacted dimension. He distinguishes between a symbolized dimension and a non-verbal enacted dimension, which is a form of unconscious, non-verbal communication and the carrier of unconscious fantasies. "In Ann's analysis", according to Katz, "what found symbolic actualization within the transference-countertransference matrix was both the dissociated and un-symbolized existential anxieties of the Holocaust, as well as the non-verbal and unacknowledged arrangement with her mother that maintained the dissociation." Once more this transformation of structure was rendered possible only when the analyst was able through a countertransference enactment to put words into the patient's consciousness.

* * *

The interpretive mode of psychoanalytic thinking is also evident in Hurvich's contribution through his concept of Annihilation Anxiety. Before addressing the substance of his paper it is necessary to situate his work more broadly. It is a vision that is rooted in a specific emphasis of Freud's early anxiety theory; it is a concept that he has translated into a set of empirically testable propositions; and now in the present volume this concept finds its application in difficult moments of transference.

What Hurvich designates as annihilation anxiety has its origins in Freud's early concept of the "traumatic moment" in the "Neuro-Psychoses of Defense" (1894) and becomes integrated with Freud's later depiction of "danger situations" which are anticipatory, in "Inhibitions, Symptoms and Anxiety" (1926). By thus coordinating one Freudian theory of anxiety with another, Hurvich is not simply a third generation theorist modifying a second generation theorist but attempts, historically speaking, to bridge the century.

After a thorough review of the clinical description of anxiety, Hurvich formulated clinical propositions which either confirm, or disconfirm, ideas of the analytic process. The propositional method is guided by the idea that clinically important concepts need to be corroborated through clinical generalizations rather than metapsychological formulations (Freedman, Hurvich & Ward, in press). The very designation of the patient's experiences of being destroyed, merged, invaded, overwhelmed, and abandoned can be seen as a vivid re-evocation of early traumatic episodes. Annihilation Anxiety is that quality of danger which signifies a threat to the survival of the ego or self. Such formulations have been substantiated by a body of empirical research and have, over the past two decades, been corroborated by a range of quantitatively based clinical studies.

In the present book Hurvich extends this documented concept to the sphere of psychoanalytic technique. Interpretive listening comes to life more clearly here and one can term it a diagnostic way of listening. While Talby-Abarbanel alerts us to the historical as well as cultural roots of trauma, Hurvich is on the alert to the annihilatory roots. He may or may not interpret but he looks for the signals, explores, contextualizes, pauses and probes, sensitive to the context until the infantile trauma comes to life. Annihilation anxiety is not only modified by transference but can create the conditions for transference and countertransference. Annihilation anxieties may include disintegration anxiety, a marker in Winnicott's and Kohut's writings.

In treatment the manifestations of annihilation anxiety must be explored, its biographical roots determined, traced both in transference and countertransference. In this process of exploration, Hurvich distinguishes between a passive and active mode of annihilation anxiety. In the passive mode, annihilation anxiety may be felt to be concretized, fragmented, dissociated, and de-symbolized. On the other hand, in the active mode, annihilation anxiety may be transformed into a new context; this is especially the case when it makes its presence felt in the transference. In the active mode annihilation anxiety may be part of the imaginary, it may be anticipated, and new ego qualities come to the fore. It is evident that through the use of active and passive forms, Hurvich links himself to some important tenets of ego psychology. The strength of the ego needs to be considered in the use of clinical interventions.

Conclusion

It is evident that the three "vehicles of transformation" are inseparably contained in the work of each of our contributors. Yet, in each one we find a particular saliency and additionally they describe a process of working through. As cited earlier, the phenomenon of primitive mental states is a central issue today but the pathways towards recovery have not been sufficiently spelled out. As we have traced the path of confrontation with the terror of object loss, the pivotal moment of selected self-disclosure and the implementation of an interpretive mode of listening, we begin to articulate the contribution of the third generation of Freudian analysts. While to a large extent this emphasis is rooted in the work of the second generation in its particularity it is innovative.

I believe in its totality this vision has replaced the crucial role of interpretation of compromise formations as the "vehicle of transformation" in analytic work. This spectrum of contributions gives substance to Druck's initial emphasis on the guiding role of modern structural theory. In fact in each of the clinical papers spelling out the process of change we have found evidence for the phenomenon of structural change. To me, it is a phenomenon of progressive symbolization and with it the creation of new forms. Each of these clinical papers has noted a change from experiences that were at first implicit and unformulated and then became formulated and in my language had become symbolized. While this is a phenomenon observed in clinical reports by our analyst contributors, it is an observation that has now been independently corroborated in other quarters. In a specimen study of recorded psychoanalysis, the phenomenon of progressive symbolization has been documented. Shifts in mental organization, arising in successive phases of analysis, have been found to be mirrored in levels of cognitive-linguistic functioning. Indeed, what was observed was a spiralling effect revealing not only new depths but new heights as well (Freedman, Hurvich & Ward, in press).

Freud had initially suggested that working through involves the inevitable confrontation with the compulsion to repeat. In the light of this work we can re-formulate this statement to read "working through is repetition transformed".

REFERENCES

Abend, S.A. (2005). Analyzing intrapsychic conflict: Compromise formation as an organizing principle. *Psychoanalytic Quarterly*, 74: 5–25.

Abend, S.M. (2007). Therapeutic action in modern conflict theory. *Psychoanalytic Quarterly*, 76S: 1417–1442.

Abend, S.M., Porder, M.S. & Willick, A.S. (1983). *Borderline Patients: Psychoanalytic Perspectives*. New York: International Universities Press.

Adler, E. & Bachant, J.L. (1996). Free association and analytic neutrality: The basic structure of the psychoanalytic situation. *Journal of the American Psychoanalytic Association*, 44: 1021–1046.

Adler, G. & Buie, D.H., Jr. (1979). Aloneness and borderline psychopathology: The possible relevance of child development issues. *International Journal of Psychoanalysis*, 60: 83–96.

Akhtar, S. (1998). From simplicity through contradiction to paradox: The evolving psychic reality of the borderline patient in treatment. *International Journal of Psychoanalysis*, 79: 241–252.

Akhtar, S. (2000). From schisms through synthesis to informed oscillation: An attempt at integrating some diverse aspects of psychoanalytic technique. *Psychoanalytic Quarterly*, 69: 265–288.

Allen, J.G., Fonagy, P. & Bateman, A.W. (2008). *Mentalizing in Clinical Practice*. London: American Psychiatric Publishing.

Alvarez, A. (1992). *Live Company: Psychoanalytic Psychotherapy with Autistic, Borderline, Deprived, and Abused Children*. London: Routledge.
Appelbaum, A.H. & Stein, H. (2009). The impact of shame on the psychoanalysis of a borderline child. *Psychoanalytic Psychology*, 21: 26–41.
Arlow, J.A. (1963). Conflict, regression, and symptom formation. *International Journal of Psychoanalysis*, 44: 12–22.
Arlow, J.A. (1969). Unconscious fantasy and disturbances of conscious experience. *Psychoanalytic Quarterly*, 38: 1–27.
Arlow, J.A. (1975). The structural hypothesis—theoretical considerations. *Psychoanalytic Quarterly*, 44: 509–525.
Arlow, J.A. (1981). Theories of Pathogenesis. *Psychoanalytic Quarterly*, 50: 488–514.
Arlow, J.A. (1991). A new look at Freud's "Analysis Terminable and Interminable". In: Sandler, J. (Ed.), *On Freud's "Analysis Terminable and Interminable"* (pp. 43–55). New Haven: Yale University Press.
Arlow, J.A. (1995). Stilted listening: Psychoanalysis as discourse. *Psychoanalytic Quarterly*, 66: 567–595.
Arlow, J.A. & Brenner, C. (1964). *Psychoanalytic Concepts and the Structural Theory*. New York: International Universities Press.
Aron, L. (1996). *A Meeting of Minds: Mutuality in Psychoanalysis*. Hillsdale, NJ: The Analytic Press.
Aron, L. (2006). Analytic impasse and the third: Clinical implications of intersubjective theory. *International Journal of Psychoanalysis*, 87: 349–368.
Asch, S.S. (1976). Varieties of negative therapeutic reaction and problems of technique. *Journal of the American Psychoanalytic Association*, 24: 383–407.
Bach, S. (1977). On the narcissistic state of consciousness. *International Journal of Psychoanalysis*, 58: 209–233.
Bach, S. (1985). *Narcissistic States and the Therapeutic Process*. Northvale, NJ: Jason Aronson.
Bach, S. (1994). *The Language of Perversion and the Language of Love*. Northvale, NJ: Jason Aronson.
Bach, S. (2006). *Getting from Here to There: Analytic Love, Analytic Process*. Hillsdale, NJ: The Analytic Press.
Bach, S. (2008). On digital consciousness and psychic death. *Psychoanalytic Dialogues*, 18: 784–794.
Balint, M. (1958). Sandor Ferenczi's last years. *International Journal of Psychoanalysis*, 39: 68.
Balint, M. (1968). *The Basic Fault: The Therapeutic Aspects of Regression*. New York: Brunner-Mazel.

Baranger, M., Baranger, W. & Mom, J.M. (1988). The infantile psychic trauma from us to Freud: Pure trauma, retroactivity and reconstruction. *International Journal of Psychoanalysis, 69*: 113–128.

Bass, A. (2002). *Difference and Disavowal: The Trauma of Eros.* Palo Alto, CA: Stanford University Press.

Bateson, P. (2005). The role of play in the evolution of great apes and humans. In: Pellegrini, A.D. & Smith, P.K. (Eds.), *The Nature of Play: Great Apes and Humans* (pp. 13–24). New York: Guilford.

Bekoff, M. & Byers, J.A. (1998). *Animal Play: Evolutionary, Comparative, and Ecological Perspectives.* Cambridge, UK: Cambridge University Press.

Beebe, B. & Lachmann, F.M. (1988). The contribution of mother–infant mutual influence to the origins of self- and object representations. *Psychoanalytic Psychology, 5*: 305–333.

Bellak, L., Hurvich, M. & Gediman, H.K. (1973). *Ego Functions in Schizophrenics, Neurotics, and Normals: A Systematic Study of Conceptual, Diagnostic, and Therapeutic Aspects.* New York: Wiley.

Benjamin, J. (2004). Beyond doer and done to: An intersubjective view of thirdness. *Psychoanalytic Quarterly, 73*: 5–46.

Benjamin, J. (2006). Our appointment in Thebes: Acknowledging the analyst's fear of doing harm. [Paper presented at the Relational Orientation Colloquium, New York University Postdoctoral Program (September)].

Benveniste, P., Papouchis, N., Allen, R. & Hurvich, M. (1998). Rorschach assessment and ego functioning. *Psychoanalytic Psychology, 15*: 536–566.

Bird, B. (1972). Notes on transference: Universal phenomenon and hardest part of analysis. *Journal of the American Psychoanalytic Association, 20*: 267–301.

Bion, W.R. (1959). Attacks on linking. *International Journal of Psychoanalysis, 40*: 308–315.

Bion, W.R. (1962). The psychoanalytic study of thinking. *International Journal of Psychoanalysis, 43*: 306–310.

Blanck, G. & Blanck, R. (1974). *Ego Psychology: Theory and Practice.* New York: Columbia University Press.

Blanck, G. & Blanck, R. (1979). *Ego Psychology II: Psychoanalytic Developmental Psychology.* New York: Columbia University Press.

Blum, H.P., Kramer, Y., Richards, A.K. & Richards, A.D. (1988). *Fantasy, Myth, and Reality.* Madison, CT: International Universities Press.

Boesky, D. (1990). The psychoanalytic process and its components. *Psychoanalytic Quarterly, 59*: 550–584.

Boesky, D. (1994). Dialogue on the Brenner paper between Charles Brenner, M.D. and Dale Boesky, M.D. *Journal of Clinical Psychoanalysis, 3*: 509–543.

Brenner, C. (1953). An addendum to Freud's theory of anxiety. *International Journal of Psychoanalysis*, 34: 18–24.

Brenner, C. (1976). *Psychoanalytic Technique and Psychic Conflict*. New York: International Universities Press.

Brenner, C. (1979). Working alliance, therapeutic alliance, and transference. *Journal of the American Psychoanalytic Association*, 27S: 137–157.

Brenner, C. (1982). *The Mind in Conflict*. New York: International Universities Press.

Brenner, C. (1986). Discussion of the various contributions. In: Rothstein, I.A. (Ed.), *The Reconstruction of Trauma: Its Significance in Clinical Work* (pp. 195–203). Madison, CT: International Universities Press.

Brenner, C. (1994). The mind as conflict and compromise formation. *Journal of Clinical Psychoanalysis*, 3: 473–488.

Brenner, C. (1997). Current view on anxiety [discussion of M. Hurvich]. *Psychoanalytic Review*, 84: 513–515.

Britton, R. (1989). The missing link: Parental sexuality in the Oedipus complex. In: Britton, R. Feldman, M. O'Shaughnessy, E. & Steiner, J. (Eds.), *The Oedipus Complex Today: Clinical Implications* (pp. 83–102). London: Karnac.

Britton, R. (2003). *Sex, Death, and the Superego: Experiences in Psychoanalysis*. London: Karnac.

Britton, R. & Steiner, J. (1994). Interpretation: Selected fact or overvalued idea? *International Journal of Psychoanalysis*, 75: 1069–1078.

Bromberg, P.M. (1994). "Speak! That I may see you": Some reflections on dissociation, reality, and psychoanalytic listening. *Psychoanalytic Dialogues*, 4: 517–547.

Bromberg, P.M. (1995). Psychoanalysis, dissociation, and personality organization: Reflections on Peter Goldberg's essay. *Psychoanalytic Dialogues*, 5: 511–528.

Broucek, F.J. (1982). Shame and its relationship to early narcissistic developments. *International Journal of Psychoanalysis*, 63: 369–378.

Broucek, F.J. (1991). *Shame and the Self*. New York: Guilford.

Bruner, J.S. (1976). Nature and uses of immaturity. In: Brunner, J.S. Jolly, A. & Sylva, K. (Eds.), *Play: Its Role in Development and Evolution* (pp. 28–64). New York: Basic.

Bucci, W. (1985). Dual coding: A cognitive model for psychoanalytic research. *Journal of the American Psychoanalytic Association*, 33: 571–607.

Buie, D.H. & Adler, G. (1982). Definitive treatment of the borderline personality. *International Journal of Psychoanalysis*, 9: 51–87.

Burghardt, G.M. (2005). *The Genesis of Animal Play: Testing the Limits*. Cambridge, MA: MIT Press.

Busch, F. (1993). "In the neighborhood": Aspects of a good interpretation and a "developmental lag" in ego psychology. *Journal of the American Psychoanalytic Association*, 41: 151–177.

Busch, F. (1995). Beginning a psychoanalytic treatment: Establishing an analytic frame. *Journal of the American Psychoanalytic Association*, 43: 449–468.

Busch, F. (2001). Are we losing our mind? *Journal of the American Psychoanalytic Association*, 49: 739–751.

Busch, F. (2005). Conflict theory/trauma theory. *Psychoanalytic Quarterly*, 74: 27–45.

Busch, F. (2006). Countertransference in defense enactments. *Journal of the American Psychoanalytic Association*, 54: 67–85.

Canestri, J. (2003). The logic of psychoanalytical research. In: Leuzinger-Bohleber, M. Dreher, A.U. & Canestri, J. (Eds.), *Pluralism and Unity? Methods of Research in Psychoanalysis* (pp. 207–221). London: International Psychoanalytic Library.

Chodorow, N.J. (2003). The psychoanalytic vision of Hans Loewald. *International Journal of Psychoanalysis*, 84: 897–913.

Chodorow, N.J. (2004). The American independent tradition: Loewald, Erikson, and the (possible) rise of intersubjective ego psychology. *Psychoanalytic Dialogues*, 14: 207–232.

Chused, J.F. (1982). The role of analytic neutrality in the use of the child analyst as a new object. *Journal of the American Psychoanalytic Association*, 30: 3–28.

Chused, J.F. (1991). The evocative power of enactments. *Journal of the American Psychoanalytic Association*, 39: 615–639.

Chused, J.F. (1992). The patient's perception of the analyst: The hidden transference. *Psychoanalytic Quarterly*, 61: 161–184.

Coleridge, S.T. (1816). Kubla Khan. In: Gardner, H. (Ed.), *The New Oxford Book of English Verse* (pp. 544–546). New York: Oxford University Press, 1972.

Compton, A. (1980). A study of the psychoanalytic theory of anxiety, III: A preliminary formulation of the anxiety response. *Journal of the American Psychoanalytic Association*, 28: 739–773.

Cranefield, P.F. (1958). Josef Breuer's evaluation of his contribution to psycho-analysis. *International Journal of Psychoanalysis*, 39: 319–322.

Davies, J.M. (1994). Love in the afternoon: A relational reconsideration of desire and dread in the countertransference. *Psychoanalytic Dialogues*, 4: 153–170.

Deutsch, H. (1942). Some forms of emotional disturbance and their relationship to schizophrenia. *Psychoanalytic Quarterly*, 11: 301–321.

Di Pellegrino, G., Fadiga, L., Fogassi, L., Gallese, V. & Rizzolatti, G. (1992). Understanding motor events: A neurophysiological study. *Experimental Brain Research*, 91: 176–180.

Druck, A.B. (1989). *Four Therapeutic Approaches to the Borderline Patient*. Northvale, NJ: Jason Aronson.

Druck, A.B. (1998). Deficit and conflict: An attempt at integration. In: Ellman, C. Grand, S. Silvan, M. & Ellman, S.J. (Eds.), *The Modern Freudians* (pp. 209–233). Northvale, NJ: Jason Aronson.

Druck, A.B. (2002). Transformations in psychoanalytic treatment and theory. In: Lasky, R. (Ed.), *Symbolization and Desymbolization* (pp. 182–203). New York: Karnac.

Eisold, K. (1994) The intolerance of diversity in psychoanalytic institutes. *International Journal of Psychoanalysis*, 75: 785–800.

Ellman, C., Grand, S., Silvan, M. & Ellman, S.J. (Eds.). (1998). *The Modern Freudians: Contemporary Psychoanalytic Technique*. Northvale, NJ: Jason Aronson.

Ellman, S.J. (1991). *Freud's Technique Papers: A Contemporary Perspective*. Northvale, NJ: Jason Aronson.

Ellman, S.J. (1998). Enactment, transference, and analytic trust. In: Ellman, S.J. & Moskowitz, M. (Eds.), *Enactment: Toward a New Approach to the Therapeutic Relationship* (pp. 183–205). Northvale, NJ: Jason Aronson.

Ellman, S.J. (2005). Rothstein as a self and object Freudian: Commentary on paper by Arnold Rothstein. *Psychoanalytic Dialogues*, 15: 459–471.

Ellman, S.J. (2007). Analytic trust and transference: Love, healing ruptures and facilitating repairs. *Psychoanalytic Inquiry*, 27: 246–263.

Epstein, M. (1998). *Going to Pieces Without Falling Apart: A Buddhist Perspective on Wholeness*. New York: Broadway.

Fagen, R. (1981). *Animal Play Behavior*. New York: Oxford University Press.

Ferenczi, S. (1915). Psychogenic anomalies of voice production. In: Rickman, J. (Ed.), *Further Contributions to the Theory and Technique of Psycho-Analysis* (Trans. J Suttie) (pp. 87–109). London: Karnac, 1980.

Ferenczi, S. (1928). The elasticity of psycho-analytic technique. In: *Final Contributions to the Problems and Methods of Psycho-Analysis* (pp. 87–101). London: Hogarth, 1955.

Ferenczi, S. (1929). The unwelcome child and his death instinct. In: *Final Contributions to the Problems and Methods of Psycho-Analysis* (pp. 102–107). London: Hogarth, 1955.

Ferenczi, S. (1930), The principle of relaxation and neocatharsis. In: *Final Contributions to the Problems and Methods of Psycho-Analysis* (pp. 108–125). London: Hogarth, 1955.
Ferenczi, S. (1931), Child-analysis in the analysis of adults. In: *Final Contributions to the Problems and Methods of Psycho-Analysis* (pp. 126–142). London: Hogarth, 1955.
Ferenczi, S. (1932). *The Clinical Diary of Sandor Ferenczi* (J. Dupont, ed.). Cambridge, MA: Harvard University Press, 1988.
Ferenczi, S. (1933). Confusion of tongues between adults and the child. In: *Final Contributions to the Problems and Methods of Psycho-Analysis* (pp. 156–167). London: Hogarth, 1955.
Ferro, A. (2005). *Seeds of Illness, Seeds of Recovery: The Genesis of Suffering and the Role of Psychoanalysis.* New York: Brunner-Routledge.
Fine, B.D., Joseph, E.D. & Waldhorn, H.F. (Eds.) (1969). The manifest content of the dream. In: *Monograph III: The Kris Study Group of the New York Psychoanalytic Institute.* New York: International Universities Press.
Fisher, M., Goodwin, J. & Shay, L. (1950). When you're smiling. *When You're Smiling.* Mills Music Inc.
Flavell, J.H. (1963). *The Developmental Psychology of Jean Piaget.* Princeton, NJ: D. Van Nostrand.
Flescher, J. (1955). A dualistic viewpoint on anxiety. *Journal of the American Psychoanalytic Association*, 3: 415–446.
Fonagy, P. (1991). Thinking about thinking: Some clinical and theoretical considerations in the treatment of a borderline patient. *International Journal of Psychoanalysis*, 72: 639–656.
Fonagy, P. (1993). Psychoanalytic and empirical approaches to developmental psychopathology: An object-relations perspective. *Journal of the American Psychoanalytic Association*, 41S: 245–260.
Fonagy, P. (2000). Attachment and borderline personality disorder. *Journal of the American Psychoanalytic Association*, 48: 1129–1146.
Fonagy, P. (2003). Some complexities in the relationship of psychoanalytic theory to technique. *Psychoanalytic Quarterly*, 72: 13–47.
Fonagy, P. & Target, M. (1996). Playing with reality: I. Theory of mind and the normal development of psychic reality. *International Journal of Psychoanalysis*, 77: 217–233.
Fonagy, P. & Target, M. (2000). Playing with reality. *International Journal of Psychoanalysis*, 81: 853–873.
Fouts, R. (1997). *Next of Kin: My Conversations with Chimpanzees.* New York: Avon.
Frankel, J. (1998). Ferenczi's trauma theory. *American Journal of Psychoanalysis*, 58: 41–61.

Frankel, J. (2001). A witness breaks his silence: The meaning of a therapist's response to an adolescent's self-destruction. *American Journal of Psychoanalysis, 61*: 85–99.

Frankel, J. (2002a). Exploring Ferenczi's concept of identification with the aggressor: Its role in trauma, everyday life, and the therapeutic relationship. *Psychoanalytic Dialogues, 12*: 101–139.

Frankel, J. (2002b). Identification and "traumatic aloneness": Reply to commentaries by Berman and Bonomi. *Psychoanalytic Dialogues, 12*: 159–170.

Frankel, J. (2006). Diagnosis-of-the-moment and what kind of good object the patient needs the analyst to be: Commentary on paper by Neil Skolnick. *Psychoanalytic Dialogues, 16*: 29–37.

Frankel, J. (2008). The concept of play and the psychoanalytic process. [Paper presented to the American Psychological Association Division of Psychoanalysis (Division 39) Spring Meeting, New York (April)].

Freedman, N. (1985). The concept of transformation in psychoanalysis. *Psychoanalytic Psychology, 2*: 317–339.

Freedman, N. (1997). On receiving the patient's transference: The symbolizing and desymbolizing countertransference. *Journal of the American Psychoanalytic Association, 45*: 79–103.

Freedman, N., Barroso, F., Bucci, W. & Grand, S. (1978). The bodily manifestations of listening. *Psychoanalysis and Contemporary Thought, 1*: 157–194.

Freedman, N. & Berzofsky, M. (1995). Shape of the communicated transference in difficult and not-so-difficult patients: Symbolized and de-symbolized transference. *Psychoanalytic Psychology, 12*: 363–374.

Freedman, N., Hurvich, M. & Ward, R. (In press). *Another Kind of Evidence*. London: Karnac.

Freedman, N., Lasky, R. & Webster, J. (2009). The ordinary and extraordinary countertransference. *Journal of the American Psychoanalytic Association, 57*: 303–331.

Freedman, N. & Ward, R. (2011). Specimen of working through. In: Freedman, N. Hurvich, M. Ward, R. with Geller, J.D. & Hoffenberg, J. (Eds.), *Another Kind of Evidence*. London: Karnac.

Freud, A. (1936). *The Ego and the Mechanisms of Defense: The Writings of Anna Freud, Vol. II*. New York: International Universities Press.

Freud, A. (1952). Notes on a connection between the states of negativism and of emotional surrender. In: *The Writings of Anna Freud, Vol. 4*. New York: International Universities Press, 1968.

Freud, S. (1894a). The neuro-psychoses of defense. *S.E., 3*. London: Hogarth.

Freud, S. (1900a). *The Interpretation of Dreams*. S.E., 4. London; Hogarth.
Freud, S. (1905). Fragment of an analysis of a case of hysteria (Dora). S.E., 7. London: Hogarth.
Freud, S. (1912a). Recommendations to physicians practicing psychoanalysis. S.E., 12. London: Hogarth.
Freud, S. (1912b). The dynamics of transference. S.E., 12. London: Hogarth.
Freud, S. (1914). Remembering, repeating and working-through. S.E., 12. London: Hogarth.
Freud, S. (1915). Observations on transference love. S.E., 12. London: Hogarth.
Freud, S. (1916–1917). Introductory lectures on psycho-analysis: Lecture XVI, anxiety. S. E., 16. London: Hogarth.
Freud, S. (1923). *The Ego and the Id*. S. E., 19. London: Hogarth.
Freud, S. (1926d). Inhibitions, symptoms and anxiety. S.E., 20. London: Hogarth.
Freud, S. (1940a). An outline of psycho-analysis. S.E., 22. London: Hogarth.
Friedman, L. (1969). The therapeutic alliance. *International Journal of Psychoanalysis*, 50: 139–153.
Friedman, L. (1978a). Treatment puzzles and training paradigms. *Contemporary Psychoanalysis*, 14: 456–467.
Friedman, L. (1978b). Trends in the psychoanalytic theory of treatment. *Psychoanalytic Quarterly*, 47: 524–567.
Friedman, L. (1992). How and why do patients become more objective? Sterba compared with Strachey. *Psychoanalytic Quarterly*, 61: 1–17.
Friedman, L. (1997). Ferrum, ignis, and medicina: Return to the crucible. *Journal of the American Psychoanalytic Association*, 45: 13–36.
Friedman, L. (2002). What lies beyond interpretation, and is that the right question? *Psychoanalytic Psychology*, 19: 540–551.
Friedman, L. (2005). Flirting with virtual reality. *Psychoanalytic Quarterly*, 74: 639–660.
Frijling-Schreuder, E.C. (1969). Borderline states in children. *Psychoanalytic Study of the Child*, 24: 307–327.
Fry, D.P. (2005). Rough-and-tumble social play in humans. In: Pellegrini, A.D. & Smith, P.K. (Eds.), *The Nature of Play: Great Apes and Humans* (pp. 54–85). New York: Guilford.
Furst, S. (Ed.) (1967). *Psychic Trauma*. New York: Basic.
Gabbard, G.O. & Westen, D. (2003). Rethinking therapeutic action. *International Journal of Psychoanalysis*, 84: 823–841.
Gillett, E. (1990). The problem of unconscious affect: Signal anxiety versus the double-prediction theory. *Psychoanalysis and Contemporary Thought*, 13: 551–600.

Glover, E. (1924). Active therapy and psycho-analysis: A critical review. *International Journal of Psychoanalysis,* 5: 269–311.

Goldberger, M. (Ed.) (1996). *Danger and Defense.* Northvale, NJ: Jason Aronson.

Gosso, Y., Otta, E., Salum, E., Morais, M.D.L., Ribiero, F.J.L. & Bussab, V.S.R. (2005). Play in hunter-gatherer society. In: Pellegrini, A.D. & Smith, P.K. (Eds.), *The Nature of Play: Great Apes and Humans* (pp. 213–253). New York: Guilford.

Gottlieb, R.M. (2003). Psychosomatic medicine: The divergent legacies of Freud and Janet. *Journal of the American Psychoanalytic Association,* 51: 857–881.

Gray, P. (1973). Psychoanalytic technique and the ego's capacity for viewing intrapsychic activity. *Journal of the American Psychoanalytic Association,* 21: 474–494.

Gray, P. (1987). On the technique of analysis of the superego—An introduction. *Psychoanalytic Quarterly,* 56: 130–154.

Gray, P. (1991). On transferred permissive or approving superego functions: The analysis of the ego's superego activities, part II. *Psychoanalytic Quarterly,* 60: 1–21.

Gray, P. (1994). *The Ego and Analysis of Defense.* Northvale, NJ: Jason Aronson.

Green, A. (2004). Thirdness and psychoanalytic concepts. *Psychoanalytic Quarterly,* 73: 99–135.

Green, A. (2006). The central phobic position: With a model of the free association method. In: Green, A. (Ed.), *Resonance of Suffering* (pp. 41–73). London: The International Psychoanalytic Library.

Greenberg, J.R. (1986). Theoretical models and the analyst's neutrality. *Contemporary Psycho-Analysis,* 24: 268–704.

Greenberg, J.R. (1995). Psychoanalytic technique and the interactive matrix. *Psychoanalytic Quarterly,* 64: 1–22.

Greenson, R.R. (1965). The working alliance and the transference neurosis. *Psychoanalytic Quarterly,* 34: 155–181.

Grotstein, J. (2007). *A Beam of Intense Darkness: Wilfred Bion's Legacy to Psychoanalysis.* London: Karnac.

Grunes, M. (1984). The therapeutic object relationship. *Psychoanalytic Review,* 17: 123–144.

Grunes, M. (1998). The therapeutic object relationship-II. In: Ellman, C. Grand, S. Silvan, M. & Ellman, S. (Eds.), *The Modern Freudians: Contemporary Psychoanalytic Technique* (pp. 129–140). Northvale, NJ: Jason Aronson.

Guntrip, H. (1969). *Schizoid Phenomena, Object Relations and the Self.* New York: International Universities Press.

Guntrip, H. (1971). *Psychoanalytic Theory, Therapy, and the Self*. New York: Basic.

Hartmann, H. (1964). *Essays on Ego Psychology: Selected Problems in Psychoanalytic Theory*. New York: International Universities Press.

Hopper, E. (1991). Encapsulation against a fear of annihilation. *International Journal of Psychoanalysis, 72*: 607–624.

Huizinga, J. (1955). *Homo Ludens: A Study of the Play Element in Culture*. Boston: Beacon.

Hurvich, M. (1989). Traumatic moment, basic dangers and annihilation anxiety. *Psychoanalytic Psychology, 6*: 309–323.

Hurvich, M. (1991). Annihilation anxiety: An introduction. In: Siegel, H. Barbanel, L. Hirsch, I. Lasky, J. Silverman, H. & Warshaw, S. (Eds.), *Psychoanalytic Reflections on Current Issues* (pp. 135–154). New York: New York University Press.

Hurvich, M. (1996). Annihilation anxieties and psychic trauma. [Second World Conference of the International Society for Traumatic Stress Studies, Jerusalem, Israel, June].

Hurvich, M. (1997). Classics revisited: "The Ego in Anxiety" (Schur, M. 1953) and "An Addendum to Freud's Theory of Anxiety" (Brenner, C. 1953). *Psychoanalytic Review, 84*: 483–504.

Hurvich, M. (1998). History and current status of the concept of annihilation anxieties. [13th International Congress of Group Psychotherapy, London, August].

Hurvich, M. (2000). Fears of being overwhelmed and psychoanalytic theories of anxiety. *Psychoanalytic Review, 87*: 615–649.

Hurvich, M. (2002a). A proposed expansion of the danger series: Annihilation as present or potential threat. [Pre-circulated paper for January 2003 Mid-Winter Meetings of the American Psychoanalytic Association].

Hurvich, M. (2002b). Symbolization, desymbolization and annihilation anxieties. In: Lasky, R. (Ed.), *Symbolization and Desymbolization: Essays in Honor of Norbert Freedman* (pp. 347–365). New York: Karnac.

Hurvich, M. (2003). The place of annihilation anxieties in psychoanalytic theory. *Journal of the American Psychoanalytic Association, 51*: 579–616.

Hurvich, M. (2004). Psychic trauma and fears of annihilation. In: Knafo, D. (Ed.), *Living with Terror, Working with Trauma: A Clinician's Handbook* (pp. 51–66). Northvale, NJ: Jason Aronson.

Hurvich, M., Beneviste, P., Howard, J. & Coonerty, S. (1993). The assessment of annihilation anxiety from projective tests. *Perceptual and Motor Skills, 77*: 387–401.

Hurvich, M., Allen, R., & Mcguire, H. (2006a). *Hurvich Experience Inventory/50: Manual. Unpublished.*

Hurvich, M. & Freedman, N. (2006b). The Propositional Method for the study of psychoanalytic concepts. [IPTAR Investigative Psychoanalysis, New York Academy of Science, 15 May].

Hurvich, M. & Freedman, N. (In preparation). The propositional method. In: N. Freedman, M. Hurvich & R. Ward, *Another Kind of Evidence.*

Hurvich, M. & Simha-Alpern, A. (1997). Annihilation anxiety in psychosomatic disorders. In: Finel, J. (Ed.), *Mind-Body Problems: Psychotherapy with Psychosomatic Disorders* (pp. 57–91). Northvale, NJ: Jason Aronson.

Jacobs, T.J. (1986). Countertransference enactments. *Journal of the American Psychoanalytic Association, 34*: 289–307.

Jacobs, T.J. (1991a). *The Use of the Self.* Madison, CT: International Universities Press.

Jacobs, T.J. (1991b). The interplay of enactments: Their role in the analytic process. In: *The Use of the Self: Countertransference and Communication in the Analytic Situation* (pp. 31–49). Madison, CT: International Universities Press.

Jacobs, T.J. (1993a). Insight and experience: Commentary on Morris Eagle's "Enactments, transference, and symptomatic cure". *Psychoanalytic Dialogues, 3*: 123–127.

Jacobs, T. (1993b). The inner experience of the analyst: Their contribution to the analytic process. *International Journal of Psychoanalysis, 74*: 7–14.

Jacobs, T.J. (1994). Nonverbal communications. *Journal of the American Psychoanalytic Association, 42*: 741–762.

Jacobs, T.J. (1997). In search of the mind of the analyst: A progress report. *Journal of the American Psychoanalytic Association, 45*: 1035–1059.

Jacobs, T.J. (1999a). Countertransference past and present: A review of the concept. *International Journal of Psychoanalysis, 80*: 575–594.

Jacobs, T.J. (1999b). On the question of self-disclosure by the analyst: Error or advance in technique. *Psychoanalytic Quarterly, 68*: 159–183.

Jacobs, T.J. (2001a). On misreading and misleading patients: Some reflections on communications, miscommunications and countertransference enactments. *International Journal of Psychoanalysis, 82*: 653–669.

Jacobs, T.J. (2001b). On unconscious communications and covert enactments: Some reflections on their role in the analytic situation. *Psychoanalytic Inquiry, 21*: 4–23.

Jacobson, E. (1964). *The Self and the Object World.* New York: International Universities Press.

Johan, M. (1992). Panel report: Enactments in psychoanalysis. *Journal of the American Psychoanalytic Association*, 40: 827–841.

Kaplan, D.M. (1984). Some conceptual and technical aspects of the actual neurosis. *International Journal of Psychoanalysis*, 65: 295–305.

Katz, G. (1998). Where the action is: The enacted dimension of analytic process. *Journal of the American Psychoanalytic Association*, 46: 1129–1167.

Katz, G. (2002). Missing in action: The enacted dimension of analytic process in a patient with traumatic object loss. In: Lasky, R. (Ed.), *Symbolization and Desymbolization: Essays in Honor of Norbert Freedman* (pp. 407–430). New York: Karnac.

Kern, J. (1987). Transference neurosis as a waking dream: Notes on a clinical enigma. *Journal of the American Psychoanalytic Association*, 35: 337–366.

Kernberg, O. (1967). Borderline personality organization. *Journal of the American Psychoanalytic Association*, 15: 641–685.

Kernberg, O.F. (1975). *Borderline Conditions and Pathological Narcissism*. New York: Jason Aronson.

Killingmo, B. (1989). Conflict and deficit: Implications for technique. *International Journal of Psychoanalysis*, 70: 65–79.

Klein, M. (1946). Notes on some schizoid mechanisms. *International Journal of Psychoanalysis*, 27: 99–110.

Klein, M., Heimann, P., Isaacs, S. & Riviere, J. (1952). *Developments in Psychoanalysis*. London: Hogarth.

Knight, R.P. (1953). Management and psychotherapy of the borderline schizophrenic patient. *Bulletin of the Menninger Clinic*, 17: 139–150.

Kohut, H. (1971). *The Analysis of the Self*. New York: International Universities Press.

Kohut, H. (1972). Thoughts on narcissism and narcissistic rage. *Psychoanalytic Study of the Child*, 27: 360–400.

Kohut, H. (1977). *The Restoration of the Self*. New York: International Universities Press.

Kohut, H. (1984). *How Does Analysis Cure*. Goldberg, A. & Stepansky, P. (Eds.). Chicago: University of Chicago Press.

Kohut, H. & Wolf, E.S. (1978). The disorders of the self and their treatment: An outline. *International Journal of Psychoanalysis*, 59: 413–425.

Kris, A.O. (1985). Resistance in convergent and in divergent conflicts. *Psychoanalytic Quarterly*, 54: 537–568.

Krystal, H. (Ed.) (1968). *Massive Psychic Trauma*. New York: International Universities Press.

Krystal, H. (1988). *Integration and Self Healing: Affect, Trauma & Alexithymia*. Hillsdale, NJ: The Analytic Press.

LaFarge, L. (2006). The wish for revenge. *Psychoanalytic Quarterly*, 75: 447–475.
Laing, R.D. (1959). *The Divided Self: An Existential Study in Sanity and Madness*. London: Tavistock.
Lansky, M.R. (1997). Envy as process. In: Morrison, A. & Lansky, M. (Eds.), *The Widening Scope of Shame* (pp. 327–338). Hillsdale, NJ: Analytic Press.
Lasky, R. (1993). *Dynamics of Development and the Therapeutic Process*. Northvale, NJ: Jason Aronson.
Lasky, R. (2002). Countertransference and the analytic instrument. *Psychoanalytic Psychology*, 19: 65–94.
Lazarus, R.R. (1966). *Psychological Stress and the Coping Process*. New York: McGraw-Hill.
LeDoux, J. (1996). *The Emotional Brain*. New York: Touchstone.
Lennon, J. (1980). Beautiful Boy (Darling Boy). *Double Fantasy*. Gefen Records.
Levin, R. & Hurvich, M. (1995). Nightmares and annihilation anxiety. *Psychoanalytic Psychology*, 12: 247–258.
Levy, S.T. & Inderbitzin, L.B. (1997). Safety, danger, and the analyst's authority. *Journal of the American Psychoanalytic Association*, 45: 377–394.
Lewin, R.A. & Schulz, C. (1992). *Losing and Fusing: Borderline Transitional Object and Self Relations*. Northvale, NJ: Jason Aronson.
Lewis, H.B. (1971). Shame and guilt in neurosis. *Psychoanalytic Review*, 58: 419–438.
Lewis, K. (2005). Social play in the great apes. In: Pellegrini, A.D. & Smith, P.K. (Eds.), *The Nature of Play: Great Apes and Humans* (pp. 27–53). New York: Guilford.
Libbey, M. (2007). On narcissistic mortification. *The Round Robin*, 22: 5.
Libet, B., Gleason, C.A., Wright, E.W. & Pearl, D.K. (1983). Time of conscious intention to act in relation to onset of cerebral activity (readiness-potential). The unconscious initiation of a freely voluntary act. *Brain*, 106: 623–642.
Lipton, S. (1977). The advantages of Freud's technique as shown in his analysis of "the Rat Man". *International Journal of Psychoanalysis*, 58: 255–273.
Little, M. (1958). On delusional transference (transference psychosis). In: *Transference Neurosis and Transference Psychosis: Toward Basic Unity* (pp. 88–91). New York: Jason Aronson, 1981.
Loewald, H.W. (1951). Ego and reality. *International Journal of Psychoanalysis*, 32: 10–18.
Loewald, H.W. (1960). On the therapeutic action of psycho-analysis. *International Journal of Psychoanalysis*, 41: 16–33.

Loewald, H.W. (1966). Psychoanalytic concepts and the structural theory: By Jacob A. Arlow and Charles Brenner. New York: International Universities Press, 1964.

Loewald, H.W. (1973). On internalization. *International Journal of Psychoanalysis*, 54: 9–17.

Loewald, H.W. (1978). Instinct theory, object relations, and psychic structure formation. *Journal of the American Psychoanalytic Association*, 26: 493–506.

Loewald, H.W. (1979). The waning of the Oedipus complex. *Journal of the American Psychoanalytic Association*, 27: 751–775.

Loewald, H. (1980). *Papers on Psychoanalysis*. New Haven, CT: Yale University Press. Mahler, M. & McDevitt, J. (1982). Thoughts on the emergence of the sense of self, with particular emphasis on the body self. *Journal of the American Psychoanalytic Association*, 30: 827–848.

Mahler, M.S., Pine, F. & Bergman, A. (1975). *The Psychological Birth of the Human Infant: Symbiosis and Individuation*. New York: Basic.

McLaughlin, J. (1987). The play of transference: Some reflections on enactment in the psychoanalytic situation. *Journal of the American Psychoanalytic Association*, 35: 557–582.

McLaughlin, J. (1991). Clinical and theoretical aspects of enactment. *Journal of the American Psychoanalytic Association*, 39: 595–614.

McLaughlin, J. (1993). Countertransference enactment and the psychoanalytic process. In: Horowitz, M.J. Kernberg, O.F. & Weinshel, E.M. (Eds.), *Psychic Structure and Psychic Change: Essays in Honor of Robert Wallerstein, S. M.D.* (pp. 135–158). Madison, CT: International Universities Press.

Meares, R. (1995). *The Metaphor of Play: Disruption and Restoration in the Borderline Experience*. Northvale, NJ: Jason Aronson.

Milgram, S. (1974). *Obedience to Authority: An Experimental View*. New York: Harper & Row.

Mitrani, J. (1998). Never before and never again: The compulsion to repeat, the fear of breakdown, and the defensive organisation. *International Journal of Psychoanalysis*, 79: 301–316.

Mitrani, J.L. (2001). "Taking the transference": Some technical implications. *International Journal of Psychoanalysis*, 82: 1085–1104.

Modell, A.H. (1965). On having the right to a life: An aspect of the superego's development. *International Journal of Psychoanalysis*, 46: 323–331.

Modell, A.H. (1976). The "holding environment" and the therapeutic action of psychoanalysis. *Journal of the American Psychoanalytic Association*, 24: 285–307.

Modell, A.H. (1988). The centrality of the psychoanalytic setting and the changing aims of treatment—A perspective from a theory of object relations. *The Psychoanalytic Quarterly*, 57: 577–596.

Moore, B. & Fine, B. (Eds.) (1995). *Psychoanalysis: The Major Concepts*. New Haven, CT: Yale University Press.

Myerson, P. (1979). Issues of technique where patients relate with difficulty. *International Review of Psycho-Analysis, 6*: 363–375.

Myerson, P. (1981a). The nature of the transactions that enhance the progress over phases of a psychoanalysis. *International Journal of Psychoanalysis, 62*: 91–103.

Myerson, P. (1981b). The nature of the transactions that occur in other than classical analysis. *International Review of Psycho-Analysis, 8*: 173–189.

Nersessian, E. & Kopff, R.G. (Eds.) (1996). *Textbook of Psychoanalysis*. Washington, DC: American Psychiatric Publishing.

Ogden, T.H. (1991). Analyzing the matrix of transference. *International Journal of Psychoanalysis, 72*: 593–605.

Ogden, T.H. (1994). The analytic third: Working with intersubjective clinical facts. *International Journal of Psychoanalysis, 75*: 3–19.

Ogden, T.H. (2004). The analytic third: Implications for psychoanalytic theory and technique. *Psychoanalytic Quarterly, 73*: 167–195.

Person, E., Cooper, A. & Gabbard, G. (2005). *The APA Textbook of Psychoanalysis*. Washington, DC: American Psychiatric Publishing.

Pine, F. (1979). On the pathology of the separation-individuation process as manifested in later clinical work: An attempt at delineation. *International Journal of Psychoanalysis, 60*: 225–241.

Pine, F. (1988). The four psychologies of psychoanalysis and their place in clinical work. *Journal of the American Psychoanalytic Association, 36*: 571–596.

Pine, F. (1994). Some impressions regarding conflict, defect, and deficit. *Psychoanalytic Study of the Child, 49*: 222–240.

Poland, W.S. (1992). Transference: "An original creation". *Psychoanalytic Quarterly, 61*: 185–205.

Poland, W.S. (2000). The analyst's witnessing and otherness. *Journal of the American Psychoanalytic Association, 48*: 17–34.

Poland, W.S. (2002). The interpretive attitude. *Journal of the American Psychoanalytic Association, 50*: 807–826.

Power, T.G. (2000). *Play and Exploration in Children and Animals*. Mahwah, NJ: Lawrence Erlbaum.

Racker, H. (1968). *Transference and Counter-Transference*. New York: International Universities Press.

Rangell, L. (1955). On the psychoanalytic theory of anxiety: A statement of a unitary theory. *Journal of the American Psychoanalytic Association, 3*: 389–414.

Renik, O. (1993). Countertransference enactment and the psychoanalytic process. In: Horowitz, M.J. Kernberg, O.F. &

Weinshel, E.M. (Eds.), *Psychic Structure and Psychic Change: Essays in Honor of Robert Wallerstein, S. M.D.* (pp. 135–158). Madison, CT: International Universities Press.

Renik, O. (1999). Playing one's cards face up in analysis: An approach to the problem of self-disclosure. *Psychoanalytic Quarterly,* 68: 521–539.

Roughton, R.E. (1993). Useful aspects of acting out: Repetition, enactment, and actualization. *Journal of the American Psychoanalytic Association,* 41: 443–472.

Rey, H. (1979). Schizoid phenomena in the borderline. In: Spillius, E.B. (Ed.), *Melanie Klein Today, Vol. I, Mainly Theory* (pp. 203–229). London: Routledge, 1988.

Richards, A.D. & Richards, A.K. (1995). Notes on psychoanalytic theory and its consequences for technique. *Journal of Clinical Psychoanalysis,* 4: 429–564.

Richards, A.D. & Willick, M.S. (1986). *Psychoanalysis: The Science of Mental Conflict.* Hillsdale, NJ: The Analytic Press.

Rosegrant, J. (2005). The therapeutic effects of the free-associative state of consciousness. *Psychoanalytic Quarterly,* 74: 737–766.

Rothstein, A. (Ed.) (1986). *The Reconstruction of Trauma: Its Significance in Clinical Work.* Madison, CT: International Universities Press.

Rothstein, A. (2002). Reflections on creative aspects of psychoanalytic diagnosing. *Psychoanalytic Quarterly,* 71: 301–326.

Rothstein, A. (2005). Compromise formation theory: An inter subjective dimension. *Psychoanalytic Dialogues,* 15: 415–431.

Sandler, J. (1960). The background of safety. *International Journal of Psychoanalysis,* 41: 352–356.

Sandler, J. (1976). Countertransference and role-responsiveness. *International Review of Psycho-Analysis,* 3: 43–47.

Sandler, J., Dreher, A.U. & Drews, S. (1991). An approach to conceptual research in psychoanalysis illustrated by a consideration of psychic trauma. *International Review of Psycho-Analysis,* 18: 133–141.

Schachter, S. (1964). The interaction of cognitive and physiological determinants of emotional state. In: Berkowitz, L. (Ed.), *Advances in Experimental Social Psychology* (pp. 49–79). New York: Academic Press.

Schafer, R. (1979). On becoming a psychoanalyst of one persuasion or another. *Contemporary Psychoanalysis,* 15: 354–360.

Schafer, R. (1983a). Danger situations. In: *The Analytic Attitude* (pp. 96–112). New York: Basic.

Schafer, R. (1983b). *The Analytic Attitude.* New York: Basic.

Schlesinger, H.J. (1969). Diagnosis and prescription for psychotherapy. *Bulletin of the Menninger Clinic,* 33: 269–278.

Schur, M. (1953). The ego in anxiety. In: R.M. Loewenstein (Ed.), *Drives, Affects and Behavior* (pp. 67–103). New York: International Universities Press.

Schwaber, E.A. (1998). From whose point of view? The neglected question in analytic listening. *Psychoanalytic Quarterly*, 67: 645–661.

Silber, A. (1989). Panic attacks facilitating recall and mastery: Implications for psychoanalytic technique. *Journal of the American Psychoanalytic Association*, 37: 337–364.

Silverman, L.H. (1984). Beyond insight: An additional necessary step in redressing intrapsychic conflict. *Psychoanalytic Psychology*, 1: 215–234.

Singer, J.L. (1995). Imaginative play in childhood: Precursor of subjunctive thoughts, daydreaming and adult pretending games. In: Pellegrini, A.D. (Ed.), *The Future of Play Theory: Multidisciplinary Inquiry into the Contributions of Brian Sutton-Smith* (pp. 187–219). Albany, NY: State University of New York Press.

Smith, H.F. (1993a). Engagements in the analytic work. *Psychoanalytic Inquiry*, 13: 425–454.

Smith, H.F. (1993b). The analytic surface and the discovery of enactment. *Annals of Psychoanalysis*, 21: 243–255.

Smith, H.F. (1997). Resistance, enactment, and interpretation: A self-analytic study. *Psychoanalytic Inquiry*, 17: 13–30.

Smith, H.F. (2000). Countertransference, conflictual listening, and the analytic object relationship. *Journal of the American Psychoanalytic Association*, 48: 95–128.

Smith, H.F. (2004). The analyst's fantasy of the ideal patient. *Psychoanalytic Quarterly*, 73: 627–658.

Smith, H.F. (2006). Analyzing disavowed action: The fundamental resistance of analysis. *Journal of the American Psychoanalytic Association*, 54: 713–737.

Smith, P.K. (2005). Social and pretend play in children. In: A.D. Pellegrini & P.K. Smith (Eds.), *The Nature of Play: Great Apes and Humans* (pp. 173–209). New York: Guilford.

Sperry, R.W. & Gazzaniga, M.S. (1967). Language following surgical disconnection of the hemisphere. In: Milikan, C.H. (Ed.), *Brain mechanisms underlying speech and language*. New York: Grune & Stratton.

Sroufe, L.A. & Wunsch, J.P. (1972). The development of laughter in the first year of life. *Child Development*, 43: 1326–1344.

Steingart, I. (1995). *A Thing Apart: Love and Reality in the Therapeutic Relationship*. Northvale, NJ: Jason Aronson.

Stern, D.N. (1985). *The Interpersonal World of the Infant: A View from Psychoanalysis and Developmental Psychology*. New York: Basic.

Stern, D.N., Sander, L.W., Nahum, J.P., Harrison, A.M., Lyons-Ruth, K., Morgan, A. C., Bruschweilerstern, N. & Tronick, E.Z. (1998). Non-interpretive mechanisms in psychoanalytic therapy: The "something more" than interpretation. *International Journal of Psychoanalysis*, 79: 903–921. Stern, M.M. (1988). *Repetition and Trauma: Toward a Teleonomic Theory of Psychoanalysis*. Hillsdale, NJ: The Analytic Press.

Stewart, W.A. (1967). *Psychoanalysis: The First Ten Years 1888–1898*. New York: Macmillan.

Stolorow, R.D. & Lachmann, F.W. (1980). *Psychoanalysis of Developmental Arrests*. New York: International Universities Press.

Stone, R. (1961). *The Psychoanalytic Situation: An Examination of its Development and Essential Nature*. New York: International Universities Press.

Strachey, J. (1934). The nature of the therapeutic action of psychoanalysis. *International Journal of Psychoanalysis*, 15: 127–159.

Strenger, C. (1989). The classic and the romantic vision in psychoanalysis. *International Journal of Psychoanalysis*, 70: 593–610.

Strenger, C. (1997). Further remarks on the classic and the romantic visions in psychoanalysis: Klein, Winnicott, and ethics. *Psychoanalysis and Contemporary Thought*, 20: 207–243.

Sugarman, A. (2006). Mentalization, insightfulness, and therapeutic action. *International Journal of Psychoanalysis*, 87: 965–987.

Sullivan, H.S. (1953). *The Interpersonal Theory of Psychiatry*. New York: Norton.

Sutton-Smith, B. (1997). *The Ambiguity of Play*. Cambridge, MA: Harvard University Press.

Tarachow, S. (1962). Interpretation and reality in psychotherapy. *International Journal of Psychoanalysis*, 43: 377–387.

Tolstoy, L. (1877) *Anna Karenina*. (Pevear, R. & Volokhonsky, L. Trans.). New York: Penguin, 2004.

Tronick, E., Brushweller-Stern, N., Harrrison, A., Lyons-Ruth, K., Morgan, A., Nahum, J., Sander, L. & Stern, D. (1998). Dyadically expanded states of consciousness and the process of therapeutic change. *Infant Mental Health Journal*, 19: 290–299.

Tuch, R.H. (2007). Thinking with, and about, patients too scared to think: Can non-interpretive maneuvers stimulate reflective thought? *International Journal of Psychoanalysis*, 88: 91–111.

Tuckett, D. (1994). The 75th volume. *International Journal of Psychoanalysis*, 75: 1–2.

Vygotsky, L. (1978). The role of play in development. In: Cole, M. (Trans.), *Mind in Society* (pp. 92–104). Cambridge, MA: Harvard University Press.

Waelder, R. (1967). Inhibitions, symptoms and anxiety, forty years later. *Psychoanalytic Quarterly, 36*: 1–36.

Wallerstein, J. (1997). Transference and countertransference in clinical interventions with divorcing families. In: Solomon, M. & Siegel, J. (Eds.), *Countertransference in Couples Therapy*. New York: Norton.

Wallerstein, R.S. (1986). *Forty-Two Lives in Treatment: A Study of Psychoanalysis and Psychotherapy*. New York: Guilford.

Wallerstein, R.S. (2002). The growth and transformation of American ego psychology. *Journal of the American Psychoanalytic Association, 50*: 135–168.

Winnicott, C. (1980). Fear of breakdown: A clinical example. *International Journal of Psychoanalysis, 61*: 351–357.

Winnicott, D.W. (1951). Transitional objects and transitional phenomena. In: *Through Paediatrics to Psycho-Analysis* (pp. 229–242). New York: Basic, 1975.

Winnicott, D.W. (1953). Transitional objects and transitional phenomena—A study of the first not-me possession. *International Journal of Psychoanalysis, 34*: 89–97.

Winnicott, D.W. (1954). Metapsychological and clinical aspects of regression within the psycho-analytical set-up. In: *Through Paediatrics to Psycho-Analysis* (pp. 278–294). New York: Basic, 1975.

Winnicott, D.W. (1955). Metapsychological and clinical aspects of regression within the psycho-analytical set-up. *International Journal of Psychoanalysis, 36*: 16–26.

Winnicott, D.W. (1956). Primary maternal preoccupation. In: *Through Paediatrics to Psycho-Analysis* (pp. 300–305). New York: Basic, 1975.

Winnicott, D.W. (1958). The capacity to be alone. In: *The Maturational Processes and the Facilitating Environment: Studies in the Theory of Emotional Development* (pp. 29–36). New York: International Universities Press, 1965.

Winnicott, D.W. (1960a). The theory of the parent-infant relationship. *International Journal of Psychoanalysis, 41*: 585–595.

Winnicott, D.W. (1960b). Ego distortion in terms of true and false self. In: *The Maturational Processes and the Facilitating Environment: Studies in the Theory of Emotional Development* (pp. 140–152). New York: International Universities Press, 1965.

Winnicott, D.W. (1963a). Dependence in infant-care, child-care, and in the psycho-analytic setting. In: *The Maturational Processes and the*

Facilitating Environment: Studies in the Theory of Emotional Development (pp. 249–259). New York: International Universities Press, 1965.

Winnicott, D.W. (1963). Communicating and not communicating leading to a study of certain opposites. In: *The Maturational Processes and the Facilitating Environment: Studies in the Theory of Emotional Development* (pp. 179–192). New York: International Universities Press, 1965.

Winnicott, D.W. (1965a). The maturational processes and the facilitating environment: Studies in the theory of emotional development. *The International Psycho-analytic Library*, 64: 1–276.

Winnicott, D.W. (1965b). The psychology of madness. *Paper prepared for the British Psychoanalytic Society*. In: Winnicott, C., Shepherd, R. & Davis, M. (Eds.), *D.W. Winnicott: Psycho-Analytic Explorations* (pp. 119–129). Cambridge, MA: Harvard University Press, 1989.

Winnicott, D.W. (1965c). *The Maturational Process and the Facilitating Environment*. London: Hogarth.

Winnicott, D.W. (1967). The concept of clinical regression compared with that of defence organisation. [Paper given at a psychotherapy symposium at Mclean Hospital, Belmont, Massachusetts]. In: Winnicott, C., Shepherd, R. & Davis, M. (Eds.), *D.W. Winnicott: Psycho-Analytic Explorations* (pp. 193–199). Cambridge, MA: Harvard University Press, 1989.

Winnicott, D.W. (1969). The use of an object. *International Journal of Psychoanalysis*, 50: 711–716.

Winnicott, D.W. (1971). The use of an object and relating through identifications. In: *Playing and Reality* (pp. 86–94). New York: Basic.

Winnicott, D.W. (1974). The fear of breakdown. *International Review of Psycho-Analysis*, 1: 103–107.

Winnicott, D.W. (1975). Through paediatrics to psycho-analysis. *The International Psycho-analytic Library*, 100: 1–325.

Wolson, P. (2006). Working with the relational unconscious: An integration of intra-psychic and relational analysis. [Paper presented at Los Angeles Institute and Society for Psychoanalytic Studies, Los Angeles].

Zetzel, E.R. (1949). Anxiety and the capacity to bear it. In: *The Capacity for Emotional Growth* (pp. 33–52). New York: International Universities Press, 1970.

Zetzel, E.R. (1956). Current concepts of transference. *International Journal of Psycho analysis*, 37: 369–375.

INDEX

Analyst-induced enactment 169
Analyst-patient
  interaction 21
  object relationship 14
  relationship 18, 40
Analyst's
  actual behaviour 17
  insensitivity 186
  objectivity 20
  personal psychology 193
  selected self-disclosure 256
  self-protective evasions 181
  subjectivity 21
Analytic relationship, play and
  structure of 192–196
Analytic self-disclosure,
  analytic authority, analytic
  responsibility 187
Angry feelings 3
Annihilating shame 139

Annihilation anxiety (AA) concept
  31, 66, 262
  abandoned 73–75
  carnival dream 82–83
  carnival dream associations
    83–84
  case summary to 89–92
  childhood traumatic experience
    82
  clinical application section 77–78
  compensatory mechanisms 70
  course of treatment 79–80
  dead girls in closet dream 80–82
  destroyed 73–75
  developments in theory and
    clinical application 65–95
  dimensionalizing 68
  disorganized 73–75
  external events facilitation
    85–89

288 INDEX

invaded 73–75
manifestations 75
masturbation fantasies 84–85
merged 73–75
overwhelmed 73–75
presenting complaints 78–79
propositions related to 72–73
psychic danger 71
psychic trauma 68–69
psychoanalytic theory of 66, 68
psychoanalytic treatment 79
sexual relationship 92
six annihilation dimensions 89
six dimensions 66–67, 70
six dimensions and sub-
  dimensions 73–75
transference aspects 92–95
traumatic anxieties 70
Zetzel, anxiety tolerance 76
Annihilation apprehensions 72
Annihilation fantasies and
  anxieties 65, 67
  anticipations 69
  apprehensions 68
Annihilation-related themes/
  fantasies 72
Ann's
  core object relationship 226
  frustration 234
  growing ability 225
  separateness 229, 233
Anonymity
  blank screen or black hole
    157–172
  in dynamic sense 160
Anxiety-fear-ridden identification
  181
Anxiety-filled opportunity 17
Anxiety-provoking impulses 58
Anxiety theory 66
  Freud's 68
Apocalyptic fantasies 220

Authentic voice 148–153
Authenticity 145
Authenticity and spontaneity 214
Autonomic dysregulation 126
Auxiliary superego 204

Bach, Sheldon 51, 132, 179
  subjective sense of self 137
Balint, Michael 178
Bion's ideas 206
  selected fact 256
Bion's model 208
Bionian 167
Bi-sexual experiences 164
Black hole 157–172
Blank screen 157–172
Blast furnace 154, 255
Bleulerian diagnostic
  thinking 251
Bohemian style 219
Boston change group 53
Breakdown and recovery 114–118
  growing stability 109
  in relation to true and false self
    99–103
  mother's anxieties 111
  tachycardia 112
  transference feelings 107
Breakdown and recovery, Ms R's
  analysis 105–129
  dream eight—November
    123–125
  dream five—May 121–122
  dream four—March 120–121
  dream one—December 118
  dream seven—October 123
  dream six—June 122–123
  dream three—January 119–120
  dream two—three weeks later
    118–119
Breakdown phenomena and
  symptoms 98–99

INDEX

Brenner, Arlow 2
   led Freudian psychoanalysis 4
   unconscious conflict 7
British contemporary Kleinians 206
British object-relations theorists 177
Britton, Ron 202, 206
   technical recommendation 207
Broucek, Francis 156
   continuous sense of self 133
   subjective self awareness 137

Casual acquaintance 167
Child's psychic world 207
Childhood neurosis 40
Classical Freudian and Kleinian
   theory 58
Classical psychoanalysis 4, 16
Classical psychoanalytic
   formulation 45
Classical structural theory 3
Clinical Diary 180
Clinical generalizations 67
Clinical psychoanalysis 66, 173
Cognitive-linguistic functioning
   264
Coherent process of working 117
Coleridge 53
Complex connection 49
Compromise formation 3
Concrete experience 148
Consciousness
   narcissistic states of 132
   obsessive-compulsive state
     of 52
   patient's state of 53
   shame in narcissistic states
     131–156
   shared states of 57
   states of 51–64
Consequential incongruity 65
Contemporary Freudian
   analysts 240
   concept of enactment 239
   psychoanalysis 46
   theory 23, 26
Contemporary Kleinians 28
   theory 216
Contemporary neuroscience 58
Contemporary psychoanalysis 26
Contemporary psychoanalytic
   thought 253
Continuous unconscious effort 213
Convergent conflict 60
Countertransference 19–21, 50, 88,
   159
Countertransference disclosure,
   mutuality and contemporary
   views of 183–185
Cultivating meaning
   space 201–217
Customary symbolic meanings 62

Dangerously emotional
   relationship 235
De-animation 108
Defensive hypervigilance 190
Deficit pathology 188
Depressive affect 19
Deutsch, Helena 58
De-vitalization 108, 116
Diagnostic and dynamic
   sensitivity 28
Diagnostic formulations 24
Disavowed exploitation 188
Discrete self-states 137–141
Disruptive effect 19
Dissociative defence 82
Divergent conflict 15, 60
Dream imagery 80
Dreaming and symbolization 125
Drive theory 10
Druck, Andrew B. 1, 25
Druck, Beverly Goldsmith 24, 50
Dysphoric affect 19

Ego
    annihilation anxiety to 71
    capacities 9
    defensive efforts 4
    development 10
    functioning 41
    functions 10
    inability to effect 11
    integration 97
    organization 98–99
    psychologist 23, 27, 29
    strengths 88
Ego psychology 27, 263
    intersubjective 26
Ellman, Carolyn 157
Emotional
    boundaries 225
    disengagement 182
    experience and objective self-
        reflection 154
    reality and interpersonal
        capabilities 198
    relationships 134
    responses 221
    self-regulation 102
Empty mind 137
Enacted dimension 36
Evocative constancy 179, 194

Ferenczi, therapeutic environment
    178
Ferenczi's concepts of identification
    with aggressor and play
    active technique 174–175
    effects of trauma, and
        relaxation technique 177
    foundational processes in
        analytic relationship 173–199
    mutuality stance 189
    providing safety 176
    relaxation technique and
        mutual analysis 176

successors to relaxation
    technique 177–179
Ferenczi's emphasis 179
Ferenczi's technical experiments
    176, 179
    identification with aggressor 176
Ferenczi's thinking 192
    play in 196
Ferro, Antonio 167
Fragment psychoanalytic listening
    251
Frankel, Jay 173
    analytic stance 257
    unique understanding
        of Ferenczi's notion 258
Freedman, Norbert 249
Freud, Anna
    anxiety theory 77
    behavioural recommendations
        160
    defence-analysis focus 203
    defence-focused theory of
        therapeutic action 203
    defense mechanisms 3
    early anxiety theory 262
    revolutionary focus 23
    structural hypothesis 9
    the neuro-psychoses of defense
        251
Freud's structural theory 2
Freudian analysts 17, 22, 157
    contributions 250
Freudian and neo-Kleinian
    conceptions of therapeutic
    action 201–217
    clinical example 210–214
Freudian clinical theory 26
Freudian concept
    excluded or revised 250–251
    traditional 20
Freudian group, contemporary 203
Freudian "mainstream" 23

Freudian psychoanalysis
    1, 20, 26
    Brenner led 4
    contemporary 46
Freudian psychoanalysts 5
Freudian spectrum 42
Freudian synthesis, new
    analyzing instrument 259
    conflictual listening 259
    implicit interpretive
        engagement 259–263
    innovative 251
    psychoanalytic theory 260
    reflections and perspective
        249–264
    third generation 253
Freudian theory 20, 203
    contemporary 26
Freudians, classical structural 202

Gay Pride Parade 164
Gray, Paul 14
Green, Andre 66

Hall, G. Stanley 249
Holocaust survivor, third
        generation 219–237
    analytic process 239–247
Holocaust trauma 244
Homosexuality 165
Hurvich, Marvin 65

Ideal therapeutic relationship 15
Idealization and hatred to sense of
    self 142–148
Identification with aggressor and
    play 173–199
Idiosyncratic formulation 2
Illness syndrome 98
Indigestible non-verbal terror 230
Infantile omnipotence 100
Influential theory 4

Interactive stance and diagnosis
    185
Internal complexity 44
Internal object relations 12
Internal systems theory 3
Internalization processes 155
Intersubjective capacities 207
Intrapsychic conflict 5, 9, 11, 59
    and concomitant development
        36
Introjected reliability 103
Introjective/projective cycles 208

Jacobs, Ted 239
James, Henry 156
Johnny Got His Gun 137
Joyce, James
    Ulysses 54

Katz, Gil 24, 239
Kernberg 8
King Lear 136
Klein, Melanie 60, 204
Kleinian ideas contemporary 204
Kleinian theorists 46
Kleinian theory 259
Krystal
    alexithymia 76
    massive psychic trauma 66, 76

Lacking internal structure 211
Lennon, John 241
Libbey, Mary 131
Libidinal conflict 175
Libidinal object relationship 42
Life-or-death struggle 59
Loewald stresses 33
Loewald's conception 216

Masturbation fantasies 84–85
Matter-of-fact-ness 151
Maturational processes 105

Maturational processes and
    recovery 126
Mental conundrum 138
Mental topography 136
Mentalness of mind 216
Metapsychological formulations
    262
Mirror-transference 108
Mitrani, Judith 97
Modern conflict analysts 17
Modern conflict theory 1–24
    analyst's role in 13–18
    critique of 5–13
    recent developments in 18–24
Modern conflict theorists 4, 37–38
    Boesky 20
    Greenberg 21
    Jacobs 20–21
Modern Kleinian concept 216
Modern (post-Bionian) Kleinians
    206
    therapeutic action 206–210
Modern structural theory 25–50
    analyst's role 36–45
    deficit and conflict 28–36
Moment-to-moment relationship
    43
Mutual analysis 176
Mutual idealizations 156

Narcissism 140, 155
Narcissism-self-consciousness 136
Narcissistic
    anxieties 185, 190
    difficulties 27
    disequilibrium 133, 186
    disorders 188
    sensitivity 186
    vulnerability 154
    withdrawal 162
Neo-Kleinian
    conceptions of therapeutic
        action 201–217
    perspectives 202
Neuroscience 58
Neurotic vicious circle 204
Neutrality, Chused's definition
    of 195
Neutrality and abstinence 48
New Freudian synthesis reflections
    and perspective 249–264
Nodal transference representations
    117
Non-gratifying object 161
Non-intrusive listening 258
Non-intrusiveness 163
Non-verbal communication 24

Object-related transference 184
    situation 40
Object-relational difficulties and
    anxieties 190
Object-relational disturbances 195
Object relations theory and self
    psychology 203
Obsessive-compulsives 55
    neurosis 256
Oedipal fantasies 161
Oedipal situation 45
Oedipal triangulation 251
Oedipal victory 87
Oedipal-dominated premises 24
Oedipus complex 207, 251
Optimal analytic environment 46
Optimal frustration 48
Optimal self esteem regulation 29

Paranoid-schizoid position
    10, 253
Parental internalization 11
Pathological human development
    23
Patient-analyst
    boundaries 36

experience 14, 19, 24, 25
object relationship 42
Patient-analyst relationship 16–19,
  24, 28, 36, 39
  moment-to-moment
    relationship 43
Patient's
  ability 188
  boundaries and maintaining
    158
  capacity 40
  conscious experience 208
  curiosity 158
  ego 16
  idiosyncratic construction 16
  idiosyncratic moulding 16
  illuminating self reflections
    132
  internal object 193
  motivation 39
  narcissistic anxiety 194
  natural identification 40
  pathological object-relational
    needs 179
  (possibly traumatic) denial 184
  self-consciousness 154
  self-object transference 184
  sensitivity 188
  sex life 161
  siphoning 174
  stabilizing self-object
    transference 186
  structural requirements 34
  subjective awareness 153
  transference 21, 241
  transference and associations
    174
  traumatizing experiences 182
  unconscious transference
    fantasies 37, 240
  unconscious world of self and
    object representations 242

Patient's idiosyncratic transference
  17
  disposition 37
Permeable barrier 161
Personal categorization 52
Personal continuity 100
Phenomenal death 99
Play for psychotherapy,
  implications of empirical
  research 197–199
Play theory 196
  provisional quality 197
Positive nature of neutrality 40
Post-traumatic environment 230
Post-traumatic stress disorder 75
Pre-Oedipal
  issues 8, 18
  factors 12
Pre-Oedipal developmental issues
  23
Pre-structural model 174
Primitive agonies 77, 98
Primitive mental states 252
Professional hypocrisy 181
Progressive symbolization 264
Projective identification 167
Projective—introjective states 253
Psychic equivalence state 133
Psychic fragmentation 71
Psychic growth 206
Psychic possibility and psychic
  space 49
Psychic process-structures 12
Psychic reality 100, 125
Psychic trauma to pathogenesis 75
Psychoanalysis 137
Psychoanalytic
  diagnosis 9
  interaction 46
  pluralism 1
  schools 26
  situation 13–14, 21

theory 1
therapy 13
thought 29
treatment 97
Psychoanalytic theorists 76–77
Psychoanalytic theory and practice 65
   psychic trauma 70
Psychoses 71
Psychosomatic symptoms 220
Psychotherapeutic factors 12
Pumpkin head dream 151

Real relationship 15
Reality interactions 16
Recovery processes 105
Referential activity 189
Reflective self-awareness 64
Relational analysts 193
Relational theorists
   Bromberg 58
   Sullivan 58
Relaxation technique and mutual analysis 176–177
Replacement therapy 12
Resurgence of sexual feelings 155
Re-symbolization 255
Run-of-the-mill self-delusion 188

Sado-masochism 56, 58
Sadistic-masochistic fantasies 171
Schachter, Stanley 54
Schur, Max 76
Secretly attached, secretly separate 219–237
   discussion of 239
Self psychological 23
Self psychology 177
Self-absorption 163
Self-and-object Freudian group 203

Self-awareness and reality adherence 64
Self-consciousness 132, 139, 145, 154
Self-conciousness and feelings 110
Self-disclosing stance 184
Self-realization 120
Sense of authenticity 26
Sense of self 149
Sensori-motor organization 126
Sensori-motor patterns 100
Separation-individuation process 256
Sexual
   arousal 85
   dynamics 85
   orientation 164
   promiscuity 8
   traumata 84
Sexuality 124, 164
Shame in narcissistic states of consciousness 131–156
   case illustration: Dev 133–153
   discrete self-states 137–141
   finding an authentic voice 148–153
   idealization and hatred to sense of self 145–148
   shame to idealization and hatred 142–144
Shame to idealization and hatred 142–144
Share emotional things 220
Signal anxiety 74
Significant stressors 125
Social-constructivist epistemology 241
State of Absolute Subjectivity 138
State of Heightened Objective Self-Awareness 137
State of Transition—A State of Shame 139

Strachey, James 204
Structural deficit 29
Subjective self-awareness 64
Subjectivity 21
Superego 3, 30
    annihilation anxiety to 71
    capacities 9
    pressure 3
    unconscious 14
Superego conflict, internal
    unconscious 14
Swami molestation 81
Swami's sexual advances 92
Symbiotic relationship 224
Symbolic actualization 245
Symbolic representation 247
Symbolization 173, 254
Symptomatic behaviour 204

Talby-Abarbanel, Michal 219, 239, 244, 246
    countertransference issues 246
Thaler, Aaron 97
The Diving Bell and the Butterfly 137
Therapeutic
    barrier 15
    matrix 21
    strategy 13
Tidal wave dream 123
Tolstoy's *Anna Karenina* 55
Traditional Freudians 48
Transference
    concept 250
    cure 14
    development 18
    dreams 117
    fantasy 14
    interpretations, premature 37
    neurosis 40, 45, 48
    objects 172
    of authority 17
    regression 254
Transference and
    countertransference 68, 215, 219–237, 240–241, 262
    interpenetration of 240
    matrix 132, 245, 247
    narcissistic configurations 132
    reasons 169
    relationship 237
    unconscious 241
    wrapper 236
Transitional phenomena 132
Transmuting internalization 44
Trauma in action 239–247
Traumatic anxiety 74
Traumatic memory surfaces 83
Traumatic neurosis 75
Traumatic pathogenesis 197
Treatment process, Strachey's description 204

Unanalysed internalization 14
Unconscious
    communication 22, 140
    conflict 30
    conflict, ubiquity of 9
    conflict and defence 13
    conscious 201
    factors 21
    fantasy 2–3, 15
    mental functioning 34
    object relational component 8
    transference 38
    transference-
        countertransference process 241
Un-integration and disintegration, inevitable agony of abyss of 253–256
Unthinkable anxieties 98
Unwelcome necessity 77

Vehicles of transformation 251–252, 263
Verbal symbolization 240, 243
Vorus, Neal 201

Wandering Jew 231, 244
Winnicott, Clare 97
    ideas about true and false self 99
    primitive agonies 98
    transitional phenomena 12

Winnicott's notion of transitional space 178
Winnicott's sense of the word 189

Young woman, breakdown and recovery in analysis 97–129

Zetzel, anxiety tolerance 76